A DICTIONARY OF
NICKNAMES

Also by L. G. Pine

The Stuarts of Traquair
The House of Wavell
The Middle Sea
The Story of Heraldry
Trace Your Ancestors
The Golden Book of the Coronation
They Came with the Conqueror
The Story of the Peerage
Tales of the British Aristocracy
The House of Constantine
Teach Yourself Heraldry and Genealogy
The Twilight of Monarchy
A Guide to Titles
Princes of Wales
American Origins
Your Family Tree
Ramshackledom, A Critical Appraisal of the Establishment
Heirs of the Conqueror
Heraldry, Ancestry and Titles, Questions and Answers
The Story of Surnames
After Their Blood
Tradition and Custom in Modern Britain
The Genealogist's Encyclopedia
The Story of Titles
International Heraldry
The Highland Clans
Sons of the Conqueror
The New Extinct Peerage
The History of Hunting
A Dictionary of Mottoes

A DICTIONARY OF
NICKNAMES

L. G. PINE

ROUTLEDGE & KEGAN PAUL

London, Boston, Melbourne and Henley

First published in 1984
by Routledge & Kegan Paul plc

14 Leicester Square, London WC2H 7PH, England

9 Park Street, Boston, Mass. 02108, USA

464 St Kilda Road, Melbourne,
Victoria 3004, Australia and

Broadway House, Newtown Road,
Henley-on-Thames, Oxon RG9 1EN, England

Set in Palatino and Helvetica
by Input Typesetting Ltd, London
and printed in Great Britain
by T. J. Press (Padstow) Ltd
Padstow, Cornwall

© L. G. Pine 1984

Library of Congress Cataloging in Publication Data

Pine, L. G. (Leslie Gilbert), 1907–

A dictionary of nicknames
1. Biography.   2. Nicknames.   I. Title
CT108.P56   1984   920'.02   84–3263

ISBN 0–7100–9582–1

Do, dico, et dedico
hunc librum nepti meae
Emily Ruth Alice Pine

PREFACE

In his *Outline of History*, H. G. Wells lamented that we did not know the name of any human being until some 5,000 years ago. It was hardly possible for us to do so before writing was invented in order to assist and perpetuate human memory. History, it is said, begins at Sumer and with it, about 3500 B.C., the written record. One can hardly perhaps conceive of unwritten tradition persisting some 5–6,000 years. Writing did, however, give to Ozymandias and his like the opportunity to be grandiloquent about themselves. King of Kings was a mild form of description for the high and mighty ones among the forked radishes. They did not hesitate to assume godlike attributes and even to bestow upon themselves divine honours. They did not always suffer the retribution given to King Herod Agrippa (Acts xii) smitten by God and eaten of worms. The empty sarcophagus, the Great Pyramid, is a lasting monument of human vanity, unless Kurt Mendelssohn's idea is right, that Cheops designed it as a necessary work project, similar to the American space mission ordered by President Kennedy (*The Riddle of the Pyramids*, Book Club Associates 1975).

Whatever the facts, the great ones of the world bestowed descriptions or epithets on themselves which one may term self-bestowed nicknames. The habit has persisted, though to some extent the theistic religions, Christianity and Islam, did check the most high-sounding titles. To some extent only, for although ascriptions of divinity are not found in Europe or in the Moslem world, one wonders how titles such as His Holiness, the All Highest, or even the Sublime Porte really sort with the recognition of Divine Omnipotence.

Passing for a moment from these self-chosen epithets, and coming to what are commonly called nicknames, we find terms which are bestowed on a man or woman by his or her fellows. They reflect usually some quality which has seized the popular imagination. They resemble in some ways the art of the caricaturist. In his cartoons he touches upon a characteristic of his subject which he draws out to an exaggerated extent, while preserving a likeness to his original which enables the viewer to recognize the subject of the cartoon. So with nicknames, some are humorous, some unpleasant, and a few downright nasty. Our medieval ancestors never hesitated to give a man a name derived from some unfortunate feature, something crippling. Mercifully, most of these have died out. There are also the well-known sobriquets which can only be described as silly: Nobby Clark, Chalky White, Dusty Miller, Dinger Bell. They may originate from the stupidity of human beings when congregated in crowds. Half a soldier's life is waiting, in the Polish proverb, and while waiting, e.g. on pay day, one is bound to hear such gems of inanity as 'let the dog see the rabbit' or 'gangway for a naval officer' about on a par with the use of Nobby or Chalky, etc.

One is inclined to wish the perpetrators of this rubbish the same fate as the American naval officer in Herman Wouk's *The Caine Mutiny*. When asked by his commanding officer for the name of one of the seamen, he realizes with horror that he knows only the man's nickname of Chaddan. There was, too, an amusing instance two generations ago in my own family. A businessman of a somewhat excitable disposition was known to his colleagues as Mr Fireworks. By some weird accident that is how he was welcomed by the wife of a colleague at a social function.

No one could pretend to have collected all known nicknames. There are bound to be omissions of some nicknames well known to a particular inquirer which have been passed on colloquially. I felt it advisable to include many descriptive terms which have great interest. Some of these were bestowed by the bearers on themselves, as with cases among the Greek sovereigns, the Diadochi; others, like the frequent Great, or Pious, or Catholic, were the tribute of subjects and admirers of the monarch concerned. I think that the attribute 'the Great' provides a rich field as regards human nature which is too tempting for a commentator to avoid. The fact that some monsters of iniquity should be so termed provides a searchlight on human nature. I hope that the bringing together of these descriptive words with what are normally regarded as nicknames will be of use to the reader. Incidentally, long lists of kings or any other lengthy pedigrees always prompt thoughts, at least to a genealogist, similar to those so caustically expressed by Swift in the 3rd Book of his immortal tale. One can but wish, *requiescant in pace*.

To anyone writing in 1984 it is curious to reflect that even humanity has acquired a nickname, *Homo Sapiens*. Carolus Linnaeus was a highly skilled scientist, but he was also a happy, simple soul. He fell on his knees to thank God when he first saw gorse in England. Perhaps he really did think that *Sapiens* was the correct adjective for *Homo*. The eighteenth century was relatively calmer and less troubled than our century, which has seen two world wars of unprecedented destruction; the post-war 'peace' with a war on every continent except Australia; half the human race undernourished if not starving, while enormous sums are spent to discover if there are microbes on Jupiter. What should be the adjective to qualify the horrible being who is responsible for the world's suffering? *Insipiens*? *Barbarus*? or simply *Malus*? To use an ancient source of wisdom, Fallen Man.

I wish to express my thanks to one of my American friends and correspondents, Mrs Linda J. La Rosa, for her kind assistance with some American nicknames.

Nicknames form one of the four divisions of surnames

– patronymics, place names and occupational names being the other three – all of which I have handled in my book *The Story of Surnames* (David & Charles, Newton Abbot, 1972). All students of surnames must acknowledge their indebtedness to the profoundly learned works of the late Dr P. H. Reaney, *A Dictionary of British Surnames* (London, Routledge & Kegan Paul, 1961) and the late Dr G. F. Black, *The Surnames of Scotland* (New York, New York Public Library, 1962), to both of which I have referred in these pages.

Leslie G. Pine

A

ABBOT

found originally, of course, as the title of the head of a monastery, but in later times a nickname, coming from, for instance, the Abbot of Misrule, the player in a medieval festival game, a good example occurs in Scott's *The Abbot*, ch. 14 where the election of the last genuine Abbot is interrupted by a crowd of buffoons led by the Abbot of Unreason.

ABELITES

also Abelians and Abelonians, a small sect in North Africa mentioned only by St Augustine (*De Haer*, LXXXVII) as existing in his diocese of Hippo (the modern Bone in Tunisia). This sect professed to follow the example of Abel (Genesis iv) whom they regarded as having lived in total continence. The Abelites enjoined matrimony as obligatory but to be lived in complete chastity. The sect was perpetuated by adoption by each married couple of a boy and a girl. There is an inevitable reminiscence of Edward Gibbon's famous account of the Christian virgins of the fiery clime of Africa who so gloried in their chastity that they occasionally ventured to share their beds with the deacons. Outraged nature, said Gibbon, sometimes took her revenge, so it may have happened with the Abelites.

ABIGAIL

description used for a lady's maid. The term is frequent in older English literature and may have gained something from the position of Abigail Hill, Mrs Masham, the influential lady-in-waiting to Queen Anne. Mrs Masham was first cousin to Sarah Churchill, Duchess of Marlborough, who introduced her to Queen Anne as a bed-chamber woman. Abigail succeeded in supplanting Sarah and in 1712 became Lady Masham, as her husband was one of the twelve Tory peers who were required in a peer-packing operation to secure passage through the House of Lords of Tory policy.

ABSALOM

a Christian name from the Hebrew, 'father of peace', the name of King David's favourite son (II Samuel xiv. 26) used by Chaucer as a nickname for a man with a fine head of hair.

ACCIDENCY, HIS

historical term applied to President of the USA, Chester Alan Arthur because he succeeded President Garfield who had been assassinated; also used of President Andrew Johnson because he succeeded Lincoln in the same way in 1865.

ACHILLES

Albert III (1414–86), Elector of Brandenburg 1470–86, was called Achilles after the celebrated hero of the *Iliad* because of his energy, strength and bravery.

Likewise, the Achilles statue in Hyde Park refers to the Achilles of England, the Duke of Wellington.

ADAMITES

an early Christian sect, at first in North Africa which advocated nudity and avoided marriage, on the example of Adam at his creation. In later times a similar sect arose in the excesses of the Reformation period which practised various kinds of sexual promiscuity.

ADIAPHORISTS

a party in German Protestantism which held that some parts of Catholic doctrine and practice were indifferent (from Greek α'διάφορα, things indifferent) and would not therefore interfere with Protestant principles.

ADMIRABLE CRICHTON, The

James Crichton (1560–85), Scots scholar and swordsman, so termed by Sir Thomas Urquhart; the subject title of one of Harrison Ainsworth's romances.

ADOPTIANISM

heresy of the eighth century in Spain which regarded Jesus Christ as only the adopted Son of God. Like many other formerly regarded as defunct heresies it is extensively held (perhaps unconsciously) by modern clerics.

ADULLAMITES

those who seceded from the Reform party in 1866. John Bright said that in effect they retired to the cave of Adullam like David who then gathered to himself all disaffected men (1 Samuel xxii. 1 and 2).

ADVENTISTS

more often called Second Adventists, a Christian sect which holds the belief that the Second Coming of Christ is imminent; usually an actual date is given, for example by the founder of the sect William Miller (1782–1849) who fixed the Coming in 1843–4 (quite contrary to Christ's own declaration in St Matthew xxiv. 36). In the present century dates have been given and passed.

AELURUS

Greek α'ίλουρος, 'weasel'; name given to Timothy (died 477) Monophysite Patriarch of Alexandria. The name was conferred by his enemies because he was short of stature.

AFRICAN, The

Hadrian, who died in 709 was so called, being an African by birth. He was offered the see of Canterbury by the Pope. He arrived in England in 670 where he became Abbot of the monastery of SS Peter and Paul and master of the school, thus working in England until his death. A great promoter of education.

AGNOSTIC

a person professing the impossibility of knowledge beyond that provided by the senses, supposed to have been coined by T. H. Huxley. The term has become very loosely used, often by people ignorant of its meaning, and is now more or less equivalent to atheism.

AHENOBARBUS

'yellow beard', originally a nickname which became the surname of a distinguished plebeian family of the Roman *gens Domitia*. The last of the Ahenobarbi was the Emperor Nero, who was adopted by the Emperor Claudius into the house of the Caesars.

AIGLON, L'

the Eaglet; term used by Bonapartists of Napoleon II (q.v.).

A JESU, Thomas

name of Diaz Sanchez de Avila (1564–1627), a Spanish Carmelite and a writer on mysticism.

À KEMPIS

i.e. from Kempen, near Cologne, the name of the famous spiritual writer Thomas à Kempis (c. 1380–1471), the author of the great Christian classic, *The Imitation of Christ*.

ALBIGENSES

from the city of Albi, in South-Western France, a large sect of heretics against whom a crusade was directed in 1209 which destroyed them. The father of Simon de Montfort was a principal leader in the Crusade. An excellent account is in Achille Luchaire's *Innocent III*, 6 vols, Paris 1904–8.

ALBIN

'white', from Latin *albinus* derivative of *albus*, similar to the well-known nickname, White.

ALCIBIADES

name given to Albert II (1522–57), Margrave of Brandenburg-Kulmbach, possibly because of the versatility of his career which resembled that of his Greek namesake whose undoubted brilliance ended in disaster. See E. F. Benson, *Alcibiades*, London, Benn, 1928.

ALCOFRIBAS, Nasier

the anagrammatic pseudonym under which were published some of François Rabelais's (c. 1494–1553) works.

ALEMANNI

or All-men. 'To denote at once their various lineage and their common bravery'; Edward Gibbon thus refers to the great swarm of the Suevi who in the reign of the Emperor Caracalla invaded the Roman Empire. 'The hasty army of volunteers gradually coalesced into a great and permanent nation, and as it was composed from so many different tribes, assumed the name of Alemanni' (*Decline and Fall*, ch. X).

ALEXANDER THE CORRECTOR

Alexander Cruden (1701–70) who compiled a work of encyclopedic detail in his *Concordance to the Bible*. He was a proofreader, sometimes experiencing a spell of lunacy, who went around wiping out wall writings.

ALEXANDER OF THE NORTH

Charles XII of Sweden (1682–1718), whose career is described very engagingly by Voltaire (*History of Charles XII*) and who was the subject of some caustic verses by Dr Johnson.

ALEXANDRIA, St Peter of

died c. 311, Bishop of Alexandria, a martyr under Emperor Maximin.

ALLMARK

also in the forms Almach and Hallmark is found in the thirteenth century as Halfmark, being derived from the coin, possibly a term for a miser or parsimonious person.

ALMANZOR

the victorious by the Grace of God, the title taken by Ibu Aby-Amir who in the tenth century contrived to make himself the real ruler of Moorish Spain under Husham II, one of the last Cordovan Caliphs.

Almanzor died in 1002 when a Monkish chronicler stated that he was 'buried in hell'. An interesting account of Almanzor is in S. Lane-Poole's *The Moors in Spain* (1897). One of the Abbasid Caliphs, Abu Ja'far, took the name of Al-Mansur, the divinely aided. He reigned as Caliph from 754 to 775.

ALOGI
a word coined from Greek ἄλογοι, to denote unreasonableness or disbelief in the Logos or Word of God (St John's Gospel, i). The name was applied by the Church to some heretics in Asia Minor in the second century, but their actual heresy is not clear.

ALP
a nickname from the name of the bullfinch, M.E. *alpe* c. 1400.

ALUMBRADOS
Spanish, 'enlightened'. A group of persons in sixteenth-century Spain of deep spiritual life.

AMANA SOCIETY
a name given to a small community at Amana, Iowa, where a settlement was made in 1855, but which originated in Germany in 1714, being known as the Community of True Inspiration.

AMBASSADOR OF THE AIR
Charles Augustus Lindbergh, aviator, also known as Lone Eagle and Lucky Lindy.

AMBLER
one with an ambling gait; in 1386 found as denoting an ambling horse or mule.

AMERICAN FABIUS, The
George Washington (1732–99), but a doubtful ascription as Washington's success against the British was really due to Sir William Howe's failure to follow up his two great victories over Washington at the White Hills and at Brandywine Creek.

AMOROUS, The
referring to King Philippe I of France (1052–1108) who sought to annul his marriage to his wife Berthe in order to marry Bertrada, the wife of Fulk, Count of Anjou, thus necessitating the annulment of the latter's marriage. The king succeeded in going through a form of marriage with Bertrada, was twice excommunicated for his marital adventures but managed to live with Bertrada till death did them part.

ANABAPTISTS
literally those who baptize a second time. Such a practice is unorthodox in both Catholic and Protestant religion in which baptism is a once for all not to be repeated sacrament. The Anabaptists arose soon after the opening of the Reformation. They were persecuted by both Protestants and Catholics. Some of them under John of Leiden set up a communistic, polygamous state at Munster (Greek α'να, and βαπτίζω).

ANACREON
of the twelfth century. Walter Map (c.1140–1210) author of *De Nugis Curialium* (trans. M. R. James, London, Hon. Soc. of Cymmrodorions, 1923) so termed because he wrote in praise of wine as Anacreon the ancient Greek poet had done. Hence the adjective anacreontic.

ANACREON MOORE — Thomas Moore (1779–1852), who translated Anacreon.

ANGEL or ANGELL — derived from the O.Fr. *angel*, Latin *angelus* and ultimately *angellos* (Gr.), a messenger, possibly used as nickname from one of the numerous players of angels in the Mystery Plays.

ANGEL OF THE SCHOOLS — St Thomas Aquinas; see Doctor Angelicus.

ANGELIC DOCTOR — St Thomas Aquinas, from the almost angelic quality of his intellect (*Motu Proprio* of Pope Pius X, *Doctoris Angelici*, 29 June 1914).

ANGLO-CATHOLIC — a term used first in 1838 to describe members of the High Church (q.v.) section in the Church of England. The word was used to describe the works of many Anglican divines in the seventeenth century, in the publication *The Library of Anglo-Catholic Theology* (1841), but the usage was retrospective.

ANIMOSUS — *see* The Courageous.

ANOTHER PLACE — the common form of reference in the House of Commons to the House of Lords.

ANOTHER ROSCIUS — Camden thus terms Richard Burbage (died 1619) a contemporary actor with Shakespeare who wrote the part of Hamlet with him in mind. 'He is fat and scant of breath', said of Hamlet, is thought to refer to Burbage's stoutness. See Roscius.

ANTINOMIANS — those who considered that by Christ's grace they were set free from observance of any moral law. This view existed among the Gnostics (q.v.) and like many other erroneous concepts of the early centuries, appeared again after the Reformation, e.g. among the Anabaptists (q.v.).

APE-CLOGGE — *see* Jack-a-Napes.

APOLLINARIANISM — term applied to teachings of Apollinarius (c. 310–90), Bishop of Laodicea, who taught views of Christ's manhood which made it incomplete, and not a perfect example for humankind.

APOSTATE, The — Emperor Julian who ruled the Roman Empire 361–4; brought up as a Christian, he reverted to paganism and tried to re-establish the classical pagan cult. He died while in warfare against the Persians. See G. W. Bowersick, *Julian the Apostate*, 1978.

APOSTLE OF ANDALUSIA — St John of Avila (1500–69) a Spanish mystic, an effective preacher.

APOSTLE OF AUSTRIA — St Severinus (died 482) a monk who worked at Noricum Ripense, and had great influence with the barbarians. A most appreciative account of him is in Charles Kingsley's *The Hermits*, 'St Severinus the Apostle of Noricum'. A man of God, come from the East, and ultimately from Roman Africa.

APOSTLE OF ENGLAND — St Augustine of Canterbury, c. 597 and first Archbishop of that See.

APOSTLE OF FRISIA	St Willibrord (658–739) a Northumbrian whose missionary exertions spread the gospel in Denmark and Thuringia.
APOSTLE OF GERMANY	St Boniface (680–754) an Englishman whose name Winfrith=Boniface, born at Crediton, Devon. Converted many Germans; hewed down Thor's Oak at Geismar and was martyred by German pagans.
APOSTLE OF HOLSTEIN	St Vicelin (c. 1090–1154) Bishop of Oldenburg 1149.
APOSTLE OF POMERANIA	St Otto, Bishop of Bamberg (1062–1139); canonized 1189.
APOSTLE OF ROME	St Philip Neri (1515–95), founder of the Oratorians (q.v.); canonized 1622.
APOSTLE OF TEMPERANCE	Father Theobald Matthew (1790–1856), an Irish Roman Catholic priest who preached among the Irish total abstinence from alcohol.
APOSTLE OF THE ARDENNES	St Hubert, died 727, the patron saint of huntsmen. He was Bishop of Liège. The story of his conversion is well known and often illustrated in art.
APOSTLE OF THE FRANKS	St Remigius (c. 438–533). He converted Clovis, King of the Franks.
APOSTLE OF THE GENTILES	St Paul; see Romans xi. 13.
APOSTLE OF THE GOTHS	Ulphilas (c. 311–83) born among the Goths, and their missionary bishop. He translated the Bible into Gothic, omitting, it is said, the books of Kings as he thought their warlike character would be a bad influence on his converts. He was led into Arianism through his connection with Eusebius of Nicomedia, with the result that the Goths remained in the Arian heresy for a long time. As Ulphilas's version of the Bible was the only book in the Gothic language, the remains of his translation from Greek form an important part in English linguistic studies. See Wright's *Grammar of the Gothic Language*, 2nd edn by O. L. Sayce, Oxford University Press, 1972, which contains the Gospel of St Mark, selections from the other Gospels and the 2nd Epistle to Timothy.
APOSTLE OF THE IRISH	St Patrick (c. 390–460).
APOSTLE OF THE NEGROES	St Peter Claver (1581–1654), who devoted himself to the care and conversion of the negro slaves.
APOSTLE OF THE NORTH	St Hyacinth (1185–1257); canonized in 1594. He was a Dominican, born in Poland (where he is known as St Iaacho), who undertook extensive missionary work in Scandinavia. St Anskar (801–65). He began the conversion of the Scandinavian countries. Bernard Gilpin (1517–83) who made many successful journeys in the north of England in the post-Reformation breakdown in religion.

APOSTLE OF THE RUSSIANS AND RUTHENIANS

St Vladimir (956–1015), a military evangelist who employed force in the work of conversion.

APOSTLE OF VIENNA

St Clement Mary Hofbauer (1751–1820), worked zealously in Warsaw, and from 1800 in Vienna where he had great success. Canonized 1909.

APOSTOLIC KING, The

the King of Hungary. The title is supposed to have been given by Sylvester II to the first Hungarian king, Stephen I (died 1038) on account of his apostolic zeal. He was also called His Apostolic Majesty.

APRIL

derived from the name of the month. When used as a surname it is usually a nickname with reference to changeableness, i.e. April weather. Latin *Aprilis*.

AQUARIANS

a sect in the early Church which used water in place of wine in the Holy Communion.

ARABIAN, The

Philip, Emperor of Rome 248. He celebrated the secular games now renewed for the fifth time, on the accomplishment of the full period of a thousand years from the foundation of Rome (Gibbon, *Decline and Fall*, ch. VII). He reigned only until 250 when he was either killed in battle or murdered soon after.

AREOPAGITE, The

referring to Dionysius who is mentioned in Acts xvii. 34, as having been converted by St Paul when the Apostle preached to members of the Areopagus. The latter was a council which met on a hill north west of the Acropolis at Athens. In medieval times he was confused with a mystical theologian (c. 500) of the same name. The original Christian Areopagite was described by Dionysius, Bishop of Corinth c. 170, as having been the first Bishop of Athens.

ARGENT, HARGENT, LARGENT

Latin *argentum*, silver. Found in the twelfth century denoting a person with silver white hair. Still in use as a surname.

ARIANS, ARIANISM

followers and teachings of Arius (c. 250–336), a priest of Alexandria who denied the real Deity of Christ. Arius taught that while Christ was higher than any other created being, He was still created. Condemned by the Church in the first Ecumenical Council at Nicaea in 325. The Nicene Creed is the Catholic answer to Arianism.

ARIOSTO OF THE NORTH

Lord Byron's description of Sir Walter Scott (*Childe Harold's Pilgrimage*, iv. 40).

ARLISS, HARLISS

from O.E. *eare* and *leas* – earless, a somewhat crude jibe at a deprived person, probably by mutilation.

ARMAGNACS

the name of a party in the fourteenth century in France which arose when the Duke of Burgundy arranged the murder of Louis, Duc d'Orléans, brother of Charles VI of France in 1407. Charles, son of Louis, married Bonne, daughter of Bernard VII, Count of Armagnac, who led the coalition against the murderer and his followers the Bourguignons (q.v.). Later troops of Gascon mercenaries were known as Armagnacs.

ARMINIANS those who agree with Jacobus Arminius, Dutch theologian (1560–1609) who opposed the Calvinistic doctrine of predestination and who taught that Christ died for all men, not simply for the elect.

ARTHUR THE GENTLEMAN President of the USA Chester Alan Arthur.

ARUNDEL from O.Fr. *arondel*, little swallow, modern Fr. *hirondelle*. When used as nickname this is its origin. The place name in Sussex was stronger than the nickname, but the latter supplied the reference in the arms of the extinct Lords Arundell of Wardour who bore six swallows in their coat. (Arundell of Wardour cr. 1605, ext. 1944 (L. G. Pine, *New Extinct Peerage*, 1972).)

ASCETIC, The St Nilus (died c. 430) Bishop of Ancyra, founder of a monastery near Ancyra. A considerable writer.

ASSASSIN a name derived from *haskiski* and used in Syria of the local branch of the Ismaili Sect of Shi'ite Moslems founded in Persia at the end of the eleventh century by Hassan-ben-Sabah. He founded and organized the religious body known later as the Hashishiyan or Assassins. He established his headquarters in 1090 in Khorassan in the impregnable citadel of Alamut, the Eagle's Nest (Sir Steven Runciman, *A History of the Crusades*, Cambridge University Press, 1951–4, vol. 2, ch.vi). At first ben-Sabah's attacks were directed against the Fatimid Caliphs, but were extended over many lands of the east. His terrorist followers were marked by the most complete indifference to their own fate.

ASTROPHEL AND STELLA Sir Philip Sidney and Penelope Devereux. He lived from 1554 to 1586 when he died at the battle of Zutphen in Holland. His life and writings were as brilliant as his death was heroic. His name of Astrophel is composed from the Greek *astron* (star) plus *philos* (lover), the star being Penelope.

ATATÜRK Father of the Turks, the title given by the Grand National Assembly to Mustapha Kemal, who brought Turkey out of the disorders of the 1914–18 war and made it a unified and modern state. He lived 1881–1938 and was President of Turkey 1923–38.

ATHANASIUS OF THE WEST St Hilary of Poitiers (c. 315–67) Bishop of Poitiers, who upheld the teachings of St Athanasius, the great opponents of the Arians (q.v.).

ATHENS OF THE NORTH Edinburgh, partly from physical appearance, but mainly for the brilliance of intellect which graced the city in the eighteenth and nineteenth centuries.

ATTER O.E. *ator*, M.E. *atter*, meaning poison, gall, venom, bitterness. An early example is Edwin atre.

ATTERDAG the name given in later time to Valdemar IV, King of Denmark (1340–75).

AUDIANI the followers of one Audius, a fourth century layman, who thought the clergy too secularized and was also accused of attributing bodily form to the Godhead.

AUGUSTUS

Philip II of France (1165–1223), so called because he was born in August, but not unworthily named, for like the Emperor Augustus he was a wise and politic ruler.

AUJI

huntsman. Mohammed IV (1642–93) Ottoman Sultan of Turkey (1648–87). Although he took part in military expeditions he preferred to devote his energies to the chase, hence his nickname. His expenditure was vast. At the battle of Mohács in Hungary in 1687 his army was defeated and he was dethroned.

AULETES

flute-player. Ptolemy XII of Egypt became king in 80 B.C. and died in 51. He was father of the famous Cleopatra, last of the Ptolemies, the Macedonian dynasty of Egypt which ruled for 300 years.

AUVERGNE, William of

(c. 1180–1249) French scholastic philosopher and theologian.

AUXERRE, William of

(died 1231) a French scholastic theologian.

AVILA, St Teresa of

the great Spanish Carmelite nun and mystic (1515–82), called more formally St Teresa of Jesus.

AVRANCHES, Hugh of

see The Fat and also Lupus.

AYRSHIRE POET

Robert Burns (1759–96).

AZTEC

comes from *Azthan* = white land, the traditional origin of the Aztecs who ruled Mexico for less than three centuries until overthrown by Hernán Cortés between 1519 and 1521. The Aztecs were also called Tenochea, a name derived from a legendary patriarch, Tenoch. Hence Tenochtitlán ('stone rising in the water'), the pre-Spanish name of Mexico City.

B

BABA

'Father of the Nation', name given to Ahmad Shah who died c. 1773 and who founded the Durrani dynasty in Afghanistan.

BABB

Babs, a diminutive or pet name from Barbara, but when occurring as le Babbe, a nickname for a young child.

'BABE' RUTH

Herman Ruth, an American baseball player (1895–1948), scored 714 regular season home runs.

BABY CHARLES

Charles I, so called by his father James I of Britain.

BABYFACE NELSON

an American gangster, George Nelson.

BACHELOR PRESIDENT

James Buchanan (1857–61).

BACK, BAX

from O.E. *balc, bakka,* meaning one with a prominent back or chin. Another source is M.E. *bakke,* a bat, referring to someone preferring darkness to light.

BAD, The

Albert, Landgrave of Thuringia and Margrave of Meissen who died in 1314.
Charles II (1332–87), King of Navarre.
William I, King of Sicily,1154–66.

BADINGUET

Napoleon III who in his pre-imperial career escaped from the fortress of Ham in 1846, in the clothes of a workman whose name was said to be Badinguet.

BAKER, The

Louis XVI, name given by the mob when they brought the King back to Versailles after his attempted escape. La Boulangère, the baker's wife, was the Queen, Marie Antoinette.

BALAFRÉ, Le

'the gashed'; said of some fighters who had received some frightful blows on the face. Henri, 2nd Duke of Guise (1550–88) and his son François, 3rd Duke. Sir Walter Scott borrowed the term for his Scottish guardsman, Ludovic Lesly, Le Balafré, uncle of the hero, Quentin Durward.

BALD

M.E. *ballede,* round-bellied, later bald; balding of same origin.

BALD, The

Charles II of France, reigned 843–77.

BALLARD

a bald-headed man, M.E. *bald* plus -ard. When Eycliff translated the famous passage about Elisha and the rude children, he used ballard where later usage was baldhead.

BALLON

sometimes denoting a little fat man, from O.Fr. *balon,* little ball or pack, more often denoting a packer by trade.

BAPTISTS

the name of some 28 million church members throughout the world. The name originated in the seventeenth century, the denomination being an offshoot from Congregationalism (q.v.). The name is derived from the church's insistence on adult baptism only, contrary to the Christian Church's practice for many centuries of infant baptism.

BARADAECUS

meaning 'beggar', nickname of Jacob Baradaecus, founder of the Syrian Jacobites (q.v.), because he wandered about from Egypt to the Euphrates dressed as a beggar to prevent himself being arrested by the Orthodox.

BARBARIANS

the Chinese and Japanese term for people from Europe. Those from Spain and Portugal were the southern barbarians; those from the northern countries like Britain were the red-haired barbarians.

BARBAROSSA

'Red Beard'. Frederick I (1122–90) Holy Roman Emperor and German King, having succeeded his uncle, Conrad III, in 1152. He became a crusader but in the Third Crusade he was drowned in the river Saleph in Cilicia.
    Khaireddin Barbarossa, a pirate who was Bey of Algiers in 1518. In 1537 appointed Admiral of the Turkish fleet (see Ernle Bradford, *The Sultan's Admiral: The Life of Barbarossa*, London, Hodder & Stoughton, 1969). There it is stated (p. ix) that it was Khaireddin's brother Aruj who had had the red beard commemorated in the nickname.

BARBE

'beard'. O.Fr. *barbe*.

BARBER POET

Jacques Jasmin, Provençal poet and barber (1798–1861).

BARD OF AVON

William Shakespeare.

BARD OF HOPE

Thomas Campbell (1777–1844) wrote *The Pleasures of Hope*.

BARD OF MEMORY

Samuel Rogers (1763–1855) banker and poet.

BARD OF OLNEY

William Cowper (1731–1800) who lived at Olney, Buckinghamshire.

BARD OF PROSE

Boccaccio (1313–75), author of *The Decameron*, so styled by Lord Byron in *Childe Harold*, iv.

BARD OF RYDAL MOUNT

William Wordsworth (1770–1850), who lived there in Westmorland.

BARD OF THE IMAGINATION

Mark Akenside (1721–70) wrote *Pleasures of the Imagination*.

BARD OF TWICKENHAM

Alexander Pope (1688–1744) lived at Twickenham.

BARE

meaning unarmed or defenceless, from O.E. *baer*.

BAREFOOT, BARFOOT

'barefooted'. O.E. *baer* and *fot*. The friars were barefooted, also in some cases pilgrims and also those doing penance. *See* Barfot.

BARFOT or BARELEG

Magnus II, King of Norway, reigned 1093–1103, subdued the Hebrides and the Isle of Man, fought in Wales and died fighting in Ireland. In the course of his expedition he came on the island of Anglesey. He quite incidentally took part with the Welsh against the

Norman Earl Hugh the Proud of Chester. 'In the midst of the conflict he fell, pierced through the eye by an arrow which was universally believed to have been aimed by Magnus himself' (Sir John Lloyd, *History of Wales*, London, Longman, 1948, p. 409).

BARNABITES   popular name of a small religious order founded at Milan in 1530 by St Antonio Maria Zaccaria, and derived from their church of St Barnabus at Milan. Official title, Clerks Regular of St Paul.

BARRATT, BARRETT   This common name comes from O.Fr. *barat*, meaning commerce or business dealing, but in M.E. came to denote deception or fraud, hence a nickname of a trickster.

BARRELL   an occupational name for a maker of barrels, but also acquired the sense of a nickname, as of a person with a large belly; as H. P. Pirie Gordon remarks (*Burke's Landed Gentry*, 1937) a 'fat chap'. From O.Fr. *baril* = barrel.

BASELEY, BAZELEY, BASIL   'Kingly' from O.Fr. *basile via* Latin *basilius* and ultimately Greek βασίλειος.

BASK   from O.N. *beiskr*, bitter or acrid, i.e. being unpleasant to the senses, probably an allusion to something unpleasant about a person, such as body odour.

BASS   O.Fr. *bas*, M.E. *bass*, of short height.

BASSET(T)   from O.Fr. *basset*, of low stature. It also acquired a meaning of lowness in a social sense, e.g. one of the most powerful Norman families in post-Conquest England had as its founder Ralph Basset of whose antecedents even Sir Bernard Burke found nothing to say. In the expressive description of a great Assyrian king, Basset was 'the son of no one' or in the words of Ordericus Vitalis, *de ignobili stirpe ac de pulvere*.

BASTARD   found as early as 1086 in Domesday Book. Its use as a stigma very much related to the social position of the bearer, e.g. William the Conqueror often referred to himself as William Bastard. Similarly in the duchy of Burgundy, *le Grand Bâtard de Bourgogne* is represented under this title (fourteenth century). Contrariwise, the poor and obscure are mentioned in English parish registers as base-born son or daughter. See also Mamzer. A notable English family owes its surname to an illegitimate man, the Bastards of Kitley.

BASTON   from O.Fr. *bastin*, a stick, used as a nickname for a slow or dull person.

BATTLER, The   Alfonso I (c. 1073–1134), King of Aragon and Navarre 1104–34.

BAUD   O.Fr. *baud*, gay or sprightly.

BAVARIAN, The   Louis IV (1282–1347), Holy Roman Emperor from 1328, also Duke of Bavaria from 1294 and German King from 1314.

BAY STATE

Massachusetts, one of the original Thirteen Colonies, when it was always known as 'The Colony of Massachusetts Bay'.

BAYARD

O.Fr. *baiart, barard,* bay coloured, applied to horses, but also in certain cases to a proud disposition. See, however, Le Chevalier Bayard.

BAYARD OF THE EAST, The

Sir James Outram (1803–63) who was called this by Sir Charles Napier at a banquet in Outram's honour. Outram was a brave and chivalrous soldier.

B. B.

Brigitte Bardot, French film actress.

BEAL (E)

O.Fr. *bele,* beautiful, found as a surname as early as 1194 in Curia Regis Rolls.

BEAN

M.E. *bene* meaning pleasant or kindly; can also come from O.E. *bean,* a bean, i.e. a thing of little worth.

BEAR, The

Albert I (c. 1100–70), Margrave of Brandenburg, was one of the leaders of German expansion in eastern Europe in the twelfth century. His name is traced to its use by Helmold, the contemporary historian of German expansion in the north.

BEARD

O.E. denoting a bearded man, found as description as early as 1100.

BEARD, The

term of ridicule applied by the inhabitants of Antioch to the Emperor Julian the Apostate. The Emperor compiled a satire *Misopogon,* beard-hater, on the licentious and effeminate manners of Antioch. This imperial reply was publicly exposed before the gates of the palace, and the *Misopogon* still remains a singular monument of the resentment, the wit, the humanity, and the indiscretion of Julian (Edward Gibbon, *Decline and Fall,* ch. XXIV).

BEARDED, The

Baldwin IV, Count of Flanders (988–1036).
Geoffrey Bouchard, crusader, of the family of Montmorency.
Henry I of Silesia (1201–38); see also Pogonatus.

BEARDED MASTER

(*Magister Barbatus*); thus Persius (Aulus Persius Flaccus), A.D. 34–62, the Latin poet and satirist, styles Socrates, the idea being that the beard is a sign of wisdom.

BEATER, BETTER

O.E. *beatere,* a fighter or champion, could also mean a quarrelsome man.

BEAU, The

Arthur Wellesley, 1st Duke of Wellington, because of his passion for neatness in dress.

BEAU BRUMMELL

George Bryan Brummell (1778–1840) an English dandy whose absorption with fashion made him the ruler of the mode. He was at first a great favourite with the Prince Regent, the First Gentleman in Europe (q.v.), but on quarrelling with the Prince, Brummell experienced vicissitudes of fortune until he died in an asylum at Caen.

BEAU NASH

real name, Richard Nash (1674–1762). He went in 1705

to Bath where he became the leader of the social round as Master of Ceremonies. His greatest interest in life was fine and elegant clothes, hence his nickname.

BEAUCLERK
a fine scholar, distinguishing name of Henry I of England (1100–35). According to Hilaire Belloc, Henry could read some Greek, knew Latin and Anglo-Saxon, but habitually spoke French (*History of England*, London, Methuen, vol. II). In Prof. V. H. Galbraith's British Academy lecture, *The Literacy of the Medieval English Kings*, the nickname is dated from the fourteenth century and some reservations are expressed on Henry's scholarship.

BEAUTIFUL PARRICIDE
Beatrice Cenci (1777–99) member of the historical Roman family of Cenci. Beatrice with her brother Giacomo and her stepmother, Lucrezia, arranged the death of her father. They were tried under the papal government, convicted and executed. The whole story abounds in horrible details. See the poet P. B. Shelley's Preface to his poem *The Cenci*.

BEAUTY OF BUTTERMERE
Mary Robinson, married in 1802 to John Hatfield an impostor and bigamist, executed for forgery at Carlisle, 1803. Mentioned as the Maid of Buttermere by Wordsworth in *The Prelude* vii, 288.

BEAVER, BEEVER
O.E. *beofor*, a beaver, referring probably to a very industrious person; modern colloquialism – person with a beard.

BECK
in sense of nickname from O.Fr. *bec*, the beak of a bird, applied to a person's physiognomy. Also gave rise to Becket.

BECKET
St Thomas usually à Becket, Archbishop of Canterbury (c. 1118–70) leader of the opposition to Henry II of England's aim to have criminous clerks tried in the secular courts. Owing to some rash words uttered by Henry II, Becket was murdered in Canterbury Cathedral by four of the King's knights. He was canonized in 1173 and his shrine became one of the great centres of pilgrimage in Europe. This pilgrimage is the motif of Chaucer's great poem. See also Dean A. P. Stanley's *Memorials of Canterbury* (London, John Murray, 1854). St Thomas is often mentioned simply as 'of Canterbury'.

BEE
O.E. *bea*, denoting very active and industrious person.

BEEFEATERS
meaning the Yeomen of the Guard, instituted in 1485 by Henry VII. They still wear the Tudor style uniform. They fed well – with beef as a principal item in their diet.

BEGUINES AND BEGHARDS
the former an organization of women, the latter of men living in community but without formal vows in the Netherlands in the twelfth century. The names were supposed to come from Lambert le Bègue (i.e.

Stammerer), a revivalist preacher in Liège who died in 1177.

BELCH
O.E. *baelce*, a belch and also stomach. In some instances this gave rise to a nickname of (a) proud person or (b) a big heavy man.

BELDAM
Anglo-Fr. *beledame*, a fine lady, in derogatory sense, becoming a synonym in sixteenth century of an aged woman.

BELHAM
O.Fr. *bel*, beautiful, and *homme*, man.

BELIAL
a Hebrew word meaning a loose and worthless person; sons of Belial is a very pejorative term in the Old Testament. In *Paradise Lost*, John Milton makes Belial one of the chief among the fallen angels, but in *Paradise Regained* he earns Satan's scorn for his obsession with women: 'A fairer spirit lost not heaven.'

BELL-THE-CAT
the name borne by Archibald Douglas 5th Earl of Angus, who died in 1514, because he had slain those he deemed the unworthy favourites of King James III of Scotland. 'Princes and favourites long grew tame and trembled at the homely name of Archibald Bell-the-Cat' (Sir Walter Scott, *Marmion*, Canto V. XIV). The name is thus explained: James III was more interested in the arts than in the exercises admired by his nobility. In particular, the Scots lords objected to the King having made Cochrane, a mason, Earl of Mar. They took the opportunity in 1482 when they were gathered ostensibly to make war on England to hold a council in the church of Lauder. All agreed that the favourites should be removed. 'Lord Gray told the assembly the apologue of the mice who had formed a resolution that it would be highly advantageous to their community to tie a bell round the cat's neck, that they might hear her approach at a distance; but which measure unfortunately miscarried from no mouse being willing to undertake the task of fastening the bell. 'I understand the moral', said Angus, 'and that what we propose may not lack execution, I will bell-the-cat.' (Scott's notes to *Marmion*).

BELLE GABRIELLE, La
(1571–99) daughter of Antoine d'Estrées, at whose chateau Henry IV stayed one night, long enough for him to be in love with Gabrielle who became one of the King's forty mistresses.

BELLETT, BELLOT
O.Fr. *bel*, beautiful, being in form of diminutive.

BELLMAINE
O.Fr. *belle* and *mains*, beautiful hands. Curia Regis Rolls 1210.

BELOVED DISCIPLE, The
St John the Evangelist, mentioned in the Fourth Gospel as the disciple whom Jesus loved.

BELOVED PHYSICIAN, The
St Luke the Evangelist, thus called by St Paul in Colossians iv. 14.

BELTED WILL
Lord William Howard (1563–1640) son of the 4th Duke of Norfolk. The term was used by Sir Walter Scott in

The Lay of the Last Minstrel, referring to the belt which he wore. The Scots called him Bould Wullie, as being warden of the western borders or marches between England and Scotland.

BENBOW
Benbaugh, from Feet of Fines in Huntingdonshire; bendbow meaning an archer; also Bender, O.E. *bendan*, to bend.

BENDIGO
name of a town in Victoria, Australia, which officially is Sandhurst, is said to be derived from the nickname of William Thompson (1811–83) a noted pugilist. His sobriquet was Abednego, the name given by the chief of eunuchs to Azariah a companion of Daniel (Daniel i. 7).

BENEDICT
Latin *benedicte*, bless you, this being a favourite saying which caused this surname.

BENEDICT
a term for a bachelor but used in Shakespeare's play *Much Ado about Nothing* of a single man who marries Beatrice.

BENEDICTINES
the monks who observe the rules of St Benedict (c. 480–550) the founder of western European monasticism; the basic rules are threefold, prayer, study and manual work. St Benedict lived at Monte Cassino in southern Italy, magnificently restored after its destruction in 1944. Survival of European civilization in the Dark Ages (500–1000) would have been unlikely without the Benedictine Order.

BENN
supposed by some to be a nickname meaning a plump person and derived from O.E. *bynna* or *beona*.

BENT
corrupt; modern slang for a corrupt policeman, for instance; also for a homosexual.

BERARD
'bear', 'strong', (O.G.) reference to physique.

BEREANS
sometimes called Barclayans, a small sect long merged in the Congregationalists, founded by J. Barclay in 1773 at Edinburgh. They were so called from the passage in Acts xvii. 10 relating to the Jews of Berea who received the word with all eagerness, examining the Scriptures daily to see if these things were so. The Bereans did not believe in natural theology, but in the absolute supremacy of Scripture and its message to the individual soul.

BERNARD OF THE NORTH
the name given to St Ailred (1109–67), Abbot of Rievaulx, who wrote many spiritual works at first by invitation of St Bernard of Clairvaux.

BERNARDINES
monks of the Order of St Bernard of Clairvaux (1090–1153) i.e. of the Cistercian Order.

BERTHE (or BERTRADA) AU GRAND PIED
the mother of Charlemagne, so called as she had a club foot.

BESS OF HARDWICK
Elizabeth (who died 13 February 1607) daughter of John Hardwick of Hardwick, Derbyshire. She had a hobby – collecting husbands – and a ruling passion – building. She married (1) Robert Barley and inherited his estate;

(2) Sir William St Loe; (3) the 6th Earl of Shrewsbury; and (4) Sir William Cavendish. She long outlived her last husband. She left to her son, Sir William Cavendish, 1st Earl of Devonshire, 'three of the most splendid seats ever raised by one hand within the same county (erected by her) namely Chatsworth, Hardwick and Oldcotes'. It was said that as long as Bess went on building she would live. A fall of snow held up the builders and she died.

BESSIE WI' THE BRAID APRON   wife of Belted Will (q.v.).

BEST(E)   O.Fr. *beste*, denoting a brutal man.

BETHLEHEMITES   the name given to (a) certain now extinct military orders designed for defence against the Turks, and (b) a reformed Order of Dominicans (c) an order established in Guatemala in 1655 to tend the sick and (d) the followers of John Huss because he preached in a church in Prague called Bethlehem.

BEVERIDGE   O.Fr. *bevrege*, a drink. In older days the word denoted a drink which bound a bargain. Dr Reaney (*Dictionary of British Surnames*, London, Routledge & Kegan Paul, 1958) gives the explanation that as a nickname it 'may well have been bestowed on a man who made a practice of getting free drinks for clinching bargains he had no intention of keeping'.

BEVIN   O.Fr. *boi vin*, a wine drinker.

BEW   O.Fr. *bel*, *beu*, beautiful.

BIANCHI   (whites) and Neri (blacks) branches of the Guelphs (q.v.).

BIBERIUS CALDIUS MERO   a punning variant of the names of the Second Roman Emperor Tiberius (reigned A.D. 14–37), Tiberius Claudius Nero; Biberius – drink loving, and Calidus (i.e. Caldius) mero, flushed with wine. Tiberius was adopted son, step-son, son-in-law and successor of Augustus.

BIBLE CHRISTIANS   a small body which originated from the work of William O'Bryan (1778–1868) a local Methodist preacher in Devon. Doctrinal differences between the Bryanites and Methodism seem not to have been of importance and in 1907 the Bible Christians were one of the bodies which formed the United Methodist Church. The term Bible Christians is used, however, in what may be termed a non-organizational sense, of persons who adopt the Bible as their sole rule of faith and conduct and are perhaps to be equated with Fundamentalism (q.v.).

BIDEFORD POSTMAN   Edward Capern (1815–94) the poet, from his occupation and abode.

BIG BEN   The large bell in the Clock Tower on the Houses of Parliament at Westminster and named from Sir Benjamin Hall, who was Commissioner of Works in 1856; used of the clock itself.

BIG FELLOW, The Michael Collins (1890–1922) the principal leader in the Irish revolt against Great Britain; accepted 1921 Treaty which set up the state of Eire, but was killed in the civil war of the Irish which followed acceptance of the Treaty.

BIG TOM the bell and clock of the tower of Bristol University.

BIGG(E) M.E. *bigge*, strong or large.

BILES, BYLES O.E. *bile* = bill or beak of a bird. Not always a nickname, but sometimes used of a place having a beaklike form.

BILIOUS BALE John Bale (1495–1563). Originally a monk at Norwich who renounced celibacy and became an ardent reformer. In 1552 was made Bishop of Ossory in Ireland but sought refuge abroad under Mary I, not returning to England until 1559.

BILLY THE KID William H. Bonney (1859–81), American outlaw and gunman who was caught in 1880 and sentenced to be hanged for three murders. He escaped from gaol in 1881 having killed two deputies, but was eventually shot by Pat Garrett, the sheriff of Lincoln County.

BIRD, BYRD, BRIDE O.E. *bridd*, bird, referring to birdlike appearance and (sometimes possibly) to a bird-catcher. As to spelling br, cf. Chaucer's 'Listen these blissful brides how they sing.'

BIRMINGHAM POET John Freeth (c. 1808).

BISHOP found in 1086 Domesday Book in form Biscop, O.E. *Bisc(e)op*. Reaney (*Dict. of British Surnames*) states, 'a nickname for one with the appearance or bearing of a bishop, or a pageant name from the custom of electing a boy-bishop on St. Nicholas's day'. It is remarkable how early it appears, before the mystery plays were in vogue.

BISHOP OF ALL OUTDOORS Sheldon Jackson (1834–1909), American missionary.

BISMIRE O.E. *bismer* or *bismor*, shame or disgrace, hence a low person, worthy of scorn.

BISS O.Fr. and M.E. *bis*, brownish or dark grey, in complexion. Cf. a diminutive Bissett, O.Fr. *biset*, dark.

BLACK, BLACKE O.E. *blaec*, dark-complexioned. Wilfricus Niger (c. 1080) as called by Dr Reaney is an instance of Black as a nickname, because (Charles Kingsley's *Hereward the Wake*, ch. 23) 'Wluncles the Blackface, so called because he once blackened his face with coal, and came unknown among the enemy and slew ten of them with one lance'.

BLACK, The Henry, Duke of Bavaria, c. 1100, married Wulfhild, daughter of Magnus Billung, Duke of Saxony.
  Henry III, German King, Emperor from 1039, reformed the papacy which had produced three rival

Popes, all of whom he arranged to depose. Nickname may be due to colour.

BLACK AGNES

the palfrey given to Mary Queen of Scots by her half-brother, Moray, and named after the famous Agnes, Countess of Dunbar.

BLACK AND TANS

members of a force recruited in 1920 for service in Ireland against Sinn Fein rebels. 'Against Sinn Fein . . . the Government fell back upon its own men who had not forgotten their fighting. They reinforced the Royal Irish Constabulary by enlisting demobilized men who had not settled down in civil life. Wearing with their khaki the dark caps of the R. I. C. they were attaining a grim notoriety as "The Black and Tans"' (P. H. Gretton, *A Modern History of the English People*, London, Martin Secker, p. 1130).

BLACK BESS

the mare ridden by the famous Dick Turpin. He is supposed to have ridden the mare from London to York. A fictitious account is in W. Harrison Ainsworth's novel *Rookwood* (1834).

BLACK COMYN or DOUGLAS

see Red Comyn.

BLACK DAN

US politician Daniel Webster (1782–1852), from his black hair and eyes, also 'the god-like Daniel' and 'the Great Stone Face'.

BLACK DOUGLAS

Sir William Douglas, Lord of Nithsdale, died c. 1392.

BLACK FRIARS

Dominicans (q.v.), called thus from the black *cappa* or mantle worn over their white habits.

BLACK JACK

the nickname earned by General John Joseph Pershing's stern bearing and rigid discipline, also because of his success in commanding black troops. Pershing was the commander in chief of the American troops in Europe in the First World War. Pershing (1860–1948) created the American Expeditionary Force. He recommended an army of 1 million men by 1918 and of 3 millions by 1919. He returned from Europe to America with a great reputation and in 1919 was given the rank of General of the Armies, a title created for George Washington in 1799, but never held by him. His organization of the A. E. F. which gave him 38 divisions for the final advance in October 1918 was a most outstanding achievement.

BLACK MAN, The

John (Jovan) Nenad had a following among the Serbs of Hungary and assumed the title of Czar (i.e. of Serbia) but was killed in 1527.

BLACK MONKS

The Benedictines who wore black habits; also known as Black Canons.

BLACK MOSES

Harriet Taberan, a black woman, US abolitionist.

BLACK POPE

the General of the Jesuits (q.v.).

BLACK PRINCE, The

Edward of Woodstock (1330–77) the eldest son of Edward III of England, who predeceased his father. The sobriquet was invented by the Elizabethans, 'for in his lifetime he was known as Edward of Woodstock (from his place of birth) or more usually as the Prince of Wales. In 1563 the chronicler Grafton was the first to refer to him as the Black Prince, claiming without substantiating it, that the French had used to call him "Le Neoir". Shakespeare read Grafton's *Chronicle of England* and used it as a source for his histories. Once Shakespeare's *Henry V* had been enjoined to emulate his great uncle, the Black Prince, previous names were cast aside' (Barbara Emerson, *The Black Prince*, London, Weidenfeld & Nicolson, 1976, p. 1). 'Allegedly from the colour of his armour, but possibly because of his fierce prosecution of war in France where he left behind him a trail of burnings' (L. G. Pine, *Princes of Wales*, Newton Abbot, David & Charles, 1970, p. 47). Bernard Shaw puts into St Joan's mouth an allusion to the Prince's ravaging in France which earned him the title of Black.

BLACK TOM
James Butler, 1st Duke of Ormonde, appointed in 1644 by King Charles I as Lord Lieutenant of Ireland. So called for harsh behaviour and grim looks. He was replaced as Lord Lieutenant in 1645 but again appointed (for the year only) in 1648.

BLACK WATCH
were originally companies of Highlanders recruited by the British government to police the Highland Line in Scotland and prevent raiding of the Lowlands by the Highland clans in pursuance of blackmail. They wore a dark tartan which can therefore be regarded as a government issue, and is hence permissible wear by those who do not belong to a highland clan. The Black Watch later became one of the most distinguished regiments in the British Army (see L. G. Pine, *The Highland Clans*, Newton Abbot, David & Charles, 1972, p. 145).

BLACKBIRD
O.E. *blace beard*, blackbeard. Cf. 'Blackbeard', Edward Teach or Thatch (died 1718) the most famous pirate, said to have been a Bristolian. Cf. also the diminutive Blackett.

BLACKFELLOW
name used of the aborigines of Australia, although they are not black, though very dark.

BLACKLOCK
O.E. *blace loce*, black hair.

BLACKMAN
O.E. *blaecmann*, darkman.

BLAMPHEY, BLAMPIED
O.Fr. *blanc pied*, whitefoot.

BLAMPHIN
O.Fr. *blanc pain*, white bread, i.e. a baker.

BLANC, BLANK
O.Fr. *blanc*, white in hair or complexion, cf. Siward le blanc (Kingsley, *Hereward the Wake*, ch. 4).

BLANCHARD
O.Fr. *blanchart*, whitish, reference to hair or complexion.

BLANCHET
O.Fr. *blankete*, M.E. *blankett*, meaning white stuff for clothing, and probably the name used as nickname for one who made or sold cloth.

BLANCHFLOWER
O.Fr. *blance fleur*, a white or fair flower as pet name for

a female; for a male it implied effeminacy.

BLENCH

O.E. *blenc*, a trick.

BLESSED, BLEST, BLISSETT

O.E. verb *bletsian*, to make sacred, in a later sense it denoted one fortunate.

BLEWETT, BLUETT

O.Fr. *bluet*, bluish, a diminutive of *bleu*.

BLIND

O.E. *blind*.

BLIND, The

Didymus the Blind (c. 313–98), an Alexandrian theologian who was blind from his infancy. He was a learned scholar who wrote many books and St Athanasius made him head of the Cathetical school at Alexandria.

Louis III (c. 880–928), Holy Roman Emperor 901–5, son of Boso, King of Provence; in 905 he was surprised at Verona by Berengan of Friuli who blinded him and sent him back to Provence.

Magnus III (1130–9), King of Norway.

BLIND HARPER, The

John Parry (died 1782) published Welsh music.

BLIND HARRY

a Scottish poet who wrote a long poem on Sir William Wallace and who lived c. 1470–92. Known as Harry the Minstrel.

BLIND MAGISTRATE

Sir John Fielding who was born blind. He served as J. P. in Middlesex, Surrey, Essex and Westminster and died in 1761.

BLISS

O.E. *bliths*, M.E. *blisse*, gladness, joy.

BLONDEL, BLUNDEL, BLUNDAL

O.Fr. *blondel*, a diminutive of *blond* = fair in hair or complexion.

BLOOD AND GUTS

American general George Smith Patton (1885–1945), a successful fighting general in both world wars, but of ungovernable temper, whose career was ended when he struck an enlisted man.

BLOODAXE, Eric

son of Harold Haarfager, King of Norway (q.v.). Eric made Norway too hot to keep him and had to leave c. 945. He settled at York where he made himself king of that area.

BLOODY, The

Otho II of Germany, Holy Roman Emperor, born 955, reigned 973–83.

BLOODY BUTCHER, The

Duke of Cumberland (1721–65), the 2nd son of King George II of Britain. Cumberland, known to his men as Royal Billy, was the victor of Culloden in 1746. There his army beat Bonnie Prince Charlie and his following of Highland clansmen, but it was his cruelties in seeking out the rebels afterwards which earned him the nickname. (For full account, see L. G. Pine, *The Highland Clans*, Newton Abbot, David & Charles, 1972.)

BLOODY MARY

the well known epithet applied to Queen Mary I (1553–8) of England because of her persecution of Protestants. 'As Bloody Mary this woman has become famous and Bloody Queen Mary she will ever be justly remembered with horror and detestation in

Great Britain' (Charles Dickens, *A Child's History of England*, ch. XXX). Five Anglican Bishops and 300 other people were burned alive because of their religious opinions in four years of Mary's reign.

BLOSSOM O.E. *blostura*, of one who is lovely and full of promise.

BLUEBEARD according to the chronicler Holinshed, the original was Gilles de Retz (or, as more usual, Rais), Marquis de Laval, who was accused of murdering six of his seven wives, and also of child murder in obscene rites. He was executed in 1440. His later behaviour is described in one of W. R. Crockett's historical novels. Gilles de Rais had been a companion in arms of Joan of Arc. He was a patron of the arts and kept a magnificent court but his extravagance led him into the practice of alchemy. 'He resorted to necromancy, satanism and finally the torture and ritual murder of kidnapped children, perhaps as many as 200' (*Encyclopedia Britannica*, 14th edn).

BLUETOOTH Harold Blaatand, King of Denmark in the tenth century, converted the Danes to Christianity and conquered Norway.

BLUFF KING HAL Henry VIII, who could be a hearty good companion but is now accused of false bonhomie.

BLUNT, BLOUNT O.Fr. *blund*, with blond or yellow hair.

BLY, BLIGH O.E. *blithe*, meaning gentle or merry.

BOANERGES the surname given by Christ Himself to two of His disciples, James and John, the sons of Zebedee. The name means 'sons of thunder' and may have reference to the two men having loud voices.

BOAR, The Richard III, whose badge was the white boar, and so sometimes called a 'hog'. Sir Richard Radclyffe K. G., who was killed at Bosworth (1485) figures as 'the rat', with the King's other advisers, Sir William Catesby and Lord Lovell in the well-known distich, 'The catte, the ratte and Lovell our dogge Rule all England under a hogge'; *Burke's Landed Gentry*, 1952, sub. Scrope of Danby), where it is added that the author of the above distich, William Collingbourne, was arrested and promptly hanged at Tyburn.

BOAST, BOST M.E. *bost*, vain talk, bragging.

BOBBY the British policeman, a nickname possibly coming from Sir Robert Peel who instituted the Metropolitan Police Force in 1828. Also called Peelers, for an obvious reason.

BOFF, LEBOFF O.Fr. *boef*, bullock, used for a big fellow.

BOGG in one meaning derived from *bog* a nickname as saucy or bold.

BOGGERS, BOGGIS, BOGGS M.E. *bogeys*, meaning bragging, blustering.

BOGOMILS the name of a heretical sect which flourished from the tenth to the fifteenth centuries in S. E. Europe, possibly named from a priest Bogomil, c. 940. Largely embraced at the same time a spiritualizing movement which rejected marriage and also practised licentious living.

BOHEMIAN BRETHREN

later known as Moravian Brethren (q.v.).

BOHEMIANS

persons of artistic professions and living a loose and irregular life. Also applied originally to the gypsies who had lived in Bohemia before reaching western Europe. The gypsies were also sometimes referred to as Egyptians.

BOLD

O.E. *bald*, M.E. *bold*, stout-hearted or brave, but some forms are place names.

BOLD, The or LE HARDI

Philip III, King of France (1270–85); see also Le Hardi. Charles, 4th and last Duke of Burgundy (1433–77), son of Philip the Good (q.v.). He could have built a powerful European state but the impetuosity of character which gave him his nickname led him into fatal error. Twice defeated by the Swiss at Granson and Morat, he was finally defeated by them on 5 January 1477. He was killed in the battle and was found naked with mortal wounds and one cheek gnawed by wolves. Excellent studies of his wild character are given in Scott's romances, *Anne of Geierstein* and *Quentin Durward*.

BOLD BRIAREUS

The great composer Handel (1685–1759), thus described by Alexander Pope in *The Dunciad* iv 65:
'Strong in new arms, lo:
Giant Handel stands
Like bold Briareus, with a hundred hands.'

BOLLANDISTS

getting their name from John van Bolland (1596–1665), who founded and first edited the *Acta Sanctorum*, a comprehensive account of the lives of the Saints. The work is done by Jesuits who are exempt from the ordinary jurisdiction of the General of the Society. Over 60 volumes have appeared. The work is one of great scholarship.

BOLSHEVIK or BOLSHEVIST

lit. the majority (from an early communist voting), the Russian party which took power in 1917. Not often used now, having been replaced by Communist or Marxist.

BOMPS, BUMPUS

O.Fr. *bon pas*, good pace, reference to swift walking.

BON CHEVALIER, Le

Bayard. See Le Chevalier sans peur, etc.

BONAMY

O.Fr. *bon ami*, good friend.

BONHAM

O.Fr. *bon homme*, good man (in some cases a place name).

BONIFANT, BULLIVANT

Fr. *bon enfant*, good child.

BONNAN

O.Fr. *bon* and O.E. *hand*. Good hand.

BONNER M.E. *boner, bonour* and O.Fr. *bonnaire*, gentle, courteous.

BONNET LAIRDS in Scotland owners of small properties whose bonnets resembled those of ordinary people.

BONNIE DUNDEE John Graham of Claverhouse, 1st Viscount Dundee, killed at Killiecrankie, 1689. The peerage was attainted in 1716.

BONNIE PRINCE CHARLIE the Young Pretender, Prince Charles Edward, died 1788, elder son of the Old Pretender (q.v.). See also Young Pretender.

BOOK OF BOOKS The Bible, also the Good Book.

BOOKLOVER, The or THE LEARNED the name of Kolman (Kaloman), King of Hungary 1095–1116, a great legislator and administrator.

BORDER MINSTREL Sir Walter Scott for his collection of ballads, *The Minstrelsy of the Scottish Border*.

BORN(E) O.Fr. *borgne*, one-eyed or squint-eyed.

BORU the name always given to Brian, who made himself in effect King of Ireland. The name comes from the ford, Beal Boruma, on the river Shannon, near Killaloe, beside which he was born. Brian Boru was killed after the battle of Clontarf in 1014, in which he had defeated the Danes and stopped them from taking over Ireland.

BOSANQUET the name of a Huguenot family which came to England in 1686 from Languedoc. The name is said to be derived from the word (in Languedoc) *bouzanguet* = dwarf. The original of the nickname must be very old as the pedigree of the family begins with Jacques Bosanquet, du mas de Bosanquet, Colognac, in the Cévennes, who was living 1540. The pedigree of Bosanquet of Dingestow, Co. Monmouth and of two related families is in *Burke's Landed Gentry*, 1952.

BOSS several derivations, one of which is a nickname from M.E. *boce, bos* and O.Fr. *boce*, meaning a swelling or lump on back, hence a cruel reference to a person so deformed. As a personal name Bose was the interrogator of St Anselm in the latter's *Cur Deus Homo*. Hence also Bossey, bossy, a hunchback.

BOSS KELLY John Kelly, nineteenth century US politician.

BOSTON STRONG BOY US boxer, John Lawrence Sullivan.

BOTT as a nickname from O.E. *bot*, a toad. Hence also, in some cases, the name Botterell, since *boterel* in O.Fr. also denotes a toad. Surname of old recorded family, Bott of Bennington (*Burke's Landed Gentry*, 1937).

BOTTOMLESS PIT, The a humorous description of William Pitt, on account of his thinness. Derived from the New Testament, Revelation xx. 3.

BOUFLER O.Fr. *beau fleur*, beautiful flower; the English sound conversion of *beau* as in Beauchamp (Beecham).

BOURGEOISIE

corresponding roughly to the middle class. The word is in frequent use by communists, one of whose favourite theories is of the necessity of class war.

BOURGUIGNONS

followers of the Duke of Burgundy against the Armagnacs (q.v.) in fourteenth century France.

BOUSTRAPA

Napoleon III; compound of the openings of Boulogne, Strasbourg, and Paris, with which his name was associated.

BOUTFLOUR

M.E. *bulte*, to sift, and flour, a nickname for a miller.

BOWDLERISM

the expurgation of a book to leave out anything which the editor thought undesirable. From Thomas Bowdler who in 1818 thus edited Shakespeare (and later Edward Gibbon). Bowdler must have been a man of fantastic and minute industry.

BOWGEN, BUDGEON

Fr. *bon Johan*, good John, familiar for good servant.

BOWIE

Gaelic *buidhe*, fair-haired. But in Black's *Surnames of Scotland*, New York Public Library, 1946, no derivation is given except a hint that it may mean bowman.

BOWLER, BOLER

O.E. *bolla*, bowl. Generally occupational, a maker of bowls, but can be also a user of bowls, a tippler.

BOX

O.E. *box*, boxtree. One meaning is of teeth being yellow as box.

BOXERS, The

a body of Chinese reactionaries who were intent upon murdering all foreigners, 'foreign devils', and native Christians, 'secondary foreign devils'. The outbreak occurred at the end of 1899 and as it was encouraged by the Empress Dowager of China, the Boxers were able to murder many thousands. The legation quarters in Peking were besieged but on 14 August 1900 an international relieving force captured Peking and suppressed the Boxer Rebellion.

BOYCOTT

the name of Charles C. Boycott, agent of Lord Erne's estate in Co. Mayo, Ireland, who for his refusal to reduce rents was sent to Coventry and refused all services in 1880. The word was afterwards used to describe a person who had been completely isolated.

BOYD

Irish Gaelic *buidhe*, yellow, referring to complexion or hair.

BOZZY

familiar term for James Boswell (1740–95), author of the *Life of Dr. Samuel Johnson*.

BRABANT, Siger of

(c. 1240–84). A philosopher of the school of Averroes, the Moslem teacher of Spain.

BRADFER

Fr. *bras de fer*, iron arm, reference to great physical strength.

BRADIE, BRADY

O.E. *brad eage*, broad eye, physical characteristic.

BRADMAN, BRAIDMAN

broad man.

BRAGG, BRAGGE

M.E. *brag(ge)*, brisk and lively.

BRAHMO SOMAJ   Society of Believers in One God. A monotheistic sect
                           founded in 1818 in Calcutta by Ramohun Roy
                           (1744–1833) to purify Hinduism.

BRAND, BRONT   O.N. and O. Danish *brand*, a firebrand, or sword.

BRANDY NAN   Queen Anne of Great Britain (1702–14), because of her
                           fondness for brandy.

BRANGHAM   Irish *bran*, raven; a diminutive.

BRANGWIN   an old Welsh name from *bran*, raven, and *(g),wen*, fair.

BRASSETT   O.E. *braes* and *heafod*, brasshead, meaning hardness
                           and lack of feeling.

BRAUN   Gaelic and Welsh, *bran*, raven.

BRAVE, The   Alfonso IV of Portugal (born 1290, reigned 1324–57).
                               Boleslaw I (c. 966–1025), the first King of Poland,
                           also termed The Great.
                               Michael (1558–1601) Prince of Walachia, who upheld
                           Rumanian aspirations against Turks and others but
                           was murdered by his Albanian colleague, General
                           Giorgio Basta. Michael is the leading Rumanian
                           national hero.

BRAVEST OF THE BRAVE   Michel Ney, Marshal of France (1769–1815); a title
                           earned from his troops at Friedland (1807). After
                           Napoleon's first exile in 1814, Ney went over to Louis
                           XVIII, the Bourbon King, from whom he received
                           many favours. However, on Napoleon's return from
                           Elba, Ney joined him and fought at Waterloo with all
                           his accustomed bravery. He was captured, tried for
                           high treason and shot in the gardens of the
                           Luxembourg. Wellington had tried to save him.

BREAKSPEAR   a nickname which would be popular to a successful
                           jouster or actual fighter. Nicholas Breakspear (twelfth
                           century) was the only Englishman ever to become Pope
                           (Adrian IV).

BREAM   O.E. *breine*, vigorous.

BREAR, BREARE   O.E. *braer*, a thorn bush; hence sharpness, prickliness.

BREESE, BREEZE   O.E. *breose*, gadfly, for a troublesome person.

BREND, BRENT   from O.E. *bearnan*, to burn, M.E. form of past
                           participle, and used as nickname for an offender who
                           had been branded, i.e. burnt.

BRENNAN, BURNAND   a burnt hand in reference to the official who burnt the
                           offender in the hand. e.g. Ben Jonson escaped the full
                           rigour of the law by pleading his 'clergy' and being
                           burnt in the hand.

**BRETHREN OF THE   an association of men in the Netherlands in the
COMMON LIFE**   fourteenth century founded by G. de Groote, the
                           object being to develop a lofty spirituality. They also
                           founded excellent schools. Thomas à Kempis, author
                           of *The Imitation of Christ*, was a member of the Brethren.
                           Not at first bound by vows, they organized
                           themselves on the lines of the Augustinian Canons.

BRETTONER, BRITNOR, BRUTTNOR

M.E. a Breton, used pejoratively as for a bragger, a boaster.

BRETWALDA

lit. Ruler of the Britons, a title used under the Heptarchy (the Old English kingdoms) to denote the nominal overlord. Curiously the term is British, not English. When the ruler of the house of Wessex became Bretwalda the family eventually developed into the royal dynasty of Britain, Elizabeth II being the sixty-third successor of Egbert, King of Wessex and Bretwalda, c. 825.

BREWER OF GHENT

Jacob van Artevelde (c. 1287–1345) member of one of the richest families of Ghent, according to tradition a brewer. Influenced by considerations of the importance of England to the Flemish wool industry, Artevelde took the side of Edward III in the Hundred Years' War. He went so far as to propose renunciation of the Flemish Suzerain, the Count of Flanders and to replace him by the Black Prince. There was a popular tumult in which Artevelde was killed (see Edouard Perroy, *The Hundred Years' War*, Eng. trans. London, Eyre and Spottiswoode, 1965, though Jacob is there called James).

BRIAREUS

a giant of Greek mythology, called also Aegeon, who had 50 heads and 100 hands. His name was given to Cardinal Mezzofant (1774–1849) who knew 58 languages, 'a walking polyglot, a Briareus of parts of speech' as Byron called him.

BRIDE OF THE SEA

Venice. On each Ascension Day, the Doge of Venice in a great ceremony threw a gold ring into the Adriatic, with the words 'We wed thee O Sea, in token of perpetual domination'. (Cf. *Venice; The Most Triumphant City* by George Bull, London, Folio Society, 1980, and Wordsworth's sonnet.)

BRIDGE OF SIGHS

in Venice, leading from the judgment hall to the prisons and execution. Also used of Waterloo Bridge in London, which at one time was a resort of suicides.

BRIGG, BRIGGS,

M.E. *brigg(e)*, bogy, or hobgoblin.

BRIGGITINES

an Order of Nuns founded by St Bridget of Sweden (c. 1303–73).

BRIGHT

O.E. *beorht*, bright, beautiful, used frequently in medieval writings of female loveliness.

BRIGHT EMPERORS

the Ming Emperors of China who reigned from 1368 to 1644. 'They believed that China was the centre of the world, and that outside the Celestial Empire were only a few barbaric tribes.

BRIGHTWEEN

O.E. *beorhtwine*, fair friend.

BRILLIANT MADMAN

Charles XII of Sweden (1682–1718).

BRISBANE, BRISBOURNE

O.Fr. *brise* = break and O.E. *ban* = bone. Hence break bone, reference either to a person prone to accidents or to a quarrelsome person indulging in heavy blows.

BRISTOL BOY

Thomas Chatterton (1752–70). Born at Bristol, one of the great city's two poets (Robert Southey being the other). His tragic story ended in suicide in Holborn, London, but he has the place of a true poet in English literature, as a forerunner of the Romantic Revival.

BRISTOL FASHION, IN, or SHIPSHAPE AND BRISTOL FASHION

Up to the eighteenth century Bristol had been for many centuries the second city in England and all its shipping was in order.

BRITISH CICERO

William Pitt, the 1st Earl of Chatham, the Great Commoner (q.v.) (1708–78).

BRITISH ISRAELITES

an association of people non-denominational, who believe that the British people are descended from the Ten Lost Tribes of Israel.

BRITISH JEREMIAH

Edward Gibbon thus described Gildas the British writer whose exhortations are almost the only document remaining for the period AD 411–597 in Britain. Gildas was wrongly described as a historian by the Venerable Bede (q.v.) and the mistake has persisted. He was really a preacher whose work contains some historical allusions. Also called the Cymric Jeremiah.

BRITISH ROSCIUS

said of Thomas Betterton (1635–1710) by Colley Cibber because of his outstanding ability as a Shakespearean actor.

BROAD, BRAID

O.E. *brad* = broad, possible reference to physical characteristic.

BROAD CHURCHMEN

persons in the Church of England who in the nineteenth century took an easy attitude towards Christian dogma. Prominent broad churchmen were Dean A. P. Stanley and Dean H. H. Milman.

BROADBELT

broad belt, nickname either for a stout man or for one very powerfully built.

BROADFOOT

O.E. *brad* and *fot* = broadfoot.

BROADHEAD

O.E. *brad* and *heafod* could refer not only to a broad head but also to a broad hood for covering same.

BROADRIBB

'broad rib', a typical M.E. nickname, marking a physical peculiarity.

BROCK

O.E. *brocc*, a badger, and still used as a term for the latter. Towards the sixteenth century the adjective stinking was often used with brock and came to denote a dirty fellow.

BROCKET

O.Fr. *broque*, hence M.E. brocket, a stag in its second year with its first horns; possibly a facetious reference to a young fellow on verge of manhood.

BROCKLESS

O.N. *broklauss*, without breeches, reference to an unfortunate condition which stuck to person so called.

BROTHER JONATHAN

an American mystical figure like Uncle Sam, who always beats his enemies by unexpected intelligence.

BROTHERS HOSPITALLERS

developed in sixteenth century Spain, with the object of tending the sick in hospitals, this being the fourth vow, added to those of poverty, chastity and obedience.

BROWN — O.E. *brun*, brown, referring to hair or complexion. Hence derivative Browning.

BROWN BESS — the old flintlock musket used formerly in the British Army.

BROWNISTS — the originals of the Independents (Congregationalists) (q.v.) named from their founder Robert Browne of Rutland, *tempore* Elizabeth I. The Brownists were, with the Papists (q.v.), the first Dissenters (q.v.) from the Established Church.

BRUDER KLAUS, BROTHER CLAUS — Nikolaus von der Flue (1417–87) a hermit who at a time when the Swiss Confederation was threatened with disunity arranged a compromise which held the Confederation together. He was beatified in 1669 and canonized in 1947. He is the patron saint of Switzerland.

BRUNGER, BROUNCKER — O.E. *brungar*, brown spear.

BRUNSDON, BRUNSDEN — O.E. *brunstan*, brown stone (possibly a place name).

BRUNWIN — O.E. *brunwine*, brown fiend.

BRYANITES — more generally known as Bible Christians (q.v.).

BRYLCREAM BOYS — a slang term in the earlier period of the Second World War (1939–45) for members of the RAF, particularly the ground-staff, as their uniforms contrasted in smartness with the battle dress of the army. The term came from a popular hair cream.

BUCCANEER — at first meant 'smoke dried meat' from the Latin American term *boucan*, but as the first practitioners of the dried meat supplemented their income by piracy, it came to mean pirates.

BUCK — O.E. a he-goat, perhaps with reference to wild behaviour. Found as early as 1055.

BUCKET — found in thirteenth century, may come from Fr. *bouquet* or *bouqueret* possible diminutives of *boue*, he-goat, having reference to wanton or lustful behaviour.

BUCKHORSE — the nickname of the boxer, John Smith, living 1740, who did not feel and so could take a severe blow (i.e. a buckhorse) without feeling it.

BUDD, BUDDS — O.E. *budda*, beetle, found in eleventh and twelfth centuries. The basic derivation is from budda, to swell, and could denote a fat person.

BUFFALO BILL — William Frederick Cody (1846–1917). One of the creators of the Wild West image of the USA. His nickname came from his work in feeding the men who built the rail road through Kansas; he did this by shooting some 4,280 bison in 17 months. He is described as a frontiersman, messenger, teamster, hunter and army scout. He starred in Wild West shows with Wild Bill Hickok (q.v.) and in 1883 he formed Buffalo Bill's Wild West show which toured America and Europe, and which must have contributed very greatly to the enormous output of juvenile romance associated with Cody's name.

BUFFARD
Thirteenth century O.Fr. *bouffard*, puffing, blowing, swelling; reference to physical characteristic but also to swelling with anger.

BULGAROCTONOS
The Bulgar Slayer (q.v.).

BULGAR SLAYER
the name of Basil II, Emperor of Byzantium. He determined to break the growing power of the Bulgars. 'It took him some 20 years of warfare which culminated in the great victory of 1014; he took 18,000 prisoners, blinded them all save one man in every hundred, left to guide the rest to Samuel the Bulgarian king. The sight broke the latter's heart and he died, while Basil offered up thanks to God for his victory in the church of the Mother of God at Athens – a building which earlier ages had known as the Parthenon' (C. A. Alington, *Europe*, London, Hollis & Carter, 1946, p. 67).

BULLED, BULLEID
O.E. *bula*, bull, and *hlafod*, head. One noted for obstinate, bullheaded behaviour.

BULLER
O.Fr. *bouleur*, M.E. *bulleu*, a deceiver or a cheat.

BULLETT, BOLLETT
twelfth century, sometimes from Bulled, bullhead, but mainly from O.Fr. *boule* = round, with reference to a person's figure.

BULLOCK
O.E. *bullue*, a bull calf.

BULLY DAWSON
a London scoundrel in the time of Charles I; Addison's Sir Roger de Coverley is described as having kicked Bully Dawson in a tavern.

BUNCH
M.E. *bunche*, a lump on the back.

BUNCLARKE
fourteenth century O.E. *bon*, *clere* = good clerk.

BUNNEY, BUNNY
possibly from O.Fr. *bugue*, a swelling.

BUNNYAN, BUNYON
of this famous surname Dr P. H. Reaney said, 'after an exhaustive discussion that it came from O.Fr. *bignon*, a diminutive of *bugue* = a bile or blane, cf. also pugnets = little round loaves or lumps made of fine meal, oil or butter and raisins, and the surname might be a nickname for one distinguished by a knob, lump or bump' (*Dictionary of British Surnames*).

BURD, BURDS
from M.E. word for a young lady. cf. Malcolm the Maiden, one of the Scots' kings, and the Lady of Christ's College, Cambridge, as applied to John Milton (q.v.).

BURDEKIN
from M.E. *burde*, young lady, being a diminutive = little young lady.

BURNARD
from combination of O.Fr. *brun* plus O.E. *hard*, denoting a person of brownish complexion or hair.

BURNELL, BRUNELL
O.Fr. *brun*, brown, referring to a person's hair or complexion.

BURNETT, BURNOTT	O.Fr. *brun*, brown, in reference to a person's colouring.
BURR	M.E. *burre*, a burr, i.e. something that sticks, e.g. tiresome person.
BURRELL, BOREL	M.E. *borel* = reddish brown, possible reference to complexion or hair, or coarse woollen cloth used in pejorative sense, borrel burgher.
BURRETT, BORIT, BORET	sometimes from O.Fr. *bourre*, rough hair, and thus used in combination with O.E. *hlafod*, head, to denote person with rough shaggy hair.
BUSHRANGERS	Australian highwaymen who lived in, and operated from the bush (see R. Boldrewood, *Robbery under Arms*).
BUTT, BUTTS	in some cases derived from M.E. *butt* = thicker end or stump, but by no means always the origin of this surname.
BUZZARD, BUSZARD	O.Fr. *busant*, M.E. *busard*, buzzard, one of the commoner British birds of prey, but not capable of being trained to falconry, hence the word used to denote stupid or ignorant person.

C

CADD, CADE

sometimes from M.E. *cade*, cash, barrel, in reference to a corpulent person.

CADDICK (OCK)

O.Fr. *caduc* = frail or decrepit.

CALAMITY JANE

an American, Martha Jane Canary, trouble always followed her, e.g. eleven of her twelve husbands died unexpectedly.

CALF

O.E. *caelf* = calf.

CALIGULA

little boots, a nickname given to the Roman Emperor Gaius Caesar (AD 12–41), in his childhood by the soldiers of his father Germanicus. He reigned 4 years and was murdered. One of the worst Caesars.

CALIXTINES

a section of the Hussites (q.v.) who thought that Holy Communion for the laity should be in both species, from *calix*, a chalice. Also known as Utraquists (in both kinds).

CALLINICUS

with glorious victory, or gloriously triumphant. Seleucus II of the Seleucid dynasty of Syria, etc. who lived c. 265–226 BC, probably so called because of a victory which he won over the Parthians c. 228. A term also used of Christian martyrs who, by their deaths for Christ, triumphed gloriously.

CALVINISTS

adherents of the theology of John Calvin (1509–64) of Geneva, hence Calvinism. Like many other names given in bad sense, it became used with approbation by Calvin's followers. The main tenet is of the absolute predestination by God of the human race, a few to heaven, and the majority to hell, and without any reference to personal merit. Calvin's theological system is expounded in his huge treatise *The Institutes of the Christian Religion* (1537), a very prolix and pleonastic work.

CAMBRIDGE APOSTLES

A debating society founded in 1826 in Cambridge University by John Sterling and which contained many distinguished members. Not mentioned by Carlyle (*Life of John Sterling*, ch. iv) except to say 'They had among them a Debating Society called The Union . . . Sterling was the acknowledged chief in this Union Club.'

CAMBRIDGE PLATONISTS

a group of philosophical divines who flourished at Cambridge between 1633 and 1688. They believed in the reason as the arbiter in both natural and revealed religion. The most important were B. Whichcote, N. Culverwel, John Smith, R. Cudworth and H. More.

CAMEL(L)   denoting in some cases a large awkward person.

CAMERONIANS   a name given by their opponents to extreme Scotch Covenanters, being followers of R. Cameron (died in 1680), killed in a fight with royal troops in Ayrshire.

CAMISARDS   fanatical French Protestants who reacted when Louis XIV tried to suppress their religion. Supposed to come from habit of wearing camisards or shirts over their clothes in night attacks.

CAMNIS, CAMOYS   in some instances derived from M.E. *camnus* = short flat nose.

CAMPBELL   can be from Gaelic *caimbeal* = crooked mouth. Surname of one of the most famous Scots families, of which the Duke of Argyll is head. There is no foundation for a derivation from *de Campo bello* as often popularly stated. On which ref. should be made to a very learned and extremely humorous account in Dr G. F. Black's *Surnames of Scotland*, 1962.

CAMPBELLITES   *see* Disciples of Christ.

CANE, KANE   M.E. and O.E. *cane* – cane or reed, used of a tall slender man.

CANNAN, CANNON   Irish, *ceann fhlonn* – whitehead.

CANTILUPE, St Thomas de   (c. 1218–82) also described as St Thomas of Hereford, a bishop, and adviser to King Edward I of England. Excommunicated by John Peckham, Archbishop of Canterbury, he appealed to the Pope, but died before judgment was pronounced. None the less his sanctity and miracles procured his canonization in 1320. Explanation of Cantilupe is not clear as he does not appear to have been much if at all at Cantalupo, a town near Rome where the first melons of this variety were grown.

CAPABILITY   the name given to Lancelot Brown (1716–83), English landscape gardener and architect, who received this name because of his habit of estimating the 'capability' of a landscape.

CAPE, COPE   O.E. *cape*, M.E. *cope*, a long cloak.

CAPET   from Latin *capa*, cope or cape, the nickname of Hugh Capet, who became first of the Capetian kings of France in 987 until 996. He was the eldest son of Hugh the Great (q.v.), and on his father's death he became Duke of the Franks and held large estates in the region of Paris and Orléans.

CAPPADOCIAN FATHERS   St Basil the Great, St Gregory of Nazianzus and St Gregory of Nyssa, in the fourth century.

CAPUCHINS   from *capouche* = a pointed cowl. A branch of the Franciscans founded by Matteo di Bassi of Urbino (died 1552), the object being to return to strict rules of life as laid down by St Francis of Assisi. The Capuchins wear pointed cowls.

CARACALLA

referring to a kind of duffle coat used in Gaul, which was habitually worn by the emperor known as Caracalla. He lived 186–217 and was emperor 211–17. He and Geta were the sons and successors of Septimius Severus, but Geta was murdered in 212 by his brother. Caracalla's real name was Marcus Aurelius Antoninus.

CARBONARI

in Italian = colliers or charcoal burners, name of some secret societies which originated in early 19th century Italy. The aim of the Carbonari was the overthrow of the despotic government which then ruled in Italy. When the Austrians crushed the rebellions of 1820 and 1821 the Carbonari lost influence and the more active members joined Mazzini's Young Italy movement (q.v.).

CARBONELL, CHARBONELL

O.Fr. *carbon, charbon* = charcoal in reference to dark hair or colouring.

CARDEN, CARDON

O.Fr. *cardon* = thistle, used perhaps for someone of an obstinate, prickly character.

CARDINAL(L)

O.Fr., this being a name derived from the bearer having acted the part in a pageant or mystery play or having a proud manner or fondness for fine garments.

CARL, KARL

M.E. *carl*, O.N. *harl* = man, in the sense of a common person or even a countryman. Dr Reaney (*Dictionary of British Surnames*) mentions that by 1300 the word had acquired the pejorative meaning of villein, a low fellow, rude in manner, a churl.

CARLESS, CARELESS, CARLOS

O.E. *carleas* = unconcerned, careless. Bardsley is kinder in his remark that Careless 'was of that happy disposition which the petty worries and anxieties of life do not easily disturb', *English Surnames*, 1969 edn, p. 471. In the form Carlos, the surname is that of one of the most illustrious English county families, who helped save King Charles II in the Royal Oak at Boscobel 1651 and was granted arms charged with an oak tree (BLG, 1952).

CARMELITES

an order of monks (later of nuns also) founded c. 1154 by St Berthold, the full title being that of Our Lady of Mount Carmel in Palestine.

CAROLINE DIVINES

see Anglo-Catholic.

CARRAN, CARINE, KARRAN

from Ciaran and finally from *ciar* = mouse-coloured. One of the MacGregors who fought at the battle of Glen Fruin, February 1603, was covered all over with grey hair, hence his nickname, the giant mouse man (Dugall Ciar Mhor, ancestor of Rob Roy). He it was who slaughtered the Glasgow students who had come to see the battle, after which the Scots Parliament outlawed the MacGregors. For an enthralling account, see William Anderson's *Scottish Nation*, Edinburgh, Fullarton & Co.

CARROTS

Lillian Gish, film star, owing to frequent eating of carrots.

CARTHUSIAN, The

Dionysius – Denys van Leewen, Denys Rychel (1402–71) a copious writer who was a member of the Carthusian Order.

Also used of Ludolf of Saxony (died 1378) a spiritual writer known, too, as Ludolf the Carthusian, he being a member of that Order.

CARTHUSIANS

the name of a contemplative order of monks founded by St Bruno in 1084 in the Grande Chartreuse, near Grenoble in France. The Carthusians established the Charterhouse (anglicization from Chartreuse) in London in 1371. Thomas Sutton founded on the site a chapel, almshouse and school. The last was removed to Godalming in Surrey and is a famous English public school.

CASBOLT

M.E. for baldhead, fourteenth century.

CASCIA, ST RITA OF

(1381–1457) a married woman who after her husband's death became a nun at Cascia in Italy.

CASEY JONES

US railroad engineer, John Luther Jones, subject of American folk ballad.

CASSINESE CONGREGATION

an offshoot of the Benedictine Order, begun by Ludovico Barla at Padua in 1409; as usual with such movements in order to correct abuses. Monte Cassino in Italy is a Cassinese congregation.

CATANACH, CATTENACH

in Gael = belonging to clan Chattan, claiming descent from Gilliecatain = servant of St Catan = little cat. Such is the nickname origin of this illustrious association of Highlanders (perhaps like the union of the six nations under the Iroquois in Canada). The honour of the headship of Clan Chattan was disputed between the Macpherson and the MacIntosh, but settled in the latter's favour in 1672 by the Lord Lyon. Both clans use the cat as crest with the motto 'touch not the cat bot a glove' thus serving as memento of the nickname.

CATCH

M.E. *cache* = act of catching

CATES, KATES

O.N. *kate* = the merry one.

CATHARI

Greek καφαροί, 'pure ones'; a very widespread heretical sect of the Middle Ages which existed in parts of western Europe from the eleventh to the fourteenth centuries. Much obsessed with apostolic poverty; the leaders, the *perfecti*, were celibate.

CATHOLIC, The

Isabella (1451–1504) Queen of Castile, who married in 1469 Ferdinand II of Aragon and who succeeded to the throne of Castile in 1474. With Ferdinand she united Spain; they expelled the Moors from Granada, their last stronghold in Spain; Isabella financed Columbus's voyage of discovery of the Americas.

Also applied to Alphonso I (739–57), King of the Asturias, from his zeal in erecting and endowing churches and monasteries.

CATHOLIC KINGS

Los Reyes Católicos, the name given to Ferdinand and Isabella who united all Spain under their rule. Their religious fervour induced them to listen to Tomás de Torquemada (died 1498), a Dominican who persuaded the sovereigns to introduce the Inquisition into Spain and who became its first Inquisitor-General.

CATHOLIC MAJESTY, His — the King of Spain; said to have been granted by Alexander VI (the Borgia Pope) to King Ferdinand of Aragon in 1494 after the conquest of Granada.

CATON — diminutive of cat.

CATT, KATT, CHATT — O.E. *catt* = the cat.

CATTEL, CATTLE — diminutive of cat.

CAUDELL, CADDELL — M.E. *caudel*, meaning a hot drink but mixed with gruel, hence applied sarcastically to a man who could not carry strong drink but had to have it diluted.

CAUDILLO, El — The Chief, General Francisco Franco (1892–1975), dictator of Spain.

CAVALIERS — meaning horsemen (like the French Chevalier and Spanish Caballero), was used in the seventeenth century in England to denote the gentry loyal to church and king.

CAYSER, KAYSER, KEYSER — M.E. *caisere* = Caesar or emperor, name derived from playing part in mystery play.

CEAN MOR — Great head, more often written as Canmore, the name given to Malcolm III of Scotland (1057–93). He was the son of King Duncan I who was murdered by Macbeth who then usurped the throne.
'Shakespeare's immortal tragedy of *Macbeth* founded on the fables of Boece has thrown an interest round the character of the principal personages concerned in it, which could never have been created by the facts of sober history' (W. Anderson, *Antiquities of the Scottish Nation*, Edinburgh, Fullarton & Co., 1863). Malcolm was an ally of England against the Normans and gave shelter to Edgar Atheling, whose sister Margaret he married as his second wife. He was slain at Alnwick in an invasion of England.

CELANO, Thomas of — (c. 1190–1260), the first biographer of St Francis of Assisi.

CELESTIALS, The — sometimes refers to the Chinese under the imperial regime, from the title 'The Celestial Empire' referring to the imperial dynasty as descended from the gods; the emperor always being known as The Son of Heaven.

CELESTINES — name of an Order founded by Pope Celestine V (described by Dante as making *il gran rifiuto* because he resigned the Papacy). Founded in 1250 as a branch of the Benedictines, it spread extensively but ended in 1785.

CENSORIOUS — the epithet of Marcus Porcius Cato (234–149 BC), owing to the rigour which he showed when Censor in Rome in 184 BC.

CEREMONIOUS, The   King Pedro IV of Aragon (1336–87).

CHAMPEAUX, William of   (c. 1070–1121) a French scholastic philosopher.

CHANCE   M.E. *cheaunce* = accident or chance. Possible reference to a gambler.

CHANTER, Peter the   (died 1197) a French medieval theologian. Precentor of Notre Dame in Paris.

CHARITY   from *caritas* = charity or, in modern rendering, love. Possible derivation as nickname by one marked by devotion to God. The use of Charity as a Christian name occurred after the Reformation among the Puritans.

CHARLES JAMES   a common term for the English fox, derived from the popular English statesman Charles James Fox (1749–1806). The latter was also known as Intrepid Fox and there is an engraving of him with this title on the wall of a public house in Soho, London.

CHARTISTS   a body of people in England in 1836 who began to agitate for several political reforms such as manhood suffrage, etc. The real cause of the movement was economic owing to the appalling conditions of the workers. There were abortive plans for revolution which came to nothing and the decade 1848–58 marked the end of the movement.

CHARTRES, Thierry of   (died post 1151) a medieval philosopher and theologian.

CHASIDIM   a Hebrew word meaning 'pious' or 'godly' applied to orthodox Jews in Palestine of the 2nd century BC who were probably the ancestors of the Pharisees (q.v.). They were also called Hasidaeans, this being the Greek form of the Hebrew.

CHAUVINISM   Chauvinism derives from the name of Nicolas Chauvin, a French soldier born at Rochefort. He was wounded many times in the Revolutionary and Napoleonic wars and although he had only a small pension he retained a simple-minded devotion to Napoleon. During the 1830s this attitude was ridiculed in popular entertainment and came to denote the attitude of 'my country, right or wrong'. The nearest English equivalent is jingo and jingoism (q.v.). It need hardly be said that the term chauvinist has no sexual connotation whatsoever. It is like many other words used incorrectly by the modern British.

CHEAL, CHEALES   in some cases from O.E. *cele* = cold, coldness.

CHEEK, CHEKE   O.E. *ceace* = jawbone, used of one with a prominent jaw. The nickname stuck, e.g. Sir John Cheke, a Greek scholar of the sixteenth century mentioned by Milton in his sonnets as teacher of King Edward VI, and Cambridge generally.

CHERONEAN SAGE   the celebrated Greek writer Plutarch (AD 46–120) author of the famous *Lives of the Noble Greeks and Romans*, who was born at Cheronea in Boeotia.

CHESTERBELLOCS
name of a series of political writings produced in 1910 by G. K. Chesterton, his brother Cecil Chesterton and Hilaire Belloc. The writings on history of G. K. C. and Belloc became known as the Chester-Belloc school which in particular regard to medieval times was provocative and inaccurate.

CHEVALIER DE ST GEORGE
a euphemism adopted in polite society in early eighteenth century to denote the Old Pretender (q.v.). This usage was employed in order to avoid offence either to Jacobites or Hanoverians.

CHEVALIER SANS PEUR ET SANS REPROCHE, Le
Pierre du Terrail, Seigneur de Bayard (c. 1473–1524). Apart from being a faultless knight, Bayard was a skilful commander who used both reconnaissance and espionage. Some of his exploits equal those of knights in romance (e.g. defence of a bridge over the Garigliano single-handed against 200 Spaniards). He did not like artillery or firearms and it was ironic that when he died in Italy he had been mortally wounded by a ball from an arquebus.

CHEW
O.E. *cio*, *ceo* = a bird of the crow species, and many chattering kinds.

CHIAN PAINTER
the most celebrated Greek painter of antiquity, Apelles (fourth century BC), born at Colophon in Asia Minor.

CHICHESTER, St Richard of
(c. 1197–1253) Bishop of Chichester, canonized 1262.

CHICK
M.E. *chike* = chicken, a term of endearment. Cf. Chicken, O.E. *cicen*.

CHILD
O.E. *cild* = child. Sometimes a pet name, at others applied to a childish or immature person; but also in the thirteenth and fourteenth centuries to a young noble who was not yet knighted. In the ballad, 'The Child of Elle' (Bishop Percy's *Reliques of Ancient English Poetry*) the child is a fully fledged knight, and Percy in his notes and glossary gives 'child' as a title sometimes given to a knight.

CHILD, The
Lewis, last of the Carolingian line in East Francia, succeeded 899, died by 911.
Otto (died 1252), grandson of Otto IV, enfeoffed by Frederick II with the duchy of Brunswick-Lüneburg.

CHILIASM
from Greek χίλιος, thousand, and referring to millenarianism (q.v.).

CHILIASTS
The Greek name for Millenarians (q.v.), from χίλιοι, thousands.

CHIN
O.E. *cin* = chin; term given to one with a long or prominent chin.

CHINESE GORDON
the term by which General Charles Gordon (1833–85) was known after a series of brilliant victories against Chinese rebels in 1863. His men regarded him as a mighty magician because in battle he carried only a cane, 'his wand of victory'. Gordon's subsequent career was one of triumph, until owing to the dilatory

behaviour of the British government, he was killed at Khartoum by the forces of the Mahdi (q.v.). For his victories over the Taiping rebels in 1863 he was made a mandarin of the first class.

CH'ING or TA CH'ING
the name adopted in 1636 by the Manchus to designate their own regime in Manchuria. They succeeded in gaining control of China from the weakened Ming dynasty (q.v.) and ruled the empire 1644-1912 when the last emperor was forced to abdicate.

CHITLOCK
M.E. *chitte* = young of an animal, 'a young cub'; chittock is diminutive.

CHLORUS
the Pale, nickname given to Constantine I (Aurelius Valerius Constantius, died 306). He was Roman emperor 293–306 and by St Helena was father of Constantine the Great (q.v.). An interesting account of Chlorus and Helena is in Evelyn Waugh's novel *Helena*.

CHOPIN, CHOPPING
O.E. *chopine* = a measure equal to an English pint, also Fr. *chopiner*, to tipple. Used of person given to over-drinking.

CHOUANS
nickname given to the Royalists who in La Vendée resisted the French Revolution. The leader Jean Cottereau was accustomed to warn his followers by imitating the screech of an owl. French *chat-haunt*, screech owl, was corrupted into chouans.

CHRISTADELPHIANS
lit. Christian brethren, a sect formed by John Thomas (1805–71) in America. As usual with sects, the doctrines professed are a mixture of orthodox tenets with private views. Thomas coined the name in place of Christian.

CHRISTIAN
originally a name given to the followers of Christ by outsiders, i.e. a nickname. Acts xi. 26, at Antioch, the disciples were first called Christians. Tacitus wrote in *Annales* XV. 44 that the name was known at the time of the Neronian persecution in AD 64. '*Christianos appellabat Auctor nominis ejus Christus, Tiberio imperitante, per procurationem Pontium Pilatum supplicio affectus erat*. The name was not immediately welcomed by Christ's followers, but soon became universal and a badge of honour. Pagans assumed Christ to be a proper name since they did not understand its Messianic meaning. They also sometimes rendered it as Chrestos from χρηστός, good, kind.

CHRISTIAN MAJESTY, His Most
Rex Christianissimus; title of Kings of France.

CHRISTIAN QUAKER
George Keith (c. 1639–1716) so called because he administered baptism and the Lord's Supper, rites not used by Quakers.

CHRISTIAN SCIENCE
founded by an American, Mrs Mary Baker Eddy (1821–1910) and inculcating a belief in spiritual healing only, and the unreality of matter.

CHRISTIAN VIRGIL   Marco Girolama Vida (died 1566), author of *Christias*,
                             in imitation of the *Aeneid*.

CHRISTIAN VIRGIL AND   Aurelius Clemens Prudentius, c. 400, one of the last
HORACE   classical Latin poets.

CHRYSOSTOM   Golden Mouth, St John, Bishop of Constantinople (c.
                             347–407), so called because of his eloquence as a
                             preacher.

CHUBB   M.E. *chubbe* = a fish, used apparently of a big, lazy
                             lumpish fellow. Now the surname of a noble family, the
                             Barons Hayter.

CHURCHES OF CHRIST   *see* Disciples of Christ.

CICERO OF FRANCE   Jean Baptiste Massilon (1663–1742), great French
                             preacher.

CICERONE   a guide whose task was to point out objects of interest
                             to strangers derived from the name of Cicero, the
                             great Roman orator, the guide being a principal
                             speaker.

CID, The   a title used by the Moors and given to Rodrigo Diaz of
                             Bivar near Burgos, the national hero of Spain, who
                             lived in the eleventh century, c. 1043–99. Also called
                             Campeador or Champion, because he proved invincible
                             in his battles. His exploits are narrated in the *Cantar*
                             (or *Poema*) *de Mio Cid* written c. 1140. This has been
                             well analysed by the great Spanish critic, Menendez
                             Pidal. There are earlier literary records of the Cid:
                             Carmen Campidoctoris, a Latin poem c. 1090 and *Historia
                             Roderici* (or *Gesta Roderici Campidocti*) a factual
                             biography c. 1110. Perhaps his greatest exploit was his
                             leading of his men against the Moors, after his death.
                             His body was tied in the saddle and the Moors who
                             knew him to be dead fled in terror at the sight of the
                             corpse on the horse.

CIMABUE   or Oxhead, the common name for Cenni di Pepi, a
                             Florentine painter (c. 1240–1302) mentioned by Dante
                             (*Purgatorio*, XI, 94–6).

CINCINNATUS OF   George Washington (1732–99) first President of the
AMERICA   USA, so named after a Roman hero, Cincinnatus of
                             the 5th century BC who was called from his farm to
                             head the state and returned to his farm afterwards.

CIRCUIT, SERKITT,   described by Reaney (*Dict. of British Surnames*) as a
SURKETT   place name but 'may also be a nickname from the
                             surcoat' (the latter being the covering worn over the
                             armour).

CIRCUMCELLIONS   lit. going around the dwellings, name given by
                             Catholic Christians to bands of fanatical peasants who
                             attached themselves to the Donatists in North Africa
                             in the fourth century. The Circumcellions called
                             themselves Agonistici or Soldiers of Christ.

CIRCUS KING   John Ringlum, an American circus owner.

CISTERCIAN ORDER   of White monks. Named from their mother house at
                             Cîteaux. A very strict variant of the Benedictines,
                             founded in 1098 by St Robert of Malesme.

CITIZEN KING King Louis Philippe (1773–1850), elected by the citizens of Paris; reigned 1830–48.

CLACK sometimes from M.E. *clacleer* = a chatterer.

CLAN-NA-GAEL United Brotherhood, a Fenian organization founded in USA, the object being the independence of Ireland to be gained by armed rebellion.

CLAPHAM SECT the name given by the famous wit Sydney Smith to a number of very earnest Anglican Evangelicals most of whom lived near Clapham. William Wilberforce was one of them.

CLAPP derived in most cases by Prof. Eilert Ekwall from O.E. *clap* = a lump, hillock or hill, but in some instances as 'le Clop' a nickname denoting a heavily built person.

CLAPPER sometimes from M.E. *clappe* = chatter, hence chatterer.

CLAPTON SECT of Anglican Churchmen in early nineteenth century, so called because a prominent member, Joshua Watson (1771–1855), lived at Clapton.

CLATER M.E. *clater* = noisy talk, hence a babbler.

CLAUDE LORRAIN name given to Claude Gelée (1600–82), French landscape painter, because he was born in Lorraine.

CLAUDIUS CLEAR contributor's name used by W. R. Nicoll (1851–1923) in writing for the *British Weekly* which he founded.

CLEMENS NON PAPA a joking reference to a Dutch composer of Church music (c. 1500–56), one Jacques Clément, facetiously to distinguish him from the contemporary Pope, Clement VII.

CLIQUOT Frederick IV of Prussia (born 1795, reigned 1840–61), so called because of his fondness for champagne.

CLITO or THE ATHELING William the son of Robert Curthose, Duke of Normandy (son of William the Conqueror) made Count of Flanders by the French king. William Clito died in 1128.

CLUNIACS members of the Order of Cluny, whose aim was to return to the strictest Benedictine rule. Cluny was a monastery near Macon in Burgundy built by William the Pious, Duke of Aquitaine, in 909. Its influence spread to other monastic houses far and wide.

COBBALD, COBBOLD, CUTBILL O.E. *Cuthbeald* = famous, bold.

COBBLER or LEATHER-SELLER Theodotus, a heretic of the second century.

COCK, COX O.E. *coce* = cock, reference to person who strutted like a cock, but also applied in partly affectionate style to a young servant, apprentice, etc.

COCK OF THE NORTH George Gordon, 5th Duke of Gordon (1770–1836) so styled on a monument to him at Fochabers in Aberdeenshire. He had in 1795 raised the Gordon Highlanders, see *Burke's Extinct Peerage*, 1883.

COCKAYNE

M.E. *cokaygne* O.Fr. *coquaigne*, the name given to an imaginary country of luxury and idleness. 'The surname was probably given to one whose habits and manner of life suggested he had come from the fabulous land of Cockaigne' (Dr Reaney, *Dict. of British Surnames*). The Cockayne family in England now represented by Lord Cullen of Ashbourne is traced in Derbyshire to the thirteenth century. Its most famous member was the distinguished G. E. C., George Edward Cockayne (his real name was Adams but in compliance with his mother's will he took the surname and arms of Cockayne in lieu of those of Adams in 1873). G. E. C. was the original founder and writer of those great works of scholarship *The Complete Peerage* and *The Complete Baronetage*.

COCKELL, COCKILL

O.E. *coccul*, *coccel* = cockle and may have pejorative reference to a weed. 'Cockle' is used in the Douai New Testament, instead of the tares in the Authorized Version.

COCKNEY SCHOOL

a contemptuous name given by John Lockhart, biographer of Sir Walter Scott, to Leigh Hunt, Hazlitt, Shelley and Keats.

CODD

O.E. *codda*, may refer to one with a body like a codfish or to a bag-like appearance of the belly.

CODOMANNUS

Darius III, Persian emperor reigning 336–330 BC; last king of the Achaemenid dynasty, who was defeated by Alexander the Great and eventually murdered by one of his satraps, Bessus.

CŒUR-DE-LION

lion heart, applied to Richard I (1189–99) of England. Apparently a contemporary description, 'that heart of his which he was pleased to hear called "a lion's" (Cœur de lion was his nickname before he died, and the right name for him for centuries) is at Rouen' (Belloc, *History of England*, London, Methuen, vol. ii). Otherwise historians have been strangely reluctant to account for the nickname. Everything about this king's reputation is peculiar. Sir Walter Scott thought that Richard's name was dear to Englishmen on the same lines as a cow, milked, exploited and finally killed by its owner might be fond of the latter. England meant to this king only a means of raising money. He was a bad son, a bad husband and a bad king, but he was very generous to the troubadours whose art he practised and who spread his fame. It can be said in his favour that he earned his nickname by his bravery in the Third Crusade. Scott did his best for him in three romances: *The Betrothed*, *The Talisman* and *Ivanhoe*.

COLCOCK

compound of col (pet form of Nicholas) and cock, diminutive.

COLE

O.E. *col* = coal, applied to someone with a swarthy appearance.

COLETTINES

a branch of the Poor Clares founded by St Colette (1381–1447).

COLFOX O.E. *col* = coal and fox, the coal fox or brant fox having more black in its fur, used unfavourably of a foxy black type.

COLLEDD O.E. *col* = coal and *hod* = hood. Someone wearing a black hood.

COLLEY, COLLIE O.E. *colis* = coal = black.

COLT O.E. *colt*, meaning someone frisky or lively.

COLUMBUS OF THE CATACOMBS the Italian archaeologist Antonio Bosio (c. 1576–1629) thus described by G. B. de Rossi. Bosio made descents into some of the Roman catacombs whose existence had been forgotten since the ninth century.

COLUMBUS OF THE SKIES Sir William Herschel (1738–1822), the discoverer of the planet Uranus.

COMESTOR, Peter (died c. 1179) a French biblical scholar, wrote a standard work on biblical history.

COMFORT M.E. strengthening, giving aid, hence someone possessing such qualities.

COMMENTATOR name used in the Middle Ages for Averroes (Ibn Rushd, 1126–98) Moorish Moslem philosopher, so called because of his commentaries on the works of Aristotle.

COMMUNISM the holding of goods in common, or the equal distribution of money, property and wealth. Several small communities have practised Communism, e.g. the Spartans in ancient Greece to some extent. Also the Essenes in second and first centuries BC in Palestine; and the earliest Christian body in Jerusalem as narrated in the *Acts of the Apostles* ch. 11. 44: 'And all who believed had all things in common and they sold their possessions and goods and distributed them to all as any had need.' Communism has also been the basis on which Plato's *Republic* was founded and the subsequent Utopias derived from it. In modern usage, Communism derives in theory, with considerable modifications in practice, from the writings of Karl Marx (1818–83). It is generally equated by its adherents with Socialism, e.g. the USSR, The Union of Soviet Socialist Republics. In practice the 14 Communist states of the world, from the Baltic to the Yellow Sea, are tyrannies, with the difference that their tyranny is impersonal and the more efficient in repression because of the all-embracing nature of the system.

COMPANIONS OF JEHU the Chouans (q.v.). Jehu whose career is given in II Kings c.ix *et seq*. Jehu's task was to destroy the family of Ahab; the Chouans' task was to destroy those who had executed Louis XVI.

COMPER O.Fr. *comper* = companion, comrade.

COMTE D'ARENENBERG name assumed by Napoleon III when he escaped from the fortress of Ham.

CONCHES, William of (c. 1080–1154) a French medieval philosopher.

CONCHIE

an extremely pejorative and slang term for a conscientious objector who refuses to serve in the armed forces or (in many cases) do any work in connection with the war effort.

CONFEDERATES

the eleven southern American states in the Civil War in America (1861–5).

CONFESSOR, The

Edward III – pre-Norman Conquest King of England 1042–66 always referred to as the Confessor. In the early ages of the Church the term meant a Christian who confessed Christ publically but was not executed. In the Middle Ages it had come to denote 'men of remarkable virtue and knowledge who confessed the faith of Christ before the world by practice of the most heroic virtue' (*Catholic Encyclopedia*, 1908 *sub* Confessor). In the Bull of 1163 which ordered the Canonization of St Edward he is referred to as the Confessor, no reason being given. For full account of the term Confessor see L. G. Pine, *Sons of The Conqueror* (Charles Tuttle Inc., 1973).

St Maximus (c. 590–662) a Greek theologian who suffered severely in physical mutilation because of his opposition to the Monothelites (q.v.).

CONGREGATIONALISTS

originated in England in the late sixteenth and seventeenth centuries, to denote a form of church organization in which each properly organized congregation is free to make its own decisions without any need to submit them to the judgment of any higher human authority. Originally known as Independents, the Congregationalists reached their greatest position of influence under the Commonwealth (1649–60) when Cromwell, Hugh Peters, Thomas Goodwin and John Owen and others held eminent positions.

CONQUEROR, The

one of the most notable nicknames in all history as borne by William I (1066–87) of England, Duke of Normandy. In 1064 William conquered the French province of Maine; from this originated his title of the Conqueror, which was amply justified by his conquest of England 1066–73.

CONSERVATIVE

the correct term for an adherent of the Conservative and Unionist Party in Britain. From approximately 1830 it began to replace Tory, now largely used by opponents only.

CONSTANT

O.Fr. *constant* = steadfast or resolute.

CONSTANTINE

said by Reaney to be derived from 'constant' (q.v.). See, however, pedigree of Constantine in *BLG*, 1952, and *The House of Constantine* by L. G. Pine (privately published by Alcuin Press, 1957) where the origin of the name is given as from Coutances in Normandy, also the view of the College of Arms.

CONVENTUALS

branch of the Franciscan Order which favoured the communal holding of property and a mitigated rule, as opposed to the Observantines (q.v.).

CONVERSE O.Fr. *convers*, Latin *conversus* = a convert. The term was applied to the converts from secular to religious life but in thirteenth century the word often denoted laymen attached to the monasteries who were anything but well behaved.

COOLE, COOLL Manx *combal* = courageous.

COOT, COOTE M.E. *cote*, *coote* = coot. Applied from the bald coot, it signified stupidity.

COPNER O.E. *copenere* = paramour or lover.

COPPER NOSE Oliver Cromwell.

COPPERHEADS adherents of the South who lived in the North in the American Civil War.

COPRONYMUS Dunger; Constantine V, Byzantine Emperor, 741. From a Greek word meaning dung, because he was said to have dirtied the font when he was baptized.

CORBET, CORBETT O.Fr. *corbet* = raven. Nickname for person with dark hair or complexion. Surname of an anciently recorded Norman family which bears ravens in its arms and was long seated in Shropshire.

CORCORAN, CORKAN Irish, the red-complexioned.

CORINTH'S PEDAGOGUE Dionysios the Younger, Tyrant of Syracuse, who on being expelled from the tyranny became a schoolmaster at Corinth.

CORINTHIAN person of dissolute life, Corinth being well known for immorality.

CORNEILLE DU BOULEVARD and even le Shakespeare du Boulevard, said of Guilbert de Pinérécourt (1773–1844) after Pierre Corneille (1606–84).

CORNELL in one of its sources from Fr. *corneille* = rook, or crow, hence a chatterer.

CORNISH CROW John Scrope, 5th Baron Scrope of Bolton, K. G., from his badge of a Cornish chough, which he adopted from the crest of his wife's family. She was Joan, daughter of 4th Baron FitzHugh.

CORNISH WONDER John Opie (1761–1807) a painter, was given this name by Dr Wolcot.

CORP O.Fr = raven.

CORPORAL VIOLET name for Napoleon I, the Little Corporal (q.v.) because when exiled in 1814 to Elba, he said that he would return with the violets.

CORRAN, CORRIN Manx, ultimately contracted from Mac Odhrain = pale faced.

CORSICAN OGRE Napoleon I (1769–1821), detested by his enemies in his lifetime, but after his death the subject of a legend or rather a myth showing him as peace-loving, benevolent, kind and opposed to war. The best summing up of Napoleon's career is in Thomas Hardy's poem *The Dynasts*.

CORTEEN   Manx, contraction of Mac Cruitin, the latter meaning hunch backed.

CORVINUS   from a raven on his shield applied to Mattias I, King of Hungary (1458–90).

CORYPHAEUS OF GERMAN LITERATURE   Goethe (1749–1832); term derived from the leader and speaker of the chorus in Greek drama.

CORYPHAEUS OF LEARNING   Richard Porson (1759–1808), one of England's greatest classical scholars. Also called Devil Dick.

COSMAS   the Indian navigator Cosmas Indicopleustes, a geographer of the sixth century whose work is valuable as showing the spread of Christianity in his time in eastern areas.

COTTAGE COUNTESS   Sarah Hoggins, who married John Jones (in reality Henry Cecil, 9th Marquess of Exeter) see *Burke's Peerage*, Exeter, M. This is beautifully told by Lord Tennyson in his poem, 'The Lord of Burleigh'.

COUNTESS   O.Fr. *Contesse* 'When applied to a woman probably meant proud, haughty as a countess; applied to a man denoted an effeminate dandy' (Reaney, *Dict. of British Surnames*).

COURAGEOUS, The or ANIMOSUS   Albert III, Duke of Saxony (1443–1500), a strong supporter of the Habsburgs.

COURTALD, COURTAULD   Huguenot name said to be diminutive of *court* = short.

COURTHOSE   'short-hose'; name bestowed by his family on Robert, Duke of Normandy, the eldest son of William I (the Conqueror) of England, because he was short in stature. Robert died 1134 in Cardiff Castle, the prisoner of his brother Henry I.

COUSE   O.N. *kause* = tom cat.

COVENANTERS   The Presbyterians of Scotland who bound themselves in the 16th and 17th centuries by covenants to maintain their religious views.

COWLEY FATHERS   Popular name for the Society of St John the Evangelist, founded in 1865 by R. M. Benson, the vicar of St James's Cowley.

COXHEAD   described as London English; cockshead a sobriquet.

COY, COEY   Fr. *coi* = quiet, shy, etc.

CRABB   O.E. *crabbe* = crab, a person walking like a crab (cf. Scrope), also M.E. *crabbe* = wild apple, i.e. as applied to a person, someone fractious or crossgrained, in colloquial terms 'crabby'.

CRAFT   O.E. *craeft* = skill, applied to mean 'cunning'.

CRAKE   M.E. *crake* = crow or raven, a reference probably to someone's croaking voice.

CRANE   O.E. *cran* = crane, possible reference to someone having long legs.

CRANK   M.E. *cranke* = high spirits, lusty.

CRASKE

M.E. meaning fat or lusty.

CRASS, CRAISE

O.Fr. fat or big, ultimately from Latin *crassus*.

CREEGOT

while usually derived from the surname, Crevecoeur, of a baronial family, can be a nickname, Fr. *crèvecoeur*, a heartbreaker, philanderer.

CRISPIN, CRIPPEN

a surname ultimately from a Roman name, Crispinus, Latin *crispus* = curly. According to Lanfranc, Archbishop of Canterbury under William the Conqueror, 'Gilbert Crispin was the first man to receive this nickname and two of his sons adopted it as their surname' (Reaney).

CROESUS

a name proverbial for vast wealth; borne by the last King of Lydia (c. 560–46 or 540 BC) who was defeated and conquered by Cyrus the Great (q.v.). Croesus found that the words of Solon, his Athenian visitor, had come true, 'If one should come with sufficient iron, he will be master of all this gold' referring to the treasury of Croesus.

CROMB, CROME

O.E. *crawb*, *cromb*, M.E. *crome*, or O.E. *crumb* = bent or stooping, the latter giving a nickname.

CROOK, CROCK

from O.N. *krokr* = hook, denoting something crooked (applied to behaviour).

CROOKED, The

Erling Skakke, father of King Magnus IV (1161–84) of Norway by the daughter of King Sigurf I.

CROUCHBACK

distinguishing term for Edmund, 1st Earl of Lancaster, the 4th son of Henry III of England. Edmund (1245–96) was ancestor of Blanche, the first wife of John of Gaunt, created Duke of Lancaster, and father of Henry IV of England. From a natural deformity of the shoulder.

The term also applies to Richard III of England (1483–85). How far a correct description in his case is not known; could have been derived from an attack of infantile paralysis. The Shakespearean portrayal of Richard III in the play of that name gives full vent to the Tudor hostility to Richard. A society exists which seeks to vindicate Richard from the numerous charges against him. See the novel *The Daughter of Time* by Josephine Tey.

CROW

O.E. *crawes* = crow.

CRUEL, Pedro the

King of Castile (1350–69). Born in 1334, legitimate son of King Alfonso XI. Described by his enemies as a monster of cruelty, he was a brave and energetic ruler who was confronted by powerful bastard half brothers, one of whom, Henry of Trastamara, eventually succeeded in defeating Pedro and killing him with his own hand. In the course of the struggle, Henry secured the help of the French, and Pedro that of the Black Prince (q.v.). The latter led an army into Spain and crushingly defeated Henry at Najera (Navaretta) in 1367. Later, owing to a quarrel with the Black Prince, Pedro was defeated. It appears that he used assassination freely as a means of getting rid of opponents, but for the generality of his people his justice was impartial. The merchant class regretted his fall. The elder of Pedro's daughters married John of Gaunt of Lancaster, fourth son of King Edward III of England. The daughter gave off an unpleasant odour which made Gaunt shy of marital relations.

CRUICKSHANK, CROOKSHANKS

a combination, according to Reaney, of O.N. *krokr*, something bent, and O.E. *sceanca* – shank. Hence a reference to a crooked leg. Bardsley concurs, but in the detailed account by Dr Black (*Surnames of Scotland*) only one instance is allowed to be possibly a nickname; the rest of the Scottish cases cited being derived from Scots place names, cruick and shank.

CRUSE, CREWES

M.E. *cruse* = bold, audacious.

CRUST

O.Fr. *crouste* – crust of bread used of one, obstinate, 'crusty'.

CTISTE

(Greek), founder, the title of Mithridates I, King of Pontus, of a family descended from Persian nobility.

CULDEES

some Irish and Scottish monks of the eighth-eleventh centuries whose name is derived from Old Irish *cele de* – companion. They appear to have been anchorites, but very little is known about them.

CULF

found in the Domesday Book, 1086, in form of *cudulf*, etc. O.E. *cuthwulf* = famous wolf.

CUNCTATOR

the delayer, strictly a surname earned by Quintus Fabius Maximus at one time appointed Dictator of Rome, and five times consul. By his delaying methods (Fabian tactics) he refused battle with Hannibal but cut off the latter's supplies. Fabius died in 203 BC. The early Roman poet, Ennius, summed up the achievement of Fabius in the celebrated line: '*Unus homo nobis cunctando restituit rem*' – 'One man by delaying restored the state to us.'

CURÉ DE MEUDON

François Rabelais (c. 1495–1553), the famous French author.

CURL, CROLL

M.E. *crulle* = curly hair.

CURLING

M.E. *crulling* = the curly one.

CURR

M.E. *curre* = cur.

CURRER BELL

assumed name of Charlotte Brontë (1816–55).

CURTIN

O.Fr. *curt* = short, cf. curt-hose.

CURTIS

O.Fr. *corteis*, *courtois* = courteous, in Middle Ages used of a man of good education.

CURTMANTLE

Henry II, King of England (1154–89) introduced the short Anjou mantle.

CUTHBERT

a term for a civil servant; also used during the First World War (1914–18) for a man of military age and physically fit who worked in an office.

CUTTERIDGE

O.E. *cuthric* = famous ruler; used in Old English as personal name but derived from a characteristic.

CYCLOPS

see Monophthalmus.

CYNIC, The

Maximus (fourth century) who was intruded into the see of Constantinople and who professed to be able to hold the cynic philosophy in conjunction with the Nicene Creed.

CYNTHIA

the moon, used of the goddess Diana, and used by the poets of her time for Elizabeth I.

CYRENE, Simon of

compelled to carry Christ's Cross (Matthew xxvii. 32 and Mark xv. 21).

D

DAFT O.E. *gedaft* = gentle or meek, becoming in M.E. = foolish, rather like 'silly', which originally meant 'holy'.

DAGG O.Fr. *dague* = dagger; applied to one who carried a dagger with perhaps Daggar as diminutive of same.

DAIN, DAYNES, DYNE M.E. *digne* = worthy or honourable.

DAINTY M.E. *deinte*, O.Fr. *daintie* = fine, pleasant.

DALAI LAMA the former priest ruler of Tibet; Lama is a Tibetan word, but Dalai is a Mongol word meaning 'ocean'. It was given to the third Dalai Lama in 1578 by Altan Khan of the Timured Mongols. The title of Dalai implied that the Lama's wisdom was wide and deep as the ocean.

DAMASCENE i.e. of Damascus; St John (c. 675–749) a distinguished Greek theologian.

DAME Fr. *dame* = lady, used in sarcastic sense as in modern American.

DAMNED, The Soyatopolk, son of St Vladimir, Grand Prince of Kiev (died 1015) who killed his brothers Boris and Gleb (both canonized as saints). Soyatopolk was defeated by another brother, Yaroslav, who then reunited the territories of the princedom of Kiev.

DAMSEL O.Fr. *dameisole* = a maiden of noble birth; also used in masculine form of a young page, probably in sense of effeminate.

DAMSEL OF BRITTANY Eleanor, daughter of Geoffrey, 2nd son of King Henry II of England. After the death of her brother Arthur of Brittany, 1203, the succession of the English throne should have devolved on her. She died unmarried in 1241. She was born two years before her father's death.

DANCING CHANCELLOR Sir Christopher Hatton (1540–91) because he was said to have danced his way into the Lord Chancellorship. He was a man of considerable attainments apart from his dancing, which undoubtedly pleased Queen Elizabeth I. His knowledge of the law was no great matter; he was admitted to the Inner Temple in 1560, but not called to the Bar. His portrait is in Inner Temple Hall.

DANGAR, DANGER O.Fr. *dangier* = power, or reluctance, hesitation.

DANISH LUTHER Hans Tausen (1494–1561), Danish reformer who had been a monk and who propagated Lutheranism in Denmark.

DARBEN M.E. *derebarne* = dear child.

DARK

found in early thirteenth century as surname from O.E. *deore* = dark, a reference to complexion.

DARK AGES

a term at one time applied by ignorant scholars to the entire 1,000 years between the fall of Rome, c. 400–500 to 1400–1500 in western Europe. Now used more properly of the period roughly from 450 to 1100 when culture had receded from its attainments in the time of classical Rome. The term must be confined to western Europe as during these Dark Ages brilliant civilizations flourished at Constantinople, in Moorish Spain and in Islam generally.

DARK CONTINENT

Africa, because it was unknown to most of the world right up to the middle of the nineteenth century, as regards the bulk of the interior. Africa did not extend in the knowledge of the Romans below the Sahara, yet they had a saying *ex Africa semper aliquid novi venit*. It is true that the eastern coast was known and used by the Chinese and later by the Arabs in the Middle Ages, but their knowledge did not extend very far into the interior.

DARLING, DEARLING, DORLING

from O.E. *dierling, dearling* and *deorling* = one dearly loved. Dr Black (*Surnames of Scotland*) said that it denoted the young noble of a family, possibly the eldest on whom all the hopes rested.

DARREE, DENRY

O.Fr. *denree* = pennyworth, probably like Pennyfather (q.v.), but with reference to poverty.

DARWINIANS and DARWINISM

followers and teaching of Charles Robert Darwin (1809–82), the famous English biologist and author of *The Origin of Species* (1859). Used sometimes in a pejorative sense by opponents of the Darwinian theory, but not correctly used as synonymous with the theory of evolution.

DASHPER, DISPER

from O.Fr. *duze pers*, twelve peers, i.e. paladins of Charlemagne, hence very brave knight.

DAVALL, DEARVILLE, DEVILLE, DIVALL, EVILL

although a place name in France, there were many cases in which the name originated as a nickname 'devil'. The father of William the Conqueror and his predecessor as Duke of Normandy was Robert the Devil.

DAVEY, DAVIE

pet form of David.

DAVID

name used in both England and Scotland, comes from the great O. T. character David (Hebrew = beloved one). Dr Black cites: 'Lord Hailes after commenting on the fact that not one of the six sons of Malcolm III (Malcolm Canmore) received the name of any of the ancient kings of Scotland, but only Anglo-Saxon names evidently chosen by Queen Margaret, says, "As David was the youngest, we may conjecture that he was born when Margaret had no hope of more children, and therefore that he received the name of the youngest son of Jesse".' (*Surnames of Scotland*, p. 202).

DAWKINS

Little David, from Dawe = David plus kin.

DAYBELL 'probably a nickname from one who turned night into day' (Reaney, *Dict. of British Surnames*).

DEACON, The James in seventh century in England who accompanied Paulinus to Northumbria where he later took a considerable part in spreading the Gospel.
Paul (c. 720–800) an Italian chronicler known as Father of Italian History.

DEAD SEA never mentioned under this name in the Old Testament and not in the New Testament at all. In the Old Testament it is the salt sea and in Hebrew tradition it was formed when the cities of the plain Sodom and Gomorrah were destroyed for their wickedness. The name θάλαδδα, νέκρα is first found in the Greek writers, Pausanius and Galen. Romans called it *Mare Mortuum*.

DEAR, DEER sometimes from O.E. *deore* = beloved or O.E. *deo* = brave, or yet again from another meaning of O.E. *deor* = wild animal.

DEARMAN O.E. *deor* and *mann*, 'dear man'.

DEATH, DE ATH, D'AETH a name derived from impersonation in the mystery and other medieval plays, e.g. in the Morality of Everyman, where the dominant influence is that of Death though he speaks little. The mythical account is that the name is that of a 'noble Norman'! Dr Reaney said of this 'The common explanation that this name derives from Ath [in Belgium, hardly Norman? L. G. P.] is just possible. One example has been noted; Gerardus de Athia 1208 Curia Regis Rolls, Glos., but the numerous other examples are certainly not topographical in origin. De Ath, etc. must be regarded as affected spellings designed to dissociate the name from death' (*Dict. of British Surnames*. p.91).

DEBBLE, DEEBLE Fr. *debile*, Latin *debilis* = weak, feeble.

DEBONNAIRE, Le Louis I, see The Pious.

DEED, DEEDES O.E. *daed* = deed.

DEFENDERS, The an eighteenth century Irish secret society formed to resist the Peepo'days boys (q.v.).

DEISTS the adherents of purely natural religion, a system which began in England in the late seventeenth and eighteenth centuries. At first the word Deism was interchangeable with Theism, but in the works of the Deists it soon became in practice undistinguishable from atheism. In England the system had little influence, its main effect being the production in reply to Deism of the classic *Analogy of Religion* by Bishop J. Butler. On the Continent Deism was received by many writers, notably the Encyclopaedists (q.v.).

DELICIAE HUMANI GENERIS Darling of the human race, the term used by the historian of *The Twelve Caesars* Suetonius, of Titus, the second of the Flavian Emperors, who reigned AD 79–81. Titus, as lieutenant of his father Vespasian, captured and destroyed Jerusalem in 70; built the Colosseum in Rome; during his reign occurred the eruption of Vesuvius which destroyed Herculaneum and Pompeii.

DEMOCRITUS JUNIOR
Robert Burton (1577–1640) who wrote *The Anatomy of Melancholy*, a somewhat unsuitable name as Democritus, who lived in the fifth century BC, was known as the laughing philosopher.

DENMARK'S SALVATION
(*Danmarks bod*), phrase used of himself by King Gorm of Denmark in the tenth century after he had reunited the whole country.

DEUTERS, DEWTERS
M.E. *douten*, O.Fr. *duter*, *douter* = to hesitate. 'Used of one who is timid, wavering in opinion, one who dilly-dallies.'

DEVIL, The
Robert II, 6th Duke of Normandy, called also the Magnificent. He died 1035 at Nicaea in Bithynia while returning from a pilgrimage to Jerusalem. He willed that his illegitimate son, William, a boy of 8, should succeed him. This boy became William the Conqueror.

DEVIL DICK
Richard Porson (1759–1808) great Greek scholar.

DEVIL'S MISSIONARY, The
Voltaire (q.v.) (1694–1778), for his infidel writings.

DEVIN, DEVINE, DIVINE
M.E. *devin*, O.Fr. *devin* = divine; reference to people of excellence.

DIABLE, Le
Oliver le Dain, minister of Louis XI of France, but hanged in 1484, after the king's death.

DIADOCHI
successors, the name given to the generals of Alexander the Great who fought over and divided his empire. They were the Seleucids (Asia Minor and Syria), the Ptolemies (Egypt), and the Antigonids (Pergamum). All their empires were absorbed into the Roman empire.

DIAMOND JIM
US financier, James Buchanan Brady.

DIAMOND LIL
and siren of the screen, Mae West.

DIAMOND PITT
Thomas Pitt (1653–1726), because he owned the Pitt Diamond. He was grandfather of the 1st Earl of Chatham.

DICE, DYCE
M.E. *dyse*, *dyce* = dice, with reference to person given to gambling.

DIETRICH VON BERN
i.e. Theodoric of Verona, see Theodoric the Great, who figures in the *Niebelungenlied* as Dietrich. (See C. Kingsley's *The Roman and the Teuton*.)

DIGGERS
seventeenth century section of the Levellers (q.v.), who believed in common ownership of land. Under Gerrard Winstanley in 1649 the Diggers began digging up some waste land at St George's Hill, Oatlands, Surrey.

DILL
in some cases from O.E. *dyl* as in Dilke, but M.E. *dull* = dull or foolish, gave rise to forms such as Dill.

DIPPER, DIAPER
in secondary meaning from M.E. *dipper* = diving bird.

DIRCAEAN SWAN
Pindar, the great Greek poet, so named from Dirce, a fountain near his birthplace, Thebes. Also called the Theban Eagle (q.v.).

DISCALCED

unshod, from Latin *discalcare*, to make unshod, a term applied to some religious orders whose members wear sandals. Originally these monks and nuns were bare-footed. Now stockings are not worn except in cold climates.

DISCIPLES OF CHRIST

a body which arose within Presbyterianism and then became separate, founded in 1811 in the USA by Alexander Campbell. Also known as Churches of Christ and Campbellites.

DISMAL SCIENCE, The

Thomas Carlyle's name for Economics.

DISMORE, DIMMER

from *de duabus marcis* = two marks, probably in reference to niggardliness.

DISSENTERS

those persons who did not assent to the Established Church of England. The first Dissenters were those who became known as Papists (q.v.); i.e. Roman Catholics who after Pope Pius V excommunicated Queen Elizabeth I in 1570 declined to attend Anglican churches. The next body of Dissenters were the followers of Robert Browne (c. 1550–1633), who was for long in and out of communion with the C. of E. He did actually receive episcopal orders, but had considerable influence on Congregationalism, Congregationalists being at first often termed Brownists. The real growth of Dissent, however, came after the Act of Uniformity 1662, when some 2000 Presbyterian clerics were ejected from their livings in the Church of England. Another term for Dissenters is Nonconformists. Now the Dissenting or Nonconformist bodies are usually referred to as Free Churches. Nor are Roman Catholics usually classed among Nonconformists, but on this see the introductory article in *Who's Who in the Free Churches*, 1950.

DIVER, DIVERS

from dive = a diving bird.

DIVINE, The

a title accorded to Ariosto (1474–1533), Italian poet, and Raphael (1483–1520), famous artist.

DIVINE MADMAN

Michelangelo (1475–1564).

DIVINE PAGAN

Hypatia (c.370–415) the head of the Neoplatonic school at Alexandria. She was murdered by a Christian mob. A full and touching account is in Charles Kingsley's novel *Hypatia*; also a very brief notice of her is in *Later Greek and Medieval Philosophy*, Cambridge University Press, 1970, p. 314, where she is described as a married woman.

DIXEY, DICKSEE

from Latin *dixi*, I have spoken; taken as name for a chorister, from the opening of a Psalm.

DIZZY

name given by admirers and opponents to Benjamin Disraeli (1804–81), Earl of Beaconsfield, twice Prime Minister, and a brilliant novelist.

DOBB, DOBBS

pet form of Robert. Cf. also Dobbie, Doby, a Scottish name, pet form of Robert. Similarly with Dobbin.

DOBEL, DOBLE

from O.Fr. *doublel* = a twin.

DOCETISTS	persons in the early church who did not believe in the reality of Christ's humanity. They were usually Gnostics (q.v.). From Greek σοκεῖν, to seem.
DOCKETT	'duckhead'.
DOCTOR ACUTUS	Gregory of Rimini who died in 1358. General of his order, the Augustinian hermits, 1357. One of his theological views was of the damnation of unbaptized infants, which gave him the nickname of *tortor infantium* (q.v.).
DOCTOR ANGELICUS	the Angelic Doctor; the description of St Thomas Aquinas (1225–74), the official theologian and philosopher of the Roman Catholic Church, author of two immense works, the *Summa Theologica* and *Summa contra Gentiles*, in which all subjects of Christian theology and morals are treated. Also the author of the most beautiful Eucharistic hymns; canonized 1323; proclaimed a doctor of the Church 1567, official position confirmed by Pope Leo XIII in *Acterni patris* (1879) and Pius XI in *Studiorem ducem* (1923).
DOCTOR CHRISTIANISSIMUS	John Gerson (1363–1429), great French spiritual writer and a proponent of the Conciliar movement. He advocated frequent Communion.
DOCTOR ECSTATICUS	John Ruysbroch (1293–1387) Flemish mystic; also Dionysius the Carthusian (q.v.).
DOCTOR INVINCIBILIS or SINGULARIS	William of Ockham (Occam) (c. 1285–1349) a celebrated philosopher and theologian best known to the general reader for Ockham's razor, *entia non sunt multiplicanda*. Also called *Venerabilis inceptor*, venerable beginner.
DOCTOR IRREFRAGABILIS	the Irrefragable Doctor (the adjective was a usage in Ecclesiastical Latin). Alexander of Hales (i.e. Halesowen in Worcestershire) (c. 1186–1245), regarded as founder of the school of theology in the Franciscan Order to which he belonged.
DOCTOR MELLIFLUUS	St Bernard of Clairvaux, the great monastic leader and preacher (1090–1153).
DOCTOR MIRABILIS	The Wonderful Doctor, Roger Bacon (c. 1214–1292), whose real position in the history of thought has still to be assessed. He was an exponent of experimental science.
DOCTOR MODERNUS	also Resolutissimus – Durandus of Saint-Pourçain (c. 1275–1334), scholastic philosopher.
DOCTOR PROFUNDUS	Thomas Bradwardine (c. 1290–1349), Archbishop of Canterbury 1349, but died same year of the Black Death. 　　Also Jacobus de Escuelo.
DOCTOR SERAPHICUS	the Seraphic Doctor; St Bonaventure, the great Franciscan theologian. He was a great spiritual writer and the fervour of his recorded prayers fully explains his title.
DOCTOR SOLEMNIS	term applied to Henry of Ghent who died in 1293 and who adhered to the teachings of St Augustine of Hippo.

DOCTOR SOLIDUS or COPIOSUS — Richard of Middleton, born c. 1249, a Franciscan philosopher.

DOCTOR SUBTILIS — the Subtle Doctor, Johannes Duns Scotus (c. 1265–1308), a great Franciscan theologian, also called Doctor Marianus because he was the first great thinker to uphold the doctrine of the Immaculate Conception of the Blessed Virgin Mary. His differences from the Doctor Angelicus, St Thomas Aquinas, show the subtlety of his thought. It is ironical that the word 'dunce' owes its origin to Duns.

DOD(D), DODS — usually from a widely used O.E. personal name, but also meaning a lumpish or stupid man, or deceiver, rascal. Cf. Dodell, Dudell = foolish fellow.

DODGE — pet name from Roger. Cf. also Dodgen, diminutive of Dodge. Dodman, Dudman would also seem to be connected.

DOGGETT — possibly a diminutive of dog.

DOLLFUSS — 'mad foot'. From *doll*, slang for *toll*, mad, and *Fuss*, foot. Nazi sneering slang for Engelbert Dollfuss, Austrian statesman (1892–1934).

DOLLING, DOWLING — O.E. *dolling*, the dull one.

DOL(L)MAN — a dull stupid person.

DOLLY MADISON — wife of James Madison (1750–1836), fourth US president. Her full name was Dorothy Payne Todd Madison, also nicknamed The Dowager, the Nation's Hostess and Quaker Dolly.

DOMESDAY BOOK — a case of a sobriquet applied in all earnestness. It was a record of land holdings in the greater part of England in 1086 by order of William the Conqueror. Its name came from O.E. *doom* or judgment because in any dispute over land appeal to the book was final.

DOMINI CANES — the hounds of the Lord, applied to the Dominican order founded by a Spaniard St Dominic (1170–1221).

DOMM — O.E. *dumb*, M.E. *domme* = mute.

DON JUAN — a term which has become proverbial for a man of unbounded gallantry. Plays, operas and poems, e.g. Byron's *Don Juan*, deal with the fictitious character's exploits, though there was an original Don Juan Tenoria, of Seville, in the fourteenth century.

DONALD — O.Fr. *domnall* = world mighty. Dr Black gave a deeply interesting account of this name which he considered that the rulers of the ancient Celtic tribes had given to themselves. He also mentioned the astonishing fact that a British tribal king of whom nothing else is known, was mentioned on the Ancyra Monument, the inscription on which was composed by the Emperor Augustus.

DONATISTS — took their name from Donatus, a schismatic bishop in Africa in the fourth century. Donatus was opposed to Caecilian, who had been consecrated by a *traditor* (i.e.

a bishop who handed over the Scriptures to the persecutors). Later the Donatists became associated with the violent Circumcellions (q.v.).

DONNELLY

Irish *donn* = brown and *gal* = valour. 'A Cenel Eoghain sept of Ballydonnelly, akin to the O'Neilly in Tyrone', Edward MacLysaght, *Irish Surnames*, p. 86. An obscure origin from some chief noted for his valour.

DOOLAN

Irish *dubbshlain* = defiance.

DOOLEY

Irish *dubb* = black, *laoch* = hero.

DO(O)LITTLE

name bestowed on an idler; cf. Shaw's character in *Pygmalion*.

DORAN

Irish *Deoradhain* = exiled person.

DORMER

Fr. *dormeur* = sleeper, sluggard.

DORMITIANUS

the nickname bestowed by St Jerome on his opponent, Vigilantius (living c. 400), as being in his opinion dormant instead of vigilant.

DOST

O.E. *dysig*, M.E. *dosye* = foolish.

DOUCE, DOUESE, DUCE

M.E. *douce*, O.Fr. *dous* = sweet or pleasant.

DOUGAL(L)

Irish *dubhgall* = black stranger, applied to Norwegians by the Irish.

DOUGHTY

O.E. *duhtig*, M.E. *doughtye* = valiant.

DOUKHOBORS

originally a Russian sect whose name meant 'spirit fighters' and which appeared among Russian peasants c. 1740. Many ideas of a communistic nature were held among them. A large number emigrated to Canada in this century.

D'OUTREMER

from overseas, the name of Louis IV, King of France, who died in 954. He had been obliged to seek refuge in England after the deposition of his father, Charles III, the Simple (q.v.).

DOVE

O.E. *dufe* = dove, as for someone gentle.

DOW(E)

can come from Gaelic *dubh* = black.

DOWSETT

M.E. *doucet*, *dulcette*, diminutive of *doux* = sweet, pleasant.

DOZME

(False) Mustafa, rival for the Turkish Sultanate to Murrad II (1404–51), but removed by the latter c. 1425.

DRABBLE

from drab = dirty woman. In Celtic languages meaning is also connected with female dirtiness.

DRABE, DRABERS

O.E. *draca* = dragon, used in M.E. of standard on which some monster was shown, hence the bearer acquired the nickname.

DRAGON

O.Fr. *dragonier* = standard-bearer, standards in pageants and plays often being blazoned with dragons.

DRAGON OF BOSNIA, The

Husein Gradascevic, of Bosnia-Herzegovina, who in 1831 led a rising against the Sultan of Turkey, but was eventually driven across the frontier into Croatia and ended in banishment.

DREAD, The   see The Terrible, Ivan IV of Russia.

DREWERY, DRURY   O.Fr. *druirie* = love, lover.

DRINGER   O.E. *drincere* = drinker.

DRINKALE, DRINKHALL   the latter recalls the origin of the name: 'drink hael', the reply to a drinking toast, hence a man fond of drinking in company.

DRINKWATER   applied to a man too poor even to purchase the very cheap medieval ale.

DRINKWELL   of a man who drank a heavy draught.

DRIVER OF EUROPE   Le Cocher de l'Europe, the Empress of Russia's name for the chief minister of Louis XV, the Duc de Choiseul (1719–85), because by means of a network of spies all over Europe he was able to exercise control.

DRON(E)   O.E. *dran* = drone, lazy man.

DROOP   M.E. *drup* = dejected, gloomy.

DUCAT   a gold coin, Latin *ducatus* = duchy, because the coins were first minted c. 1140 in the Duchy of Apulia. Probably applied to a man who appeared to have plenty of money.

DUCE, IL   The Chief. Benito Mussolini (1883–1945), Dictator of Italy and leader of the Fascist movement.

DUCK, DOOKS   M.E. *dubbe, duck* = duck.

DUCKER, DUKER   M.E. *douker* = diving bird as in Diver (q.v.).

DUCKETT   O.Fr. *ducquet*, diminutive of *duc* = leader.

DUFF   Gaelic *dubh* = black.

DUFFET   'dove foot' or 'dove head'.

DUGAN, DOUGAN   from Gaelic *dubh* = black.

DUGARD   from Fr. *Dieu te garde* = God keep you; probably derived from a customary exclamation.

DUGUID   'do good'.

DUKE(S)   from Fr. *duc* = leader of an army, probably either because of participation in a play or from warlike qualities.

DUKE, The   John Wayne, celebrated American film actor, especially in cowboy roles; a man of character, he was received into the Roman Catholic Church in his last illness.

DUMBELL   diminutive of dumb = a slow-witted person.

DUMB OX OF SICILY   St Thomas Aquinas, so called by his teacher, Albertus Magnus, because of his habitual silence; Albertus commented that the dumb ox would one day fill the world with his lowing.

DUNCALF   a nickname found from the fourteenth century.

DUNCE, DUNS

a dunce. This is one of the most strangely derived of all nicknames. It comes from the name of John Duns Scotus (1265–1308), John the Scot, possibly from Duns in Berwickshire. He was one of the most celebrated of the Schoolmen, a Franciscan and known in his own time as Doctor Subtilis (q.v.), because of the subtlety of his reasoning in philosophy and theology. After the Renaissance the scholastic philosophy fell into disrepute (until the nineteenth-twentieth centuries). 'The word "dunce" used by humanists and the Reformers to ridicule the subtleties of the Schools, is a curious testimony to its popularity' (*Oxford Dictionary of the Christian Church*).

DUNNING

son of the dark swarthy one (O.E.).

DURHAM, Simon of

(c. 1060–1130) a chronicler.

DURRAN, DURRAND

O.Fr. *durant* = obstinate.

DUST, DOUST

O.E. *dust* = dust, i.e. dust-coloured hair or complexion, or of little value; cf. phrase 'less than the dust'.

DUTCH

derived from description of immigrant workers from Holland.

DWARFS(WA)

early Chinese term for the Japanese, see Wa.

DWELLY

O.E. *dweollic* = foolish, or in error.

E

EAGLE OF BRITTANY
Bertrand Duguesclin (1320–80), Constable of France. 'That impoverished Breton knight enjoyed a popularity out of all proportion to his talents and his exploits.' Whenever 'he fought on his own account, he invited a pitched battle and got himself defeated, as he did at Auray and Naserao'. Thus Edouard Perroy, *The Hundred Years War* London, Eyre & Spottiswoode, 1948, pp. 148–9. None the less Duguesclin's tactics whittled away the English conquests in France in the latter part of Edward III's reign.

EAGLE OF DIVINES
St Thomas Aquinas (1225–74).

EAGLE OF MEAUX
Jacques Bénigne Bossuet (1627–1704), Bishop of Meaux, considered by many good judges as the first among modern Christian orators. His most important writings were *Discours sur l'histoire universelle* (1681), written primarily for his pupil the Dauphin, son of Louis XIV; and *Histoire des variations des églises protestantes* (1688), a study based on the works of the reformers themselves.

EAGLE OF THE NORTH
Count Axel Gustafson Oxenstierna (1583–1654), one of Sweden's greatest patriotic statesmen.

EARL(E), HEARLE, HURL(E)
O.E. *eorl* = earl. The only English title in the peerage, itself an anglicization of the Norse jarl. Use as surname came from characterization in pageants or medieval plays.

EARLEY, ERLEIGH
sometimes from O.E. *eorlic* = manly.

EASTMAN, ESMOND
O.E. *eastmund* = grace or favour, protection.

EASTMURE
O.E. Eastmaer = grace or favour, famous.

EBIONITES
lit. poor men, from a Hebrew word, applied whether by themselves or others to a Jewish sect extinguished by the second century AD which held unorthodox views of Christ, regarding Him merely as a prophet. The name may refer to the idea that the holders were 'poor in spirit' (St Matthew V).

ECKHARD
O.G. *eckhard* = edge, hard.

EDDOLILS
O.E. Eadwulf = prosperity wolf. The original meaning is long lost.

EDDY, EDDIE
O.E. Eadwig = prosperity war.

EDGAR, EGGERS, AGAR
O.E. Eadgar = prosperity spear.

EDGELL
O.E. Ecgwulf = sword wolf.

EDMAN, EDMANS, ADMANS
O.E. *eadmann* = prosperity man. Cf. Edmond, Edmonds, O.E. Eadmund = prosperity, protector.

EDRICH, EDRIDGE	O.E. Eadric = prosperity powerful.
EDRUPT	from Greek εὔτροπός, of proved character.
EDWARD, EDWARD(E)(S)	O.E. Eadweard = prosperity guard.
EDWIN	O.E. Eadwine = prosperity friend.
EFFEMY	Greek ἐφημία, auspicious speech.
ÉGALITÉ	the name assumed by Philippe, Duc d'Orléans (1747–93) when he renounced his title and voted for the death of Louis XVI. Égalité was the father of Louis Philippe, King of the French; his assumption of the revolutionary cause did not save him from the guillotine.
EGBERT	O.E. Ecgbeorht = sword bright, the name of Egbert of Wessex c. 825, from whom descends his 63rd successor, Elizabeth II.
ELDER, ELDERS	the elder.
ELDER, The	Apollinarius, who rewrote much of the Bible in classical metre when the last pagan Roman Emperor Julian (died 362) forbade Christians to use the pagan classics. This work Apollinarius executed in conjunction with his son, the Younger.
	Edmund Calamy (1600–66), a Presbyterian divine of Huguenot origin.
	Edward I, pre-Norman Conquest, who reigned 899–944, son of Alfred the Great. He reconquered the land occupied by the Danes up to the Humber and became overlord of Britain. Name used to distinguish him from his great-grandson Edward the Martyr (q.v.).
	Elder is applied to Gaius Plinius Secundus (AD 23–79) to distinguish him as a writer from his nephew, Gaius Plinius Caecilius Secundus (born 61 or 62) the Younger (q.v.). The elder Pliny perished in the eruption of Vesuvius in AD 79.
	Hans Holbein (c. 1466–1524) was the senior member of a family of painters which included his brother Sigismund, his son Ambrosius and the famous Hans Holbein the younger (q.v.).
	St Melania (c. 342–410) a Roman lady who as a widow adopted the ascetic life and died in Jerusalem.
	Seneca the Elder, a rhetorician of Cordoa in Spain father of Seneca the famous philosopher.
ELEGANTIAE ARBITER	arbiter of taste. Petronius, a Latin writer of the first century who held a position of influence in the court of the Emperor Nero 'until falling out of favour, he ended a strange life of mingled activity and debauchery in AD 66 by committing a leisurely suicide' (*Chambers Encyclopaedia*, Tacitus, *Annales*, xvi. 18–20).
EL GRECO	the Greek; name given to a native of Crete, Domenico Theotocopuli, who went to Italy, then to Spain, where in Toledo he produced his great paintings.
ELIA	Charles Lamb's *nom de plume*. He lived 1775–1834 and was author of the famous *Essays of Elia* which have ensured his permanent place in English literature.

ELKASITES	a Jewish Christian sect similar to the Ebionites (q.v.), existing east of the Jordan c. AD 100. As with the Ebionites, the Elkasites (*elkesal*, sacred power) were heretical on the deity of Christ, and laid emphasis on the keeping of the Mosaic Law.
ELLEN ALLEYNE	pseudonym of Christina Georgina Rossetti (1836–94), poetess.
EL(L)IOT(T)	sometimes from O.E. Aelfweald = elf ruler, cf. also Ellwood.
ELSEY, ELSIE	O.E. Aelfsige = elf victory.
ELWES	from O.E. and O.G. sources, *heluis*, *heilwides* = hale or sound-wide.
EMANCIPATOR, The GREAT	Abraham Lincoln, US President, 1809–65, also called Honest Abe, and Rail Splitter (q.v.).
ENCRATITES	from Greek ἐγκρατεις, lit. in possession of power, and meaning as here, self-controlled; a Gnostic-style sect in the early Christian centuries, having Puritanic views on food, drink and often on marriage.
ENCYCLOPEDISTS	the contributors to the French *Encyclopédie*, published 1751–80 in 35 vols under the editorship of D. Diderot. Many of the articles provided intellectual and disruptive elements for the French Revolution; the religious views expressed were akin to those of the Deists (q.v.).
ENGLAND'S DARLING	Alfred the Great (q.v.).
ENGLISH	O.E. *Englise* = English, according to Reaney (*Dict. of British Surnames*) differentiated Angles from Saxons. It is hard to understand its use in England, unless in some counties in the immediate post-Norman Conquest period, as a term of contempt for the defeated English, *Angli* in contrast with *Franci*. Cf. presentation of Englishry and Lord Macaulay's first chapter in *History of England*.
ENGLISH ACHILLES	John Talbot, 1st Earl of Shrewsbury, who was killed at the battle of Châtillon in 1453; his heroic exploits are extolled in Shakespeare's *Henry VI*. Also applied to the 1st Duke of Wellington.
ENGLISH ATTICUS	Joseph Addison (1672–1719), a finished and graceful writer so named by Alexander Pope in the *Prologue to Satires*. Atticus was an elegant Roman scholar to whom Cicero wrote and who was his friend.
ENGLISH BAYARD	Sir Philip Sidney (1554–86).
ENGLISH ENNIUS	Geoffrey Chaucer, as the first great English poet; the original Ennius was the first Latin poet of stature, only fragments of Ennius' work remain. Cicero said of him *ingenio ingens arte rudis*.
ENGLISH HOBBEMA	John Crome of Norwich (1768–1821), from Meindert Hobbema (1638–1709), Dutch landscape painter.
ENGLISH JUSTINIAN	Edward I (1272–1307) of England, because of his many legal changes, including the famous statute *Quia Emptores* on land law. The allusion is to the Byzantine

Emperor Justinian (c. 482–565), who ordered the codification of Roman Law; the Institutes of Justinian.

ENGLISH LADIES — the popular name for the Institute of the Blessed Virgin Mary, a body of religious women founded in 1609 by Mary Ward (1585–1645).

ENGLISH MERLIN — William Lilly (1602–81), an astrologer who called himself *Merlinus Anglicus*.

ENGLISH SOLOMON — James I of England (1603–25), James VI of Scotland. Renowned for his learning but very pedantic, called by the French 'the wisest fool in Christendom'.

ENGLISH ST SEBASTIAN — Saint Edmund, King of East Anglia, who was martyred by the heathen Danes on 20 November 869. So called because St Sebastian was shot to death by archers as was St Edmund. Bury St Edmunds is named after him, being his burial place. His shrine was in the abbey, now ruined.

ENLIGHTENED DOCTOR — Raymond Lull (c. 1234–1315), a lay missionary whose great object was the conversion of Jews and Moslems. His methods were far in advance of his time, including the thorough study of Arabic (which he learned in Majorca, his birthplace) and other oriental tongues, and the use of purely rational arguments in dealing with Jews and Moslems on the basis of their monotheism in common with Christians. His book *Blanquerna* sets forth his ideals and Prof. E. A. Peers's *Ramon Lull* is valuable.

ENNION — Welsh, *einion* = anvil, denoting stability, fortitude.

ENTHUSIASTIC — used with the greatest opprobriousness in eighteenth century England about anyone who was supposed to exhibit extravagance in devotion. Dr Johnson defined enthusiasm as 'a vain confidence of Divine favour or communication'. This attitude had a deadening influence on the eighteenth century C. of E. The only excuse for the depreciation was in reaction to the very great enthusiasm in 17th century England which had swept away king, nobility and church.

EPICUREANISM — a system of thought derived from the Greek philosopher, Epicurus (342–270 BC), who taught that the senses are the source of all ideas; pleasure was the highest good, but was to be attained by the use of prudence as the highest virtue. It is easy to understand how perverted such teaching could become, so that in general an Epicurean is considered to be a person seeking only sensual pleasures. Cf. Anatole France, *Jardin d'Epicure* and Walter Pater, *Marius the Epicurean*.

EPIPHANES — 'God manifest', assumed by Antiochus IV (c. 215–163 BC), King of Syria, known in history because of his enthusiasm for Greek culture. Palestine formed part of his empire and he decided to make the Jews into Greeks. The result was the war with the Maccabees (q.v.). His assumption of the name Epiphanes would incense his Jewish subjects.
Ptolemy V Epiphanes (reigned 205–181 BC) of Egypt.

ERASMUS, Desiderius   strictly not a nickname, but the rendering in Latin and Greek of Gerhard, i.e. the beloved. It was the form adopted by a boy born out of wedlock, the child of Margaret, a physician's daughter and of Roger Gerhard, a priest. He lived 1466–1536 and was the most renowned scholar in Europe. He produced in 1516 the first western European edition of the Greek New Testament. A romantic rendering of his parents' story is in Charles Reade's novel *The Cloister and the Hearth*.

ERASTIAN   the theory that the state is supreme in ecclesiastical affairs derives from the name of Thomas Erastus (1524–83) German-Swiss theologian and physician. His surname was originally Leiber. Curiously enough, his writings do not contain an exposition of the theory associated with his name. The term 'Erastian' in the modern sense appears first to have come into use in England during the debates in the Westminster Assembly, 1643.

ERRETT   O.E. *Eadraed* = prosperity counsel.

ESSENES   a Jewish sect, mentioned by Philo, Josephus and Pliny the Elder as living in Palestine from the second century BC. They were communistic and very ascetical. Many scholars think that the Essenes were the community of the Dead Sea Scrolls.

EST-IL-POSSIBLE?   Nickname given to Prince George of Denmark husband of Queen Anne (1702–14) of Britain, because this was the only remark he could make when told of the fall and flight of his father-in-law, King James II.

ETTRICK SHEPHERD   James Hogg (1770–1835), the Scottish poet, because his birthplace was in Ettrick Forest in Selkirkshire.

EUERGETES   well-doer, benefactor; borne by Mithridates V, King of Pontus c. 150 BC.
    Ptolemy III of Egypt, reigned 246–221 BC.

EUMENIDES   the kindly ones, the name given by the Greeks to the Furies whose real name was Erinnyes, avengers of wrong. It was not thought polite to call them by their real names.

EUPATOR   see Mithridates the Great. The term is allied with the other Greek form, Eupatris, meaning of noble sire.

EUSTACE   Greek ἐυδταχος, fruitful.

EUTYCHIANISM   a term applied to the teaching and followers of one Eutyches (c. 378–454), who was zealous against the Nestorians but then fell into an opposite error and confounded the two natures of Christ, meaning that Christ's manhood was not consubstantial with ours, hence redemption through Him would be impossible. Eutyches was condemned by the General Council of Ephesus in 451. He is the founder of Monophysitism (q.v.), 'but the Eutychian Christ is a compromise and in such a being were he conceivable to reason, it would be worth my while to say there is no salvation' (T. H. Passmore, *The Mediator of Life*, which gives account of the various forms of wrong thinking in Arians (q.v.), Nestorians (q.v.), etc.

EVANGELIC DOCTOR — John Wycliffe (1320–84), Morning Star of the Reformation.

EVENING — M.E. = equal or match.

EVER MEMORABLE, The — John Hales, an Anglican theologian (1584–1656), sometime chaplain to Archbishop Laud.

EVER VICTORIOUS ARMY — was commanded by Chinese Gordon (q.v.).

EXIGUUS — scanty or little, a self-assumed epithet of Dionysius, a Scythian monk, who lived in Rome c. 500–50, the name being taken for sake of humility. He was very learned and compiled a corpus of canon law. He is also responsible for a very important change in chronology by accepting 753 *ab urbe condita* (of Rome) as the basis for the year of the Incarnation i.e. 1 AD; the system of the Christian era still in use.

EXILE, The — Edward, son of Edmund II (Ironside (q.v.)) sent as a child to Hungary where he married a lady of royal birth, Agatha, daughter of the Emperor of Germany. He was brought to England by order of Edward the Confessor, but died in 1057 without ever meeting the king. He was the father of Edgar Atheling and Margaret of Scotland. Also known as the Outlaw.

EYE OF GREECE, The — Athens, for its intellectual brilliance.

F

FABIAN

Latin Fabianus = of Fabian, i.e. a bean, but this original meaning, while it led to the Roman name, probably did not produce a nickname in England, since a third century Pope was popular as a name giver.

FABIAN SOCIETY

association of middle-class socialist intellectuals founded in 1884 with Shaw and the Webbs. The name derived from Fabius Cunctator (q.v.), because of his cautious tactics. The Fabians believed not in violent revolution but in 'the inevitability of gradualness', which did indeed bring victory to socialism in Britain.

FAERIE QUEENE, The

the name of Edmund Spenser's great unfinished poem, and used often to typify Elizabeth I, as by Spenser.

FAGE

M.E. *fage* = coaxing or cheating.

FAGG, VAGG

O.E. *facg* = flat fish, but thought also to apply to a flat or clean loaf, used kindly of a good baker.

FAINÉANT, Le

do-nothing, applied to Louis V, King of France, who succeeded in 986 but died in 987, the last of the Carolingian dynasty.

FAIR

O.E. *faeger* = fair, beautiful.

FAIR, The

Edwy, King of England (995–9), 'from his beauty' (Lingard, *History of England*, London, J. Mawman, vol. 1, p. 317). A prince who fell out with St Dunstan and the monks and has been recorded by the monastic chroniclers as revelling in obscenity. It is related that he had two mistresses, mother and daughter simultaneously.

Frederick III (c. 1286–1330), German King from 1314, also Duke of Austria from 1308.

(Le Bel), Philip IV (1285–1314), King of France, so called in virtue of his outstanding good looks. A successful king, capable of using horrible cruelty to further his ends. His suppression of the Order of Knights Templars brought the odour of burning flesh to the Île-de-Paris (Malcolm Barber, *The Trial of the Templars*, Cambridge University Press, 1978). Also the name of Philip IV's youngest son, Charles IV (1322–28).

Philip, son of the Habsburg Emperor Maximilian I (whom he succeeded in 1493) who married Joan of Castile and Aragon in 1496.

FAIR GERALDINE, The

Lady Elizabeth Fitzgerald, daughter of the Earl of Kildare. She was called thus in the Earl of Surrey's poems. She died in 1589. See W. H. Ainsworth's novel, *Windsor Castle*.

FAIR MAID OF ANJOU

Lady Edith Plantaganet, married Prince David of Scotland in Scott's novel *The Talisman*, but not a real historical character. Scott says himself in his Introduction to the story: 'One of the inferior characters introduced was a supposed relation of Richard Coeur-de-Lion, a violation of the truth of history.'

FAIR MAID OF BRITTANY Eleanor, the sister of Arthur of Brittany. Arthur was murdered at the instigation of her uncle, King John of England. John imprisoned Eleanor in Bristol Castle where she died in 1241.

FAIR ROSAMUND daughter of Lord Clifford and mistress of King Henry II of England, supposed to have been mother of William Longsword (q.v.), and to have been poisoned by Queen Eleanor who penetrated the maze at Woodstock where Henry kept her. Scott's novel *Woodstock* contains details of this legend.

FAIRBAIN O.E. *ban* = bone, of a person with fine limbs.

FAIRBAIRN O.E. *bearn* = lovely child.

FAIRBARD, FAIRBEARD O.E. *beard* = fair beard.

FAIRBROTHER brother of one nicknamed fair.

FAIRCHILD O.E. *child*, a beautiful child.

FAIRER, FAYER O.E. *faeger*, fair hair.

FAIREY, FAREY O.E. *faeger*, fair; O.E. *eage*, eye.

FAIRFAX O.E. *faeger* = fair and *feax* = hair.

FAIRFOOT though often a place name, sometimes a nickname 'fairfoot'.

FAIRFOUL O.E. *fugol* = fowl, fair bird.

FAIRHAIRED, The Harold I, King of Norway (872–930), from his luxuriant golden locks.

FAIRHEAD O.E. *faeger* and *heafod* = fair or beautiful head.

FAIRLAM sometimes = fair lamb.

FAIRMAN O.E. *faeger* and *mann* = fair man.

FAIRWEATHER M.E. *fair weder*, allusion to one of a bright and happy disposition.

FAITH short for 'faithful'.

FALANGE in full Falange Española, Spanish Phalanx, a Spanish political party founded in 1933 by José Antonio Primo de Rivera, Marqués de Estella, whose father had been dictator of Spain. In 1937 all other ultra-nationalist groups were merged in it, and General Franco, El Caudillo (q.v.), became its chief.

FALCON O.Fr. *faucon*, reference to a person thought to be like a falcon.

FALLOWELL, FALLEVELL fall in the well.

FALSE PROPHET a term applied before the rise of the study of comparative religion in the 19th century to Mohammed. Bishop Charles Gore, referring to this, mentioned that in the older view 'Mohammed was distinctively the False Prophet' (*The Reconstruction of Belief*, London, John Murray, 1930, p.18). For the older Christian view of Islam, cf. St Thomas Aquinas in *Summa contra Gentiles*, book I. c. vi; *vera quae docuit multis fabulis et falsissimis doctrinis immiscuit*. The view expressed in Dante's *Inferno*, canto XXVIII, is similar except that Mohammed (and his son-in-law the 4th Caliph Ali) are shown as schismatics, i.e. cut open as punishment for rending the Church. Dante here adopted a common medieval view of Mohammed as an apostate Christian. In editions designed for Islamic countries this portion of the *Inferno* is omitted.

FALSE SEXTUS

'who wrought the deed of shame', i.e. who raped Lucretia, the faithful wife of L. Tarquinius Collatinus. She killed herself; her husband and her father moved the Roman people to expel the Tarquins and establish a republic. Shakespeare's poem, *The Rape of Lucrece*, recounts the story originally told by the Roman historian Livy; also the subject of Benjamin Britten's opera, *The Rape of Lucretia*.

FAMILISTS or FAMILY OF LOVE

a short-lived sect founded in Holland by H. Nicholas, and devoted to some vague doctrines of love to all humanity. They were the subject of a proclamation in 1580 by Elizabeth I which ordered their books to be burned and themselves imprisoned.

FAMILY OF LOVE

see Familists.

FANE, VANE

O.E. *faegen*, M.E. *fayn* = well disposed.

FANT, FONT, VANT

Fr. *L'enfant* = the child. Cf. Lenfant.

FAREWELL, VARWELL

= fare well.

FARMER GEORGE

King George III of England who reigned 1760–1820, so called from the simplicity of his manners.

FARQUHAR

Gaelic *fearchar* = very dear one.

FARRAND, FERRAND

O.Fr. *ferrant* = iron grey.

FARRAR, FARROW, FARO, PHARAOH, PHARRO

These various forms are derived by Reaney (*Dict. of British Surnames*) from ferrer, O.Fr. *ferreor* = worker in iron, a smith, an occupational name, but the form Pharao(h) is derived from a miracle play or a pageant.

FARSON

fair son.

FASCISM

the name given originally to the Italian political movement launched by Benito Mussolini from Milan in 1919. The word was taken over from Sicilian revolutionary groups in the 19th century called *fasces*, but the latter was the name given to the axe and bundle of rods carried by the Roman lictors in ancient times as symbols of the authority of the state.

FASTER, The

John IV, Patriarch of Constantinople (died 595), practised great asceticism, and when he died had no personal possessions.

FAT, The

Alfonso II of Portugal (1212–23).

Charles III, East Frankish King and Holy Roman Emperor from 881. He died in 888.

Hugh of Avranches, Earl of Chester (died 1101), described in the *Dictionary of National Biography* as *perhaps* a nephew of William the Conqueror. He was in later generations styled Lupus (q.v.) or the wolf.

Louis VI, Le Gros, of France (1108–37).

St Olave (995–1030). Olaf Haraldsson, Patron Saint of Norway, converted to the Christian Faith in England.

Sancho I who died in 965, King of Leon 956–65, described by S. Lane-Poole as so fat that he could not walk without being held up. He was cured of his corpulency by the Jewish physician, Hasdai, whom he went to consult at the court in Cordova of the Caliph Abd-er-Rahman III the Great (q.v.) (S. Lane-Poole, *The Moors in Spain*, London, T. Fisher Unwin, 1897).

FATES, LAFITTE

O.Fr. *afaitie* = affected, skilful, prudent.

FATHER DOLLING

Robert William Radclyffe Dolling (1851–1902) an Anglo-Catholic priest and missioner who achieved great improvements in the Portsmouth slums. Also known as Brother Bob from his work as warden of a fellowship for postmen. He was a friend of the Labour movement because of the appalling social conditions in Poplar, London, where he was vicar of St Saviour's Church.

FATHER IGNATIUS

the Rev. Joseph Leycester Lyne (1837–1908), a mission preacher in the Anglican Church who endeavoured to revive the Benedictine Order in the Church of England. His buildings at Capel-y-ffin, near Llanthony, passed on his death into the possession of the Anglican Benedictines at Caldey Island, which became Pershore, and finally Nashdown Abbey.

FATHER OF CHEMISTRY AND PHYSICS

Robert Boyle (1627–91), 7th son of the 1st Earl of Cork. He was a leading scientist and one of the founders of the Royal Society.

FATHER OF CONTINENTAL CONGRESS

also Sage of America and Father of Lightning, Benjamin Franklin (1706–90).

FATHER OF ECCLESIASTICAL HISTORY

Eusebius of Caesarea (c. 264–340).

FATHER OF ENGLISH PRINTING

William Caxton (1422–91), at Westminster produced in 1477 the first English printed book, *The Dictes and Sayings of the Philosophers*.

FATHER OF EPIC POETRY

Homer.

FATHER OF FRENCH HISTORY

André Duchesne (1584–1640).

FATHER OF HIS COUNTRY

George Washington, first President of the USA. Also applied to many other distinguished characters though with less justice.

FATHER OF HISTORY	Herodotus (5th century BC) wrote the history of the Persian wars with Greece. His work remains a source of great entertainment as well as of information.
FATHER OF ITALIAN HISTORY	Paul the Deacon (q.v.).
FATHER OF MEDICINE	Hippocrates of Cos (460–377 BC). Also Aretaeus, a Greek physician, born in Cappadocia towards the end of the 2nd century AD. He wrote two valuable books, on the causes and symptoms of acute and chronic pains and their cure.
FATHER OF MORAL PHILOSOPHY	St Thomas Aquinas, the Angelic Doctor (q.v.); probably because in his *Summa* he deals so extensively with ethics.
FATHER OF MUSICIANS	in Genesis iv. 21, Jubal, father of all such as handle the harp and organ.
FATHER OF THE DECLARATION OF INDEPENDENCE OF THE USA	Thomas Jefferson (1743–1826), President of the USA.
FATHER OF THE FAITHFUL or FATHER ABRAHAM	the progenitor of the Israelites.
FATHER OF THE PHONOGRAPH	Thomas Alva Edison (1847–1931), US inventor; also Wizard of Wenlo Parkin, New Jersey, where he worked.
FATHER OF THE STEAMBOAT	US inventor Robert Fulton (1765–1815).
FATHER OF TRAGEDY	the great Greek dramatist Aeschylus (died 456 BC), seven of whose plays have been preserved.
FATHER OF WATERS	the Mississippi, with the Missouri as its child. Also applied to the Irrawaddy.
FATHER SMITH	Bernard Smith (c. 1630–1708) an organ builder, born in Germany who came to England and built many famous organs.
FATHERS, FADDER	O.E. *faeder* = father, and cognate forms in allied Scandinavian languages, used to denote one who cares protectively like a father.
FATHERS OF THE CHURCH	Christian writers from the post-apostolic period up to possibly the 7th century.
FATIK	the conqueror, Mohammed II (1432–81), Ottoman Sultan of Turkey (1451–81). He captured Constantinople in 1453, thus bringing to an end the Byzantine Empire.
FAUGH	O.E. *feala* = pale brownish or reddish and yellow colour.
FAUN, FAWN(S)	O.E. *faon*, M.E. *faun* = young animal, applied to a lively, frisky young man.
FAVELL	O.Fr. *fauvel* = fallow coloured, with symbolic application of trickery or underhand behaviour.

FAY　in some cases from O.Fr. *fae* = fairy. Cf. Morgan la Faye the sorceress who figures in some of the Arthurian stories.

FEAR, PHEAR　M.E. *fere* = companion, often used in Spenser's *Faerie Queene*: also from O.Fr. *fier* = proud or fierce.

FEARLESS, The　Le Sans Peur, the second Valois duke of Burgundy who succeeded in 1404 and was assassinated in 1419 by the Armagnac faction, thus driving Burgundy to unite with Henry V of England in his struggle to secure the French crown.

Richard I, third duke of Normandy, succeeded 942, died 996.

FEATHER, FEDDER　O.E. *feder* = feather, used as nickname for one of light disposition.

FEDERAL STATES　hence the Federals; the Northern States which eventually won the American Civil War of 1861–5.

FELIX　Latin *felix* = happy, but in many cases from name of Saint Felix, the apostle of East Anglia, after whom Felixstowe was named.

FELIX　the fortunate; name given to Sulla, the Dictator of Rome, who saw himself as a new Romulus refounding Rome. Sulla died in 78 BC.

FELLOWES　O.E. *feolaza* = companion. Cf. fellowship, with reference to membership of a guild.

FENCIBLES　name of a force on the lines of the Home Guard, raised in 1759–1802, for home defence, the name being shortened from Defencibles.

FENDER　from fend = defend, a defender.

FENIANS　from *fiann*, *feinne*, a legendary band of warriors in Ireland led by Finn MacCumhaill, and used as the name of a revolutionary secret society of the 1860s. It spread its branches throughout the English-speaking world, its object being the establishment in Ireland of a republic, by violent means.

FERRET　M.E. *fyrette*, *ferette* = little pilferer.

FERRETER　in some cases of one who searches or rummages closely.

FETTERS, FAYTER　M.E. and Fr. *partour* = doer in sense of cheat.

FEUILLANTS　an order of reformed Cistercians founded in 1586 by Jean de la Barrière from the convent of Feuillans in Languedoc. The order ended at the time of the French Revolution.

FEVERAL　M.E. form of February, often symbolized as an aged man.

FIDKIN, FITKIN　from Fidd as a diminutive and pet form of Vivian.

FIELD OF THE CLOTH OF GOLD　where Henry VIII met Francis I of France in 1520 near Guisnes. The term came from the magnificent attire and display generally shown there. As Shakespeare wrote 'many have broke their backs by laying manors on them'.

FIFTEEN, The   Jacobite Rebellion of 1715, when the Old Pretender (q.v.) made an attempt to regain the throne.

FIFTH MONARCHY MEN   a very fanatical sect which arose in England in the Civil War between Charles I and his Parliament. It was based on Daniel ii. 44: 'The God of heaven will set up a kingdom which will never be destroyed.' This was to come after the four empires or monarchies – Assyria (Babylonia), Persia, Greece and Rome. Then the Fifth Monarchy would be that of Christ and His Saints reigning for 1,000 years (Revelation xx. 4 is the source of the latter view). The Fifth Monarchy Men rose against Cromwell in 1657 and against Charles III in 1661, but the rebellions were suppressed and Thomas Venner, the leader, and 16 others were beheaded.

FIGGIS   O.E. *fickets* = faithful.

FILS DE L'HOMME   the Son of the Man, one of the terms used by Bonapartists to describe Napoleon II, well in keeping with Napoleon I's disregard of Christ.

FINALITY JOHN   Lord John Russell (1st Earl Russell), who called the Reform Bill in 1832 the final, though in 1854, 1860 and 1866 other Reform Bills were brought forward.

FINCH, FINK, VINK   O.E. *finc* = finch, used to denote 'simpleton'.

FINE(S)   O.Fr. delicate.

FINGARD   possibly for a seller of fine goods.

FINLAY, FINDLAY   Gaelic *Fionnlagh* = fair hero.

FINNEMORE   O.Fr. *fin amour* = dear love.

FIONA McLEOD   assumed pen name of William Sharp.

FIREBRACE, FAIRBRASS   O.Fr. *fer*, *fier*, M.E. *feer*, *fere* = bold, proud and Fr. *bras* = arm.

FIRMIN, FIRMAN   from O.Fr. *firmin*, from Latin *firmus* = firm, strong, but used from name of St Firmin, Bishop of Metz in 5th century.

FIRST CROWNED, The   Stephen, King of Serbia, who received a royal crown from Pope Honorius III in 1217. He was known as Stephen I and was crowned by Dava the Saint in the Church of the Seven Doors at Zica in 1220.

FIRST DARK HORSE   President James Kiron Polk (1795–1849), owing to unexpected electoral win.

FIRST GENTLEMAN IN EUROPE   term applied to George IV (1820–30) of Britain without any apparent reason as his foul language and revolting general conduct would have better merited the description of the highest bred lout.

FIRST GRENADIER OF FRANCE   Napoleon gave this name to Latour d'Auvergne (1743–1800).

FISH(E)   O.E. *fisc* = fish.

FISHERMAN'S RING, The supposed to be that of St Peter and worn by the Pope on special occasions.

FIVE MEMBERS, The were five MPs – Pym, Hampden, Hazelrig, Strode and Holles, whom Charles I in 1642 entered the Commons to arrest, only to find that 'the birds had flown', thus precipitating the Civil War.

FLANDERS MARE Henry VIII's name for his fourth wife, Anne of Cleves. Her unattractiveness led to the downfall of Thomas Cromwell, who had arranged the marriage (1540).

FLEET M.E. *flete* = swift.

FLESHLY SCHOOL a term applied in hostility by Robert Buchanan in 1871 to Swinburne, Rossetti, Morris and other poets.

FLEWETT O.G. *hlodhard* = glory strong.

FLINT O.E. = hard as a rock (one of its meanings, the other being the place-name Flint = dweller by the rock).

FLITTER O.E. *flittere*, from the verb *flitan* = to wrangle.

FLORIZEL, Prince a name of a character in Shakespeare's *Winter's Tale* used by the Prince Regent, later George IV, in correspondence with Mrs Robinson, an actress who took the name of Perdita, also a character in the play.

FOALE O.E. *fole* = foal, used as by-name = frisky or rough, shaggy.

FOGARTY Irish *fogartoigh*, descendants of, given meaning of 'expelling' by Dr MacLysaght (*Irish Surnames*, Dublin, Irish University Press) who describes the bearers as a Dalcassian sept who settled in the barony of Eliogarty which was named after them in Tipperary.

FOLJAMBE O.Fr. *fol* = foolish and *jambe* = leg, i.e. a useless, maimed leg, an example of the cruel nicknaming habits of medieval times.

FOLKHARD, FANC(H)ARD O.G. *fulcard* = people brave.

FOLL O.Fr. *fol* = foolish. Cf. Follet, diminutive of *fol*.

FOLLENFANT O.Fr. *fol* = foolish, and *enfant* = child.

FOLLY O.Fr. *folie* = foolishness, but apart from such a nickname, the word came to denote a small plantation thus accounting for some of the examples.

FOOT(E) O.N. *fotr* and O.E. *fot* = foot.

FORDRED O.E. = forth-counsel.

FOREIGN DEVILS the description given by the Chinese to foreigners, especially when used out of combined fear and hatred.

FORFEIT O.E. *for* = pig and *fot* = foot, pig foot.

FORT, LEFORT O.Fr. *fort* = strong.

FORTESCUE, FOSHEW O.Fr. *fort escu* = strong shield. The name is found in the 12th century. The celebrated family of Fortescue of which the Earl Fortescue is the head begins its lineage in 1406 as first recorded date.

FORTMAN 'strong hands', but cf. also Fortnam, Fortnum, (F. *fort anon* = strong young ass'.

FORTUNATE, The Manuel I, King of Portugal (reigned 1495–1521). He reaped the reward from the work of his predecessors in encouraging overseas exploration. Vasco da Gama sailed in 1497 under his patronage. By the Treaty of Tordesillas in 1494 Pope Alexander VI had divided the New World of discovery between Spain and Portugal. King Manuel who was foolish enough to refuse the services of Magellan (who then entered the Spanish service) assumed the style of 'Lord of the Conquest, Navigation and Commerce of India, Ethiopia, Arabia and Persia'.

FORTY or THE FORTY IMMORTALS the members of the Académie Française.

FORTY-FIVE, The name of the rebellion in 1745 led by the Young Pretender (q.v.).

FOU, Le 'The Mad' Charles VI, King of France (1368–1422) whose onset of mental disturbance is so well described by Froissart. Through the instrumentality of his queen he disinherited his and her son, the Dauphin, later Charles VII, in favour of the English King, Henry V. Ironically, Charles VI defeated Henry by dying a short while after him in 1422 so preventing him from succeeding to the French Crown under the Treaty of Troyes.

FOURTH ESTATE the Press, supposed to be the 4th after Lords Spiritual, Lords Temporal and the Commons.

FOURWEATHER, FOWWEATHER M.E. *foul wedir* = wet and stormy.

FOWLE(S), VOWELS, VOWLES O.E. *fugol* = fowl or bird.

FOWLER, The Henry I (c. 876–963), German King, owed his nickname to a legend (unsubstantiated) that he was surprised in 919 by Saxon and Frankish nobles while out hawking. They had come to elect him king.

FOX a nickname from the late 13th century.

FOX, The Martin Van Buren (1782–1862), US President, also known as Little Magician and Petticoat Pet (due to fondness for women).

FRAIS, FROSE O.Fr. *freis* (m.) *fresche* (f.) = vigorous, active, healthy-looking.

FRANCISCANS members of the Order of St Francis of Assisi (1181–1226).

FRANK(S) M.E. and O.Fr. *franc* = free (to distinguish from serf or villein). Cf. Frankman, Francombe, a freeman.

FRANKENSTEIN	often taken as the name of the monster in Mrs Shelley's story of that name (1818), but in fact the young student who created the monster.
FRANKLIN, FRANKLING	O.Fr. *fraunclein*, M.E. *frankeleyn* = 'a freeman being a landowner not of noble birth', the definition of the *Concise Oxford Dictionary* which would perhaps (?) fit Chaucer's Franklin. It would not fit Sir Walter Scott's Cedric in *Ivanhoe* but then Scott wrote before much of our exact medieval scholarship.
FREEBAIRN	O.E. *freo* and *bearn* = free child.
FREEBODY	O.E. *freo* = free and *bodig* = body, a freeman.
FREEBORN	O.E. *frio* and *boren*, free-born.
FREELOVE	O.E. *frithulaf* = peace survivor.
FREEMAN	O.E. *freomann* = free-born man.
FREEMAN, Mrs	name taken by Sarah, Duchess of Marlborough, in correspondence with Queen Anne who was known as Mrs Morley.
FRENCH DEVIL	Jean Bart (1651–1702), a great French Admiral.
FRENCH ENNIUS	Guillaume de Loris (c. 1235–65), wrote the *Romance of the Rose*, from the Latin Ennius, first Roman epic poet. Also of Jean de Meung (c. 1260–1318), continuer of the *Romance*.
FRENCH FABIUS	Anne, Duc de Montmorency, Constable of France (1493–1567) defeated the Emperor Charles V by a scorched earth withdrawal which compelled Charles to evacuate Provence.
FRENCH ILIAD	*The Romance of The Rose*, an allegorical poem in 20,000 lines, begun by Guillaume de Loris in later 12th century and continued by Jean de Meung in the early 14th century. 'The small town of Meung, the birthplace of the author of the *Romance of the Rose*' (Alexandre Dumas, *The Three Musketeers*, ch. 1). *The Romance* was translated in parts by Geoffrey Chaucer, whose version takes up 80 pages in the Oxford edition of his works.
FRENCH ISOCRATES	Esprit Flécher (1632–1710), Bishop of Nismes, famous for his funeral orations. See Old Man Eloquent.
FRIARS MAJOR	the Dominicans.
FRIARS MINOR	the Franciscans.
FRIDAY	O.E. *Frigedaeq* = Friday, possibly for one whose visage was as gloomy as a Friday fast day.
FRIEND, FREND	O.E. *freond* = friend.
FRIEND OF MAN, The	the Marquis de Mirabeau (1715–89) author of *L'Ami des Hommes*, which gave him the nickname.
FRIEND OF THE HELPLESS CHILDREN	Herbert Hoover, born 1874, 30th President of USA, so called because of his relief campaign 1915–16.
FRIENDS	Religious Society of Friends, the Quakers (q.v.).
FRISIAN, The	Robert I (died 1093), Count of Flanders.

FRONDE	lit. 'catapult', was the name given by Bachanmont, *conseiller* of the Paris *parlement* to the French civil war of 1648–53. The frondeurs included many of the nobility and were opposed to the two foreigners at the head of government in the minority of Louis XIV, namely his mother, Queen Anne of Austria and the Italian Cardinal Mazarin.
FROST	O.E. *forst, frost*; of someone of cold manner, or of white, aged head.
FRY(E)	O.E. *frig* = free.
FUGERE, FUCHER, FOULGER, VOLKER	O.E. *fulchar* = people-army.
FUGGERS	German merchant bankers of the 15th and 16th centuries whose name like that of Croesus, became synonymous for wealth.
FÜHRER	leader, the title used by Adolf Hitler (real name Schickelgruber) (1889–1945), Austrian-born dictator of Germany (1933–45).
FULLALOVE	for an amorous person.
FULLER, Peter the	(died 488), Monophysite Patriarch of Antioch, who had practised the trade of a fuller in Constantinople.
FUM THE FOURTH	Byron's term in *Don Juan* xi. 78 for King George IV.
FUNDAMENTALISM	a movement originating in the USA in the late 19th century and after the First World War as a reaction against evolutionary theory and the Higher Criticism of the Bible. The term is often applied to the belief in the literal inspiration and hence the inerrancy of the Bible, but as set out in an American conference at Niagara in 1895 it includes also the doctrines of the Deity of Christ, the Virgin Birth, the Atonement, the physical resurrection and bodily return of Christ.

G

GABB

O.Fr. *gab* = deceit, therefore a gabber = deceiver or liar. Cf. 'Thou art one of the knights of France, who hold it for glee and pastime to "gab" as they term it, of exploits that are beyond human power' (*The Talisman*, ch. 2; and Scott adds the note that the verb and its meaning are retained in Scottish).

GAIN(S), DINGAIN

O.Fr. *engaigne* = trickery, yet the name of an important Norman French family which settled in England.

GAIT(ES)

sometimes from O.N. *gert* = goat.

GALAHAD

term used for a man not only brave and truthful but of pure and holy life in the world. Sir Galahad is one of the great heroes of the Arthurian cycle; one who was able to sit in the Siege Perilous of King Arthur's Table, and to achieve the Quest of the Holy Grail.

GALBRAITH

O. Gaelic *Gall-Breathnach* = stranger-Briton, according to Reaney 'a name given to Britons settled among Gauls' (*Dict. of British Surnames*). In the 5th century after the Roman withdrawal from Britain, many Britons went to Armorica (Britanny) to avoid the Saxons and Angles. Some descendants of theirs came to England at the Norman Conquest which may explain this surname recorded here from early 13th century.

GALE, GAYLE

O.E. *gal* = light or merry; also wanton, licentious.

GALEN

the most celebrated of the Greek physicians in the 2nd century AD. Tennyson in *The Princess* refers to 'our court Galen' as term for a physician.

GALILEO

the Christian name of the famous Italian astronomer Galilei (1564–1642), who for some unknown reason is not known by his surname.

GALL, GAUL, GAWL

from Celtic, *gall* = foreigner or stranger.

GALLACHER, GALLAGHER

from Irish *O'Gallchol-hair* = foreign help. In the Anglicized forms there are 23 variants. One of the principal septs of Donegal.

GALLAN

O.Fr. and M.E. *galant* = dashing or spirited.

GALLIARD, GAILLARD, GAYLORD

O.Fr. *gaillard*, also M.E. = lively, gay.

GALLICANISM

the doctrines of those in *l'Église gallicane* (hence the name) who believed in the freedom of the Roman Catholic Church from the authority of the Pope. After a long and disturbing history the movement was eventually ended by the 1870 definition of the Infallibility of the Pope.

GALLING   O.E. *gaedeling* = companion, M.E. *gadeling* = vagabond.

GALLIOT   O.Fr. *galiot* = galley-slave or pirate, also M.E. *galyot* = pirate.

GALTER, GLATOR   O.N. *gert*, M.E. *gayte* = goat (sometimes with the meaning of goatherd).

GAME   O.E. *gamen* also M.E. = game, a sobriquet for one fond of or good at games, or who won prizes at games.

GAMMON   O.Fr. *gamb* = jambe = leg; here the diminutive, little or short leg.

GANDER   O.E. *gand* = gander.

GANGER, Rolf The   or Rollo, the Viking who being outlawed from Norway, made his way into Northern France in 886. As the French king, Charles the Simple, could not drive out the Norsemen, he agreed to their settlement in what has ever since been called Normandy. This was in 911. Rollo's 'nickname was earned because he was too big for a horse to carry him and therefore had to walk. He was quite probably a big man, but as the only horses available were small breeds about the size of ponies, we need not credit him with a giant stature' (L. G. Pine, *Sons of the Conqueror*, Charles Tuttle Inc., 1973, p.53). Rollo was appointed by the French king as patrician of Normandy but is reckoned as the first Duke, this title being taken by the third in the succession. He died in 927.

GAPE(S)   O.Fr. *gape* = weak, enfeebled.

GARBETT, GARBUTT   O.G. *Gerbard*, *Gerbold* = spear bold.

GARGATE, GARGETT   O.Fr. *gargate* = throat.

GARMAN, GARMONS   O.E. *Garmund* = spear protector.

GARNON(S), GERNON, GARNHAM, GRENNAN   O.Fr. *grenon*, *gernon* = moustache. From this nickname came the name Algernons borne by William de Percy, a genuine companion of William the Conqueror and founder of the Percy family. As most Normans were cleanshaven, William was distinguished by his moustaches, probably of the 'handlebar' variety. From the 15th century in the form of Algernon, the Christian name has been borne by the Percies, the Dukes of Northumberland, William's descendants (through female lines).

GATHERCOLE   probably used for an old man, one who had gathered cold.

GAUCHE   O.Fr. *gauche* = left-handed, awkward, clumsy.

GAUNT   from M.E. *gaunt* = slender or thin; one of the derivations of this name. The other origins are from gaunter = glovemaker, or from Ghent in Flanders, e.g. John of Gaunt (q.v.).

GAUNT, John of   (1340–99), third son of Edward III, so called from Ghent his birthplace. In Shakespeare's *Richard II* he appears as old John of Gaunt, time-honoured Lancaster, but in reality his ambitions and those of his son Henry IV, led ultimately to the Wars of the Roses.

GAWKRODGER — meaning awkward Roger. Cf. popular word, gawky or gawling = looking awkwardly or rudely.

GAY — M.E. *gai*, O.Fr. *gai* = full of joy. Word now used for homosexuals.

GEAKE, JECKS, JEX — M.E. *geke* = simpleton.

GEAR, GEERE — M.E. *gere* = passion-ridden or changeful.

GEARING, GEERING — M.E. gering = villain.

GEARY — M.E. *geery* = changeable.

GEDGE — M.E. *gegge*, apparently contemptuous term for a gaggle of people.

GELDING, GILDING — O.N. *gelding* = a eunuch. But must have been used in contemptuous sense of person supposed to be sexually deficient but not really incapable or the surname could not have been passed on.

GEMBLOUX, Sigebert of — (c. 1030–1112), a medieval chronicler and monk of Gembloux, France.

GENEROUS, The or The Bold — Boleslaw II (1039–81), King of Poland.

GENEVA BULL — Stephen Marshall, died 1655, a violent Presbyterian preacher said to have bellowed like a bull of Bashan in the Old Testament.

GENGHIS KHAN — the title borne by the Mongol conqueror Temujin. He lived in the 12th and 13th centuries (1162–1227). He subjugated huge areas across Asia and eastern Europe with savage and remorseless cruelty. The exact meaning of the title by which he is known to history is not clear.

GENT — O.Fr. *gent*, M.E. *gente* = well-born. Cf. also gentle, gentleman.

GENTILES — a scriptural Hebrew term meaning 'nations' applied to non-Israelites. In Greek it is ἔθνη, nations, and *gentiles* is the Latin equivalent.

GENTLE SHEPHERD — George Grenville (1712–70), so called by the Elder Pitt from a song he narrated.

GENTLEMAN IN BLACK VELVET — a mole, toasted by Jacobites because William III's horse, by stumbling over a mole hill, brought about the king's death in 1702.

GENTLEMAN JIM — US boxer, James J. Corbett.

GENTLEMAN JOHNNY — the common name for John Burgoyne (1723–92), a British soldier who is often most unfairly described as the man 'who lost us America', a term richly deserved by Sir William Howe. Burgoyne was insufficiently supported and had to surrender at Saratoga in 1776. He was a successful politician and playwright and left an illegitimate son, Sir John Fox Burgoyne, Baronet and Field Marshal. Gentleman Johnny is a character in Shaw's play *The Devil's Disciple*.

GERISH, GARRISH M.E. *gerysshe* = changeful.

GERMAN, The Louis (c. 806–76), King of the East Franks, was the 3rd son of the Carolingian emperor Louis I, the Pious.

GERMAN CHRISTIANS (DEUTSCHE CHRISTEN) those among the German Protestants who sided with Hitler and got rid of the Old Testament and eliminated from the Gospels everything Jewish.

GERMAN ILIAD, The *Niebelungenlied*, written in the early 13th century by an unknown Austrian minstrel. It is the story of Siegfried of the Netherlands and is a full-length heroic epic.

GERMAN MILTON, The Friedrich Gottlieb Klopstock (1724–1803), who read *Paradise Lost* and then began to write his own epic, *Der Messias*, not equal in any sense to Milton.

GERONIMO the fictitious name of Don John of Austria (1547–78), born at Ratisbon 24 February 1547, the illegitimate son of the Emperor Charles V by Barbara Blomberg, a burgher's daughter. He was acknowledged as half-brother by Philip II of Spain, who then gave him the name of Don Juan de Austria (1559). He proved a brilliant commander, his greatest achievement being the destruction of the Turkish fleet at Lepanto (5 October 1571). For a somewhat exaggerated account, see G. K. Chesterton's poem, 'The Battle of Lepanto'.

GETHING(S), GITTINGS Welsh *gethin* = perhaps swarthy.

GHAZI victorious, a title bestowed on Osman Nuri Pasha (1832–1900), a Turkish soldier who defended Plevna (Pleven in Bulgaria) in the Russo-Turkish War of 1877–8. He entrenched himself at Plevna, repulsed the Russians three times and was only forced to capitulate when he tried to cut his way out.

Also used of the Ghaza or razzia, an expedition undertaken by Turkish tribes on the Byzantine border in Asia Minor, partly in quest of plunder but also as being of the *jihad* or holy war which it is incumbent on Moslems to wage against unbelievers.

GHIBELLINE the name given to those in Italy who favoured the Holy Roman Emperors. The name was an Italianization of the Hohenstaufen Emperors' battle cry, *Hie Weibling*. As one result of the strife between the Ghibellines and the other great party, the Guelphs, Dante was banished from Florence and spent the rest of his life in exile. Weiblingen was a seat of the Hohenstaufens in Swabia.

GHOR more usually given as Ghazni, placename of Mohammed who died 1206 and was conqueror of the north Indian plain.

GHOST, GAST O.E. *gaest* = ghost, perhaps used for a person of emaciated appearance.

GIDDY, GEDDIE O.E. *gydig*, possessed of evil spirit, and thus insane.

GIGG(S) M.E. *gigge* = giddy girl.

GILDED CHAMBER, The   House of Lords.

GILDON   O.E. *gylden* = golden (haired).

GILLEBRAND   O.G. *Giselbrand* = hostage-sword.

GINGER   M.E. *gingivere*, sometimes denoting a red-haired man, at others an occupational name for a dealer in ginger.

GINN   M.E. *gin*, O.Fr. *engin* = skill or snare, trap.

GIRLE   M.E. *gurle* = youth or maiden, young person.

GIRONDISTS   the more moderate republicans in the French Revolution (1791–3), from the Department of Gironde, whence some of them came.

GLADDEN   O.E. *glaed* = glad.

GLAUBER'S SALTS   take their name from Johann Glauber (1604–68), a German alchemist who discovered them accidentally. They are of sodium sulphate and a purgative even more unpleasant than many others.

GLEAVE, GLAVE   O.Fr. *glaive* = lance, M.E. *gleve* = lance; 'a name for a spearman or for a winner in a race in which the lance, set up as a winning post, was given as a prize' (Reaney, *Dict. of British Surnames*).

GLEW, GLUE   O.E. *gleaw* = wise or prudent.

GLIDE, GLEED   O.E. *glida*, M.E. *glede* = kite.

GLOOMY DEAN, The   W. R. Inge (1860–1954), Dean of St Paul's, London, 1911–34. A profound scholar and writer on Christian mysticism, much concerned with the relationship between Platonism and Christianity. He was also a writer on the problems created for religion by post-Copernican astronomy. In conjunction with his clear writing as a scholar he had also the unusual gift of incisive journalism. He wrote many articles in the London *Evening Standard*, thus causing the quip that 'if not a pillar of the Church he was at least able to provide two columns in the *Evening Standard*'. Some volumes of his essays were considered to be ultra-pessimistic as to the future of England and Europe, and of European civilization. This led to the sobriquet which was attached to his name and was even expressed after his death in a study by R. M. Helm, *The Gloomy Dean*. In fact, the nickname did not do justice to his profound thought and realistic estimate of the future.

GLORIANA   Elizabeth I (1558–1603) of England, the subject of the title of Edmund Spenser's *Faerie Queene* where he terms her 'Glory'.

GLORIOUS JOHN   the poet John Dryden (1631–1700).

GLUTTON, The   Vitellius (15–69 AD) reigned for 11 months in AD 69, the Year of the Four Emperors – Nero, Otho, Galba and Vitellius. The last who had an enormous appetite was killed on 22 December 69.

GNOSTICISM	derived from Greek γνωδις, knowledge, and the term given to extensive heretical or completely unChristian teaching which began in the 2nd century and persisted for some ages. The Gnostics claimed a superior knowledge, usually passed on by a supposed secret tradition.
GNOSTICS	from Greek γνωδις, knowledge, a name given to a body of persons who from the 2nd century appeared in all centres of Christianity. They varied very greatly but had some general features in common; (1) two Gods, the Demiurge who created the material world, and the true God; (2) a secret gnosis handed down from the Apostles and others; (3) a Puritanic view of matter. St Irenaeus, c. 200, in his *Adversus omnes haereses*, gives a careful account of the Gnostics and their curious mythology.
GOACHER	M.E. *chere*, O.Fr. *chier* = face. A person of good, cheerful countenance.
GOBELINS	name of a family of French dyers whose works became a royal establishment in the 18th century, hence Gobelin tapestries.
GOD, St John of	(1495–1550), founder of the Order of Charity for the service of the sick.
GODBEAR	God (or good) be herein.
GODBERT	O.G. *godebert* = god bright. Cf. also the following: Godbold = god-bold; Goddard = god-hard; Godfrey = god-peace.
GODDAM or GODON	a most objectionable name for the English used by the French in the Hundred Years War, owing to the blasphemous expletives used by English soldiers.
GODMAN, GOODMAN	O.E. *godmann*, and O.G. *god(e)* man = good man, also head of a household, used in the 16th century as term of moderate respect, as also good wife.
GODSAFE	M.E. *on a Godes half* = in God's name, applied to someone who frequently used the phrase.
GODSAL	good soul, an honest person.
GODSMAN	O.G. Godesman, man of God, applied to a pious man.
GODSMARK	God's mark, i.e. of the plague. Cf. the phrase, an Act of God.
GODSON, GOODSON	possibly in the sense implied as = good son or godson.
GODWARD	O.E. *Godweard* = God and protector. Cf. Godwin, from O.E. *God* and *wine* = protector or friend.
GOLD, GAULD	golden-haired, also rich.
GOLDBARD	gold-bright or golden-beard. Cf. also Goldburgh = gold fortress.
GOLDEN, GOULDEN	O.E. *gylden* = golden-haired. Cf. Goldfinch, O.E. *goldfinc* = goldfinch; Golder, Goulder, O.E. *gold*; Goldfoot, O.E. *gylden* and *fot*; Goldhawk; Goldney = golden.

GOLDEN HORN, The	the situation of Constantinople on the Bosphorus, of curved outline.
GOLDSTON	gold stone.
GOLDWIN	= good friend.
GOLIGHTLY, GALLATLY, GELLATLY	= go lightly applied to a messenger.
GONATAS	possibly a reference to some deformity of the joints. Antigonus II (c. 319–236 BC) King of Macedonia from 276 BC.
GOOD	O.E. *god* = good.
GOOD, The	Prince Albert (1817–61), of Saxe-Coburg-Gotha, Prince Consort and husband of Queen Victoria, a man of ability and very high moral purpose.

Alfonso VIII of Leon (reigned 1158–1214), the Noble and Good.

Haakon I, King of Norway, who died c. 960, a son of Harold I, was educated at court of King Athelstan of England.

Hywel, a Welsh prince, a grandson of Rhodri Mawr (see under Great) who died c. 950. 'One prince only among the many who bore rule in Wales in the Middle Ages, was honoured by posterity with the title of "Good", a circumstance which in itself imparts a peculiar interest to the reign of Hywel Dda' (Sir John Lloyd, *History of Wales*, London, Longman, 1948, p. 333; who tells, however, that paucity of records do not allow a proper account of Hywel's conduct).

Jean II, Duke of Brittany (1286–1341).

John II (1350–64), King of France; his bravery earned him the epithet, the Good. He was defeated and captured by the Black Prince (q.v.) at Poitiers in 1356. He came back to his imprisonment in England after his government failed to find his ransom. 'His former jailer [i.e. Edward III of England] held a sumptuous funeral for him in St. Paul's Cathedral' (E. Perroy, *The Hundred Years' War*, London, Eyre & Spottiswoode, 1948, p. 142).

Magnus I, the Good, King of Norway, son of Olaf II, the Saint (q.v.). He succeeded to the throne in 1035 and reigned until 1047.

St Odo, Archbishop of Canterbury (died 959), said to have been son of a Dane and originally a pagan.

Philip the Good, the third of the Valois Dukes of Burgundy, lived 1396–1476, secured control of the Netherlands and was one of the richest princes in Europe. He kept a splendid court and founded the Order of the Golden Fleece, the symbol of which alludes to the source of Netherland wealth.

René, Count of Provence, Duke of Anjou, and titular sovereign of Sicily, father of Margaret, Queen of Henry VI of England. He lived 1409–80.

Richard II, the 4th Duke of Normandy, succeeded in 996 and died in 1027; his sister Emma married (1) Ethelred II, the Unready (q.v.) and (2) Canute of England.

GOOD QUEEN BESS	Elizabeth I 'of immortal memory'.
GOOD REGENT	James Stewart, Earl of Moray (died 1570) natural son of James V of Scotland, became Regent of Scotland after Mary Queen of Scots' imprisonment.
GOODBAIRN, GOODBAND	M.E. *god barn* = good child. Cf. also Goodchild.
GOODBODY	O.E. *god* and *bodig*, a form of courteous address. Cf. Goodman.
GOODCHEAP	O.E. *god* and *ceap* = barter or price; nickname of one who offered a good bargain.
GOOD DUKE HUMPHREY	Humphrey, Duke of Gloucester (1391–1447), youngest son of Henry IV of England, a man of great piety.
GOODENDAY	M.E. *godne daere* = good day, or God give you a good day.
GOODENOUGH, GOODNOW, GOODNER, GOODANEW	said to be a nickname applied to a person easily satisfied, but in some of the later forms, a disguised version of O.E. *god* and *cnhafa* = boy, servant. Disguised because of the pejorative meaning given to *knaf* = knave.
GOODER, GOODE	O.E. Godhere = good army.
GOODEVE	O.E. *Godgifur* = God or good gift.
GOODFAR(E)	O.Fr. *aferir* = to be proper.
GOODFELLOW	M.E. *god felaw* = good fellow, applied to the fairies' Robin Goodfellow. Cf. Kipling, *Puck of Pook's Hill*. Cf. Goodgame = good sport; Goodhart.
GOODHAND	said by Reaney (*Dict. of British Surnames*) to derive from *Goudenhond* = golden hand, said of a generous person.
GOODHEAD	O.E. *god* and *heafod*, M.E. *godhede* = goodness. Cf. Goodhind, O.E. *god* and M.E. *hine* from O.E. *hiwan* (plural) = member of a household, i.e. a youth, hence good lad; Goodlad.
GOODIFF, GOODEY	M.E. *good-wife*, term of respect in 16th century for the mistress of a household.
GOODISON	O.E. Godgyth = god or good battle; here = son of Godgyth, used as woman's name, difficult to see applicability, though originating as nickname.
GOODLAKE, GOODLUCK, GULLICH, etc.	from O.E. Guthla = battle, play; the name of a celebrated O.E. saint who lived in the Fens.
GOODLAMB	O.E. Godlamb = good lamb.
GOODLIFF	O.E. Godleof = good or God dear.
GOODLUD	good lord, as in legal practice, m'lud.
GOODREAD, GOODERED	M.E. *god rede* = good counsel.
GOODRICH, etc.	O.E. Godric = good ruler.
GOODSIR	M.E. = grandfather.
GOODSPEED	God speed you, probably used so frequently by person

that it became his nickname.

GOODSWEN M.E. *god swain*, the latter from O.N. *sveinn* = good servant.

GOODYER, GOODIER M.E. *goodyear*, said to have been used as exclamation 'What the good year' and from frequency in the speaker's mouth earned him a nickname.

GOOK from O.N. *gaukr* = cuckoo, M.E. *goke, gouke*, could have been used to denote folly as in modern colloquialism or to denote a selfish use of others.

GOOSE O.E. *gos* = goose. Cf. Goosey = goose eye.

GORMAN derived from Irish *gorm* = blue, in diminutive.

GOSLING M.E. *geslyng* = gosling.

GOSSIP O.E. *godsibb* = godfather or godmother, later became address to a familiar acquaintance.

GOSSON possibly from godson.

GOTHIC, Claudius the the Roman emperor so named because of his victory over the Goths who had previously devastated the Roman Empire. He reigned two years and died in AD 270.

GOTOBED the meaning of which is clear, though Bardsley (*English Surnames*) thought it a slurred version of Godebert.

GOTT O.E. *gutt*, = guts and used of a fat or greedy person.

GOVER M.E. *faire* = gently, used of someone who walks well or uses gentle ways.

GRAMMARIAN, The Alfric (c. 955–1020), Abbot of Eynsham, wrote several books of great merit for the English rural people in their own language.

GRAMMATICUS, Saxo the first Danish historian (mid 12th to early 13th century), wrote *Gesta Danorum* in excellent Latin. It was his Latin eloquence which early in the 14th century caused him to be called Grammaticus. Shakespeare's *Hamlet* is based on Saxo's work.

GRAND CORNEILLE, Le the famous French dramatist, Pierre Corneille (1606–84).

GRAND DAUPHIN, Le Louis, Duc de Bourgogne (1661–1711), eldest son of Louis XIV of France but died before his father.

GRAND MADEMOISELLE, La The Duchesse de Montpensier (1627–93), daughter of Gaston, Duc d'Orléans and cousin of Louis XIV. 'He [i.e. Charles II] had been made to woo his cousin Mme de Montpensier, the richest heiress in France . . . on Charles she made no impression' (Sir Arthur Bryant, *King Charles II*, London, Longman, 1949, p.48).

GRAND MONARQUE, Le Louis XIV, King of France (1643 – he succeeded when he was 5, and reigned until 1715 when he was succeeded by his great-grandson). Also termed Le Roi Soleil, the Sun King (q.v.)

GRAND OLD GARDENER Adam, the first man, so termed by Tennyson in his poem *Lady Clara Vere de Vere*.

GRAND OLD MAN	the term applied by his admirers to William Ewart Gladstone (1809–98) the Victorian statesman, four times Prime Minister. Term used by Lord Rosebery in 1882.
GRAND OLD MAN OF LABOUR	US labour leader, Samuel Compers.
GRANNY, OLD	term used by Lord Rosebery in 1882 of US President William Henry Harrison (1773–1841).
GRANT, GRAND, LEGRAND	O.Fr. *grand* = great, bestowed in sense of elder or senior and also to denote tallness.
GRAY, GREY, LE GREY	O.E. *graeg* = grey, probably grey-haired.
GRAYCLOAK	Harold II Graafell, died c. 970, King of Norway, son of Eric Bloodaxe (q.v.).
GREASLEY, GREASKEY, GRESLEY	and many other variants, from O.Fr. *greslet* = marked as by hail, i.e. pockmarked. This was not the origin of the great Norman family of Gresley Bts which derived their surname from Gresley in Notts and Gresley in Derby. In England the baronet's family of Gresley which became extinct in 1976 took its name from Gresley in Derby, one of the few families in 20th century to have a genuine Norman descent, agreed by no less an authority than J. H. Round.
GREAT, The	A title bestowed on many persons who were notable for their achievements. The only Englishman to be so named is the famous King Alfred (849–99), the saviour of England, who in the toils of war and state undertook an educational programme which resulted in the establishment of written English earlier than in any other western European language. 'It is the praise of Alfred that he was not only a warrior but also the patron of the arts, and the legislator of his people' (John Lingard, *History of England*, vol. 1, p. 232); similar comment made by David Hume in his *History*. The title is sometimes given to Canute (Cnut), King of England (1016–35), Norway and Denmark.

Abd-al-Rahman or Abd-er-Rahman III, the greatest of the Omayyad rulers of Spain and the first to assume the title of Caliph. He reigned 912–61.

Akbar, third of the line of Mogul (sometimes Moghul and a corruption of Mongol), was the grandson of Babur and son of Humayun, both of whom had tried to create an empire. Akbar succeeded. He lived 1542–1605. He conquered a great part of India. In matters of religion he was very tolerant. All authorities agree on his greatness. Thus *Chambers' Encyclopedia*, 'Akbar was the greatest ruler that India has seen.'

Alexander III (356–323 BC) King of Macedonia, better known as Alexander the Great, who conquered the entire Persian empire, and was the first western conqueror to enter India where he subdued the Punjab. He died at the age of 32 and his empire broke up into sections ruled by his generals. But the effects of Alexander's conquests were lasting. Hellenism had been fairly widespread in the Orient but as a result of his conquests it acquired political power. Thus Greek became a universal language and the medium of the New Testament. He founded numerous cities, Alexandria and Kandahar being two examples. He was the first man to endow scientific research, for his old tutor Aristotle, and to some extent this was continued by his successors, the Ptolemies of Egypt. Over against these achievements, Alexander exhibited the unthinking cruelty which usually accompanies absolute power. For an interesting contrast in describing the same incidents, see Mary Renault, *The Persian Boy* and H. G. Wells's *Outline of History*.

Antiochus III (c. 242–187 BC) strengthened his kingdom in the east and against Egypt but was decisively beaten by the Romans. He is classed, however, as the most successful of the Seleucids after Nicator (q.v.).

Arnulf I (918–65) Count of Flanders.

St Basil (c. 330–79) one of the three great Cappadocian Fathers (q.v.) of the Church, a great organizer as well as thinker. The monasticism of the Eastern Orthodox Church still bears the impress of his work.

Casimir III, King of Poland (1333–70).

Catherine the Great (1684–1727), a German princess, the daughter of Christian Augustus of Anhalt-Zerbst. She was married to the future Czar Peter III and bore him a son, later Paul I. In 1762 Catherine became ruler of Russia by a *coup d'état* and Peter III died in circumstances never explained. Catherine introduced French culture into Russia and in foreign affairs gained the Crimea from the Turks and assisted in the two partitions of Poland. Catherine had many lovers, but it is assumed that Paul I was the son of Peter III as he resembled the latter in appearance and character.

Charlemagne, Charles the Great (742–814), son of Pepin the Short (q.v.), King of France and from 800 Holy Roman Emperor, the imperial dignity of the western Roman Empire having been revived in his person by action of the Pope. He ruled over a very large area in Western Europe and in addition to his many conquests, was active in initiating a considerable cultural renaissance.

Charles III (1543–1608) Duke of Lorraine from 1545; his reign greatly benefited his country in the judicial system, in finances, industry and the arts.

Constantine, the first Christian Roman Emperor (280–337), reigned 306–337. He gave toleration to the Christians but was not baptized until just before his death. He had presided at the Council of Nicaea (325), which produced the original Nicene Creed.

Cyrus II, founder of the Persian empire, who reigned from 559 to his death in 530 BC, the son of Cambyses I of Anshan. Few if any great leaders have received such unqualified praise. Herodotus wrote of him; Xenophon's account is an idealistic panygric; and the Deutero-Isaiah described him as God's Chosen, in terms that most Jewish kings came nowhere near to receiving.

Darius I, ruler of the Persian Empire 522–486 BC, son of Hystaspes, Satrap of Parthia. He belonged to a collateral branch of the royal Persian family of Achaemenids. He restored the empire which had been usurped by one Smerdis, who he said was really Gaumata, a Magian. He sent an expedition against Greece which was beaten at Marathon by the Athenians in 490 BC. He allowed the Jews to rebuild the temple at Jerusalem in accordance with the earlier decree of Cyrus the Great (q.v.).

Dionysius, Bishop of Alexandria c. 264, a pupil of Origen and a writer on theology.

Ferdinand I (1016/18–65) King of Castile and Leon, a son of Sancho III, the Great (q.v.), of Navarre, brought a large part of Spain under his control but divided his territories between his sons and so broke up the dominion which he had created.

Frederick II, King of Prussia (1712–86). It is most difficult to assess his character. His several wars resulted in much suffering for his subjects and for the lands which he attacked. This part of his greatness must be set against his French culture and efforts to improve Prussian industry.

St Gertrude (1256–c. 1302), a German mystic who was one of the first exponents of devotion to the Sacred Heart.

St Gregory I, the Great, was pope 590–604, *doctor ecclesiae*, a man great in administration, in charitable care, and in spiritual writing. He sent St Augustine to England, made him the first Archbishop of Canterbury, and this action led to the conversion of England to Christianity.

Herod the Great (73–4 BC) ruler of Palestine at the time of Christ's birth (St Matthew's Gospel) 'whether by accident or design surnamed the Great' (Dean A. P. Stanley, *Lectures on the History of the Jewish Church*, 1876, p. 410). Strangely no other writer gives any explanation of the title. Herod's greatness may be analysed into (1) superb statecraft by which in the troubled era of the Roman Empire under Julius Caesar, Antony and Augustus, he made himself King of the Jews; (2) his enormities in cruelty, e.g. killing one of his wives (the heiress of the Hasmoneans) his children, the Sanhedrin, Jewish nobles, etc.; (3) his physical and mental agonies and (4) his place in Providential workings. To quote Stanley (*op. cit*, p. 432) 'But the importance of Herod's life does not end with his personal history. He created in great part that Palestine which he left behind him as the platform on which the closing scenes of the Jewish, as the opening scenes of the Christian Church were to be enacted.' Herod's family held positions of authority in Palestine during the first five decades of the 1st century AD and one of them, Herod Agrippa I (10 BC–AD 44) was king of all the territories ruled by his grandfather, Herod the Great.

Hugh the Great, restored the Carolingians in 936; grandson of Robert the Strong (q.v.). His son, Hugh Capet (q.v.), became first of the Capetian kings.

St Isaac (c. 350–440) Catholicós of Armenia secured independence of Armenian Church from dependence on Caesarea in Cappadocia. He translated much of the Bible into Armenian.

St Leo I, Bishop of Rome 440–61, a Doctor of the Western Church, one of the very few Popes to be a theologian. His *Tome*, the expression of the Catholic Faith as against the heresy of Eutyches (Monophysitism), was accepted by the Council of Chalcedon in 451. Leo asserted strongly the primacy of the Holy See. By his moral greatness he was able at Lake Garda to turn back Attila the Hun, the Scourge of God (q.v.).

Llewelyn ap Iorwerth, Llewelyn Fawr, the Great, died in 1240, was effective ruler of North Wales which enjoyed peace and prosperity under his government (Sir John Lloyd, *History of Wales*, London, Longman, 1948).

Louis (Lajos) I, King of Hungary, the son and successor of Charles I of Hungary (1308–42), who was Charles Robert of Anjou of the Naples dynasty. Lajos was son-in-law of Casimir III, the Great, of Poland.

St Macarius (c. 300–90), an Egyptian monk of great sanctity, and according to his translators and historians, a great writer on religious matters.

Mithridates VI (died 63 BC) also called Eupator (q.v.) King of Pontus, a very able, energetic and utterly ruthless man who opposed the extension of Roman rule in Asia Minor. He had, however, to contend with three great Roman generals, Sulla, Lucullus and Pompey the Great (q.v.). He tried to poison himself but could not as he had accustomed his body to all sorts of poisons, hence the term mithridate, meaning antidote. He had therefore to order one of his mercenaries to kill him.

Otto the Great (936–73), German King, son of Henry I the Fowler (q.v.).

Peter I, (1672–1725), Czar of Russia from 1682, responsible by his personal efforts for bringing Russia out of medievalism into the status of a great power whose concurrence had to be obtained in any European settlement. As a completely despotic ruler, Peter was, of course, at times very cruel and contemptuous of human life as in the foundation of St Petersburg (later Petrograd and now Leningrad), when thousands of lives were lost.

Pompey, the distinguished Roman soldier and statesman, lived 100–48 BC, won the title of Magnus for his brilliant recovery of Sicily and Africa. In 67 he cleared the Mediterranean of pirates. He brought Judea under Roman rule, but the Jews watched the deterioration of his career after he had insisted on entering the Holy of Holies at Jerusalem. He was decisively beaten by Julius Caesar and was murdered by Egyptian assassins in 48 BC. Lucan's immortal line, *stat magni umbra nominis* is the sad monument of his career. Yet when Caesar was murdered he fell hard by Pompey's statue.

Rhodri Mawr who died in 879 was the nearest approach to a King of Wales which the Welsh rules of partition of inheritance permitted.

Sancho III Garcés (c. 992–1035), King of Pamplona (i.e. Navarre) and Aragon, established a hegemony over all the Christian states of Spain.

Theodoric, Ostrogothic King of Italy from 493 to 526. He was the historical prototype of Dietrich von Bern or of Verona in Middle High German poems (*Das Heldenbuch*). For a good account there is *The Roman and the Teuton*, a series of lectures by Charles Kingsley given to Cambridge University.

Theodosius I (c. 346–95) a Spaniard who was Roman emperor 379–95. Famous for the rebuke which he accepted from St Ambrose of Milan and for his refusal to tolerate the Arian heretical church, he made Orthodox Christianity the religion of the state in 381 and prohibited pagan sacrifice and worship.

GREAT CAPTAIN, The

(El Gran Capitano), name given to the Spanish general Gonsalvo de Cordova (1453–1515), through whose efforts Granada was united to the realm of Ferdinand and Isabella. As Lord Macaulay said of the British conquerors of India, 'they [i.e. the Indians] could show myriads of cavalry and long trains of artillery which would have astonished the Great Captain' (*Essay on Lord Clive*).

GREAT CHAM OF LITERATURE

Dr Samuel Johnson (1709–84), so called by Tobias Smollett, the novelist. Dr Johnson's position as a type of arbiter of learning and literature has never been approached by anyone else in English literature. Cham is an older spelling of Khan, the ancient sovereign prince of Tartary.

GREAT COMMONER

William Pitt, 1st Earl of Chatham (1708–78), one of the greatest statesmen in British history. He was the farseeing and administrative genius who secured for Britain the unparalleled triumphs of the Seven Years War, 1756–63. In an age when noblemen dominated English politics, Pitt was notable as a commoner but in 1766 accepted an earldom. Referred to also as William Pitt the Elder to distinguish him from his son.

GREAT CONDÉ, The

Prince Louis II of Bourbon (1621–86), one of the greatest soldiers of France, defended Alsace after Turenne's death against the imperial armies (1675).

GREAT ELECTOR

Frederick William of Brandenburg (1620–88), secured the freedom of his country from the Swedes and the terms of the Peace of Westphalia (1648) showed the success of his policy at the end of the Thirty Years War.

GREAT ELEPHANT	Chaka Zulu, the founder of the Zulus as a military organization c. 1826. Also styled The August One. Vast areas were depopulated in the course of Chaka's conquests which were also marked by appalling cruelty.
GREAT UNKNOWN	see The Wizard of the North.
GREATHEAD	O.E. *great, heafod* = bighead. Sometimes with reference to physique.
GREAT WEN	London, thus described by William Cobbett, viewing it as a tumour on the land.
GREEDY	O.E. *graedig* = gluttonous.
GREEN	can occasionally derive from O.E. *grene* = green, denoting someone young and immature.
GREENHEAD	in some cases from O.E. *grene hod* = green hood.
GREET	in some cases from O.E. *great* = big.
GREW(E)	O.Fr. *grue* = crane. The word pedigree comes from the same origin as sign used in chart pedigrees resembled a crane's foot. Cf. Grewcock, Growcott, M.E. *grew* and *cock* = a crane cock.
GREY FRIARS	the friars of Franciscan Order who wore grey habits (but now brown).
GREY NUNS	Sisters of Charity.
GRICE, GRISS, LE GRICE	M.E. *grise*, O.N. *griss* = a pig or M.E. *gris* = greyhaired.
GRIGG(S)	sometimes a nickname from M.E. *grigge* = a dwarf.
GRILL, GRYLLS	M.E. *grille* = fierce.
GRIMBLE	O.G. Grombald = helmet bold.
GRIME(S)	in some cases from O.E. *grim* = fierce.
GRIMMETT, GRIMMITT	O.N. *grimhilde* = helmet battle. Cf. Grimward, O.G. = helmet guard.
GRISSOM, GRISSON	O.Fr. *grison* = grey.
GROSS, LE GROS	O.Fr. *gros* = fat. Cf. Grosset, a diminutive of Gross.
GROSVENOR	O.Fr. *gros venour* = chief huntsman. The surname of the Dukes of Westminster, a family whose ancestry is traced to the 13th century. Their alleged descent from the Chief Hunter of Normandy is exposed in *The Ancestor*, vols I and II. The 'Chief Hunter' in question is completely mythical.
GRUBB(E)	M.E. *grubbe, grub*, applied to a short person.
GUBBINGS	the name (origin unknown) of some ultra-savage inhabitants of Brent Tor, Devon, described by Fuller in his *Worthies* (1661). In Charles Kingsley's *Westward Ho!* the hero, Sir Amyas Leigh, has an encounter with the Gubbings.
GUBELL	O.E. *gutheald* = battle-bold.

GUDGEON
O.Fr. *goujon* = gudgeon, meaning possibly greedy, or ready to take a bait, i.e. gullible.

GUELPHS, GUELFS
the name of the party in Italian medieval politics which was opposed to the Ghibellines (q.v.). The name Guelph indicated adherents of the Welf (q.v.) Otto IV and the Guelphs were generally pro-papal. The meaning of the two names early attracted the attention of Italian writers. The 14th century jurist and early writer on heraldry, Bartolus of Sassoferrato gave several contemporary explanations in his treatise *De Guelphis et Ghibellinis*. The party was also divided into factions, the Whites and the Blacks.

GUEUX, Les
Lit. the beggars. This term was used in ridicule of the Dutch nobles who joined in a confederacy against the Spaniards. This was in 1566 and these nobles went through a ceremony in which each wore the leather wallet of a mendicant. '*Vivent les gueuls*' was the cry. They were later known for their brave exploits as 'wild beggars' and 'beggars of the sea'. (The full account is given in J. L. Mottley's *Rise of the Dutch Republic*, London, Swann Sonneschein, Pt 2, ch. 6.)

GULL
M.E. *gulle* = gull, or M.E. *gull*, O.N. *gulr* = pale.

GULLING
M.E. *gulling* = pale one.

GULLIVER, GULLIFORD
O.Fr. *goulafre* = glutton.

GULLY
M.E. *golias* = giant.

GUMBEL
O.G. Gundbald = battle bold.

GUNDRY
O.G. Gundric = battle ruler.

GUNTER, GUNTHER
O.G. Gunter = battle army.

GURNETT
M.E. *gurnard* = 'a fish with a large spiny head and mailed cheeks with a throat almost as big as the rest of its body. So called because of the grunting noise it makes' (Reaney, *Dict. of British Surnames*). Applied sarcastically to an individual. Cf. Falstaff's remark about a soused gurnett.

GUYER
O.Fr. *guyour* = guide.

GUYMER, GYMER
O.G. *wignar* = battle famous.

H

HAARFAGER, FAIRHAIR	name of Harold I, the first king of Norway, died c. 940. The story was that he vowed to let his golden hair remain uncut until he had become King of all Norway. He was supposed to have been refused in marriage because the lady would marry only Norway's King and not the kinglet of a district.
HACKETT, HAGGETT, ACKETTS	said to be a diminutive of O.N. *haki*; and 'occasionally we may have a nickname from a fish = from *bacaed* (haket) a fish mentioned in a 14th century copy of the foundation Charter of the Abbey of Ramsey' (Reaney, *Dict. of British Surnames*).
HACKNEY	O.Fr. *haquenee*, M.E. *hakenel* = an ambling mount particularly for ladies to ride.
HACKWOOD	a nickname for a woodcutter.
HADDOCK	possibly a nickname from the fish.
HAGARENES	from Hagar, a bondswoman who bore to Abraham a son, Ishamel, the reputed ancestor of the Arabs. Hence the use of the term for Arabians, Saracens or Moors.
HAGGARD, HAGGART	M.E. and O.Fr. *hagard* = wild.
HAIN	M.E. *hayne*, *haine* = a mean wretch.
HAKE	O.N. Haki = hook or crook.
HAKLUYT	from 'hack little', meaning a lazy woodcutter.
HALFNIGHT(S)	O.E. *healf* and *cniht* = half a knight, referring to one who under the feudal system held half a knight's fee or used pejoratively for someone as 'half a knight'.
HAMMEL, HAMILL	O.E. meaning scarred or mutilated.
HAMMER OF THE ARIANS	St Hilary, Bishop of Poitiers (died 368).
HAMMER OF THE MONKS	Thomas Cromwell (1485–1540), Vicar General of Henry VIII, who caused the Dissolution of the English monasteries. In due course Cromwell was beheaded by order of Henry VIII.
HAMMER OF THE SCOTS,	the name of King Edward I of England (1272–1307) see Malleus Scotorum; see also Charles Martel.
HAMPOLE, Richard Rolle of	(c. 1300–49) a hermit and mystical writer who lived near the convent of Hampole.
HAND	O.E., with some skill of hand. Cf. also Hankin(s) = a diminutive of hand.
HANDSOME, The	Philip I (1478–1506), the first Habsburg King of Castile, married Joan the Mad (q.v.).

HAPPE	O.E. *gehaep* = fit.
HARBOLT, HERBOLT	O.G. *haribald*, army-bold.
HARBORD	O.E. *har* and *beard* = grey beard.
HARDHEADED PETE	Peter Stuyvesant, Dutch Governor of New Amsterdam (1647–64), now New York; also called Old Silver Leg, One-Legged Gov., and Wooden Leg.

HARDI, Le	more usually Englished as the Bold, a sobriquet of two of the four Valois, Dukes of Burgundy (who ruled from 1363 to 1477). (1) Philip le Hardi or Bold, the 4th son of King John II of France. This duke lived 1342–1404 and like all the Burgundian Valois dukes left numerous bastards, (2) Charles le Hardi, called le Téméraire or the Bold, who was killed in battle with the Swiss in 1477 at Nancy. He is a character in two of Sir Walter Scott's romances *Anne of Geierstein* and *Quentin Durward*. As to the bastards of Burgundy, more than 80 pages were required to trace them to the present day in the publications of the Brussels' Genealogical Studies.
	    Philippe III of France, born in 1245, reigned 1270–85.
	    William Douglas, died in 1302; defended Berwick.

HARDIMAN	bold man. Cf. also Hardy, bold courageous.
HARDING	O.E. *hearding* = hard. Cf. Hardman.
HARDRAADE	Hardruler or Hardcounsel, Harold III, King of Norway 1046–66. He invaded England and at the battle of Stamford Bridge in 1066 he was killed and his army annihilated. He was the last of the Vikings; the Viking age closed with his maraudings.
HARE(S)	nickname from O.E. *hare*, denoting speed or timidity (in the former meaning, King Harold Harefoot (q.v.), one of King Canute's sons), or from O.E. *haer* = hair.
HAREFOOT	Harold I (1035–40), one of the three Danish kings of England (1016–42); a nickname derived from fleetness of foot.
HARGER	O.G. = army spear.
HARKER	from M.E. *herkien* = to listen, hence an eavesdropper.
HARLEQUIN	Francis I of France thus referred to Charles V (1500–58) the Emperor.
HARLOCK	greylock, from O.E. *har* and *locc*.
HARMAN, HARMOND	O.G. *hereman* = warrior.
HARMER	O.G. *heremar* = army famous.
HARMONISTS or HARMONY SOCIETY	a sect of Communists (of the old style) founded in 1803–4 by J. G. Rapp. They settled in Pennsylvania on an estate which they called Harmony. Their views can only be described as weird. Rapp died in 1847 and the Harmonists died out soon after.
HARSANT, HASSENT	O.Fr. *hersent*, O.G. *herisint* = army truth.

HARVER, HERVEY	O.Fr. *herve*, O. Bret. *haervin* = battle worthy, the name coming from Brittany with the Bretons who formed part of William the Conqueror's army. Also 'army war' from O.G. *herewig*.
HARWIN	O.Fr. *harduin*, O.G. *hardwin* = firm friend.
HASIDAEANS	the Chasidim (q.v.).
HASMONEANS	the family name of the Maccabeans. According to Josephus, the first Maccabean mentioned in the Books of the name Mattathias, the priest of Modin, was the great-great-grandson of Hasmon.
HASSAN-BEN-SABAH	the Old Man of the Mountains (see Assassin).
HAVERS	O.E. *haefer* = he goat.
HAWK(E), HAWKES	O.E. *hafoc* = hawk, applied to one of cruel manners.
HAWKSEY	hawk's eye.
HAYDAY	O.E. *heah daeg* = high or festal day.
HAYE	can sometimes be from O.E. *heah* = tall.
HAZARD	O.E. *hals* and *ard* = neck, of a person with some peculiarity in his neck. Can also be from O.E. *hasu* = grey + *ard*, or again from O.Fr. *hasard* = gaming.
HEART OF MIDLOTHIAN	the old jail of Edinburgh demolished in 1817; the title of one of Scott's novels.
HEATHCOCK	the black grouse.
HEATHEN	see Pagan.
HECTOR OF GERMANY	Joachim II, Elector of Brandenburg (1514–71) from the Trojan hero of the *Iliad*.
HEDONISTS	adherents of the doctrine of Hedonism, i.e. that the motive and end of all moral action is pleasure.
HENN	sometimes a pet name from Henry, but also nickname from the bird.
HENRICIANS or HENRICANS	a medieval sect named from its originator, Henricus, an Italian monk of the 12th century. Mainly concerned with reform of the clergy.
HENRY SETON MERRIMAN	assumed pen name of Hugh Stowel-Scott (1862–1903).
HER LITTLE BLACK HUSBAND	the expression used by Queen Elizabeth I of John Whitgift whom she appointed Archibishop of Canterbury in 1583 and in whom she had complete confidence. He lived c. 1530–1604 and was the founder of Whitgift School at Croydon.
HERCULES SECUNDUS	the title given to himself by one of the worst Roman Emperors, Commodus (reigned AD 180–92), the son and successor of Marcus Aurelius. Claimed divine honours and was worshipped as Hercules.
HERE	O.E. *heore* = gentle.
HERMIT, The	Mark, c. 431, an ascetical writer of whom little is known, but one of whose writings, against

Justification from Works, endeared him to some
Protestants.

Peter (1050–1115) who preached the First Crusade
but escaped when those whom he led were
slaughtered in Asia Minor.

St Paul, the first of the Egyptian hermits who lived
to age of 113 and died in 341.

HERMIT OF THE SAHARA	Charles Eugène de Foucauld (1858–1916), a French officer who from a life of dissipation turned to the most severe ascetic practices in Algeria in the Sahara. He was murdered by wandering Tuaregs in 1916. He prayed earnestly for companions in his life; after his death the Little Brothers of Jesus were founded by René Voillaume, on de Foucauld's principles. They now number over one thousand.
HERO OF APPOMATTOX	Ulysses Simpson Grant, Northern General, received the surrender of the Southern General Lee. Later was President, also called Useless Grant.
HERO OF MOBILE BAY	Northern Admiral in US Civil War, Admiral David Glasgow Farragut.
HERO OF THE NILE	Viscount Nelson, for his victory there in 1798 when he destroyed the fleet with which Napoleon had invaded Egypt.
HERODIANS	a party of persons mentioned in the Gospel of St Mark xxii. 16 as being opposed to Christ. They are regarded as being supporters of the family of Herod the Great (q.v.), who for two generations ruled in Palestine.
HERON	from O.Fr. *hairon*, M.E. *heiroun* = heron, used to describe a thin man having long legs.
HICK, HICKES, HIX	from York Freemen's Register, origin Hick = pet form of Richard. Cf. Hickmott = Hick's brother-in-law; also Higgett, diminutive of Hick; Higgins, Hitch and Hitchcock.
HICKOX, HEACOCK	from Hea-coi, a diminutive of O.E. *heah* = high.
HIERAX	the Hawk. Antiochus, a prince (c. 263–226 BC) of the Seleucid dynasty who ruled independently part of his elder brother Seleucus II Callinicus' (q.v.) dominions until he was driven into exile.
HIGH CHURCH	the views of those members of the Church of England who hold exalted tenets about the Church and the Sacraments. They stress the Catholic character of the Church of England. They were first so called in the 17th century, when such outstanding men as Lancelot Andrewes and William Laud were in the Church. As they upheld the doctrine of the Divine Right of Kings they were unable to accept William III in place of James II. The Non-Jurors (q.v.) left the Church. High Church principles were still held, e.g. by Bishop Joseph Butler and Dr Samuel Johnson but it was not until the 19th century after the Oxford Movement of 1833 that High Churchmen became numerous in the Church.

HIGHLAND MARY	one of Robert Burns's many loves, but the identity is uncertain; she may have been a daughter of Archibald Campbell, a Clyde sailor.
HILDEBRAND	O.G. battle sword.
HILGER	O.G. battle spear.
HILLARY, HILARY	from Latin *hilaris* = cheerful but rather than always a nickname more often from St Hilarius of Tours (Poitiers) great champion of Catholic Faith and thought by many scholars to be author of Athanasian Creed. His funeral was attended by Jewish rabbis who admired him.
HIND OF SERTORIUS, The	a white hind was supposed to give counsel to Sertorius, the Spanish leader who resisted the Romans in last century BC and was beaten by Pompey in 72 BC and assassinated.
HIS MOST FAITHFUL MAJESTY	the title given to King John V (1706–50) of Portugal by Pope Benedict XIV in 1749.
HITCHMOUGH	brother-in-law of Hick (q.v.).
HOAR(E)	O.E. *har* = hoar, grey-haired in some of the instances, others being from common place name.
HOB, HOBBS	pet name of Robert.
HOBGEN	John and Hobb combined. There was also Hobhouchin = an owl.
HOCKADAY, HOCKERDAY	M.E. Hocedei or Hokedey, the second Tuesday after Easter Sunday, a term day for payment of rents.
HOG, The	Richard III, see the Boar.
HOGBEN, HOGBIN	from a Yorkshire dialect word, huckbone, e.g. a bent hip-bone referring to a person crippled or deformed.
HOIBERT, HULBERT	O.E. Holdbeorht = gracious, bright.
HOLDSHIP	O.E. *holdscipe* = loyalty.
HOLL(E)Y	O.E. *hol* and *eage* = hollow eye, in some cases the origin of the surname which otherwise originated as a place name.
HOLLIER, HULLYER	O.Fr *holier*, M.E. *holer* = whoremonger, debauchee.
HOLY CLUB, The	see Methodists.
HOLY CONSTABLE	Nuno Alvares Pereira (1360–1431), a most distinguished Portuguese military commander who was responsible for securing the throne for King John I of Portugal, the first of the House of Aviz (John had been Master of the Order of Aviz). Pereira secured the independence of Portugal from Castile by his victories. He had a daughter, Beatriz, who was married to Alfonso, the illegitimate son of King John I and from this marriage descended the later Portuguese royal house of Braganza. Pereira for the last 8 years of his life was a friar in the Carmelite house which he founded in Lisbon. He was beatified on 23 January 1918.
HOLY LAND	since the Middle Ages the name given to Palestine.

HOLYMAN, HOLLYMAN O.E. *halig* and *mann* = holy man. Could have been sarcastic in application.

HOLY MOUNTAIN Mount Athos in Greece, used exclusively by the Greek monks. Nothing female is allowed there.

HOME RUN BAKER John Franklin Baker, US baseball star.

HONEST ABE sobriquet of Abraham Lincoln (1809–65) President of USA, who led the Union states (the Federals) to victory in the Civil War (1861–5). Assassinated 1865. Called by his troops Father Abraham.

HONEY O.E. *hunig* = honey (the main source of sweetness in Middle Ages), used as a term of endearment, an example of the survival of older English in the American dialect.

HOODLASS, HUDLESS hoodless, one who did not wear a hood.

HOOK(E) in some cases from O.E. *hoc* = hook, applied to a person with a bent figure.

HOPKIN(S) Hobbe-kin, diminutive of Hob (q.v.).

HOPPER from O.E. *hoppian* = to hop or leap, hence a dancer.

HORRABIN, HOROBON O.E. *har* = grey and a pet form of Robert, 'grey Robert'.

HORSNALL, ARSNELL horse-nail, in some instances from a nickname for a man who shod horses.

HOSKER O.E. Osgar = god-spear.

HOSPITALLERS were originally an order of men who looked after the sick in the East c. 1099, and then later armed soldiers whose duty it was to defend the Holy Places against the Moslems. After 1291 Palestine was lost to the Christians, and the order withdrew to Rhodes and then in 1530 to Malta which the Order lost to Napoleon in 1798. After 1310 the Hospitallers were called Knights of Rhodes and after 1530 Knights of Malta.

HOT GOSPELLER a name applied by opponents to the Puritans. Allied to the distrust and dislike of enthusiasts which was common in the 18th century, and which was caused by the effusion of violent emotions in the 17th century in England.

HOTSPUR Sir Henry Percy (1364–1403), son of Henry Percy, 1st Earl of Northumberland; Hotspur rebelled against Richard II and then, dissatisfied with Henry IV, rebelled against the latter. Hotspur was killed at the battle of Shrewsbury which he lost. The nickname seems to be derived from hot pursuit of Scottish invaders of the north and a certain impetuosity in attack. Shakespeare's *Henry IV*, Pt 1 gives a good study of Hotspur.

HOUND O.E. *hund* = dog.

HUBBOLD, HUBBLE O.G. Hugibald = mind bold. Cf. Hubert, Hubbard, O.G. Higibert = mind bright. St Hubert, patron saint of huntsmen, contributed largely to the popularity of the name in medieval times.

HUDSMITH

Hudd's brother-in-law.

HUGUENOTS

the French Protestant Calvinists. The name 'is explained by Henri Estienne in his *Apologie d'Herodote* (1566) as a nickname based on a medieval romance about a King Hugo' (*Oxford Dictionary of the Christian Church*).

HUI THE FILIAL

name of the second of the Han Emperors (see Men of Han), Liu Ying, who succeeded in 196 BC. The title of Filial was added with one exception to the names of all the Han rulers posthumously. The various Han emperors usually took another regular name.

HUNN

O.N. *hunn* = young bear.

HUNTINGDONIANS

members of the Countess of Huntingdon's Connection, i.e. a sect of Methodists founded in 1718 by Selina, widow of the 9th Earl of Huntingdon, and George Whitefield who had become her chaplain when he left the brothers Wesley. For an account of the modern Connection, see *Who's Who in the Free Churches*, 1950.

HURRAN

O.Fr. *hure* = hair + suffix – and, hence, shaggy haired.

HUSSEY

from M.E. *huswieff* = housewife, mistress of a household, 'applied to a woman, a compliment, to a man derogatory . . . the surname is not to be associated with the modern meaning of hussey' (Reaney *Dict. of British Surnames*).

HUSSITES

the followers of John Huss (c. 1372–1415), the Bohemian reformer who was much influenced by John Wycliffe. Burned alive after the Council of Constance on 6 July 1415, the proceedings being reminiscent of A. O. B. (any other business) on an agenda.

HUTTERITES

from Jacob Hutter (died 1536) a branch of the Anabapists (q.v.), who made settlements in Moravia with common ownership of land. Hutterites or Hutterian Brethren are found in the USA.

HYKSOS

the Shepherd Kings of ancient Egypt who are thought to have ruled from c. 1720 to 1567 BC. They were invaders from Asia who were ultimately expelled by a native dynasty.

HYMNOGRAPHER, The

St Joseph (c. 810–86), a voluminous Greek hymn writer.

I

IBERIA'S PILOT
Christopher Columbus (c. 1446–1507), Iberia being the name given in olden times to Spain and Portugal, the Iberian peninsula.

ICHABOD
usually translated as 'the glory has departed', a Hebrew name given by the wife of Phineas to the son she had just borne (I. Samuel iv. 21). News had come while she was in labour that her husband had been killed in battle with the Philistines and that the Ark of the Covenant had been captured.

ICONOCLAST
image-breaker, sometimes applied to Leo III the Isaurian, Byzantine Emperor in 717, lived c. 680–741, who was opposed to use of icons in the Eastern Church.

IDDON
O.N. *idunn, idja* to do + *unna* = to love. Cf. Ineson = son of Iddon.

IDEALISTS
derived from Plato's concept of original ideas of which material objects are the images; in modern usage has little philosophical import but is used of persons who have certain standards of conduct which they want to see realized.

IDIOT
Greek ἰδιώτης, really a private person. It is only in the last 300 years that it has come to bear its modern meaning as of a person *non compos mentis*.

IDLE, IDEL(L)
O.E. *idel* = lazy.

IGNORANTINES
the name bestowed popularly on the Brothers of Charity, an order of Augustinian begging monks founded in Portugal in 1495 by John of Monte Major and concerned with ministering to the sick poor.

IKHNATON or AKHENATON
not a nickname but an assumed name taken early in his reign by the Egyptian Pharaoh Amenhotep (Amenophis) IV, who reigned from 1379 to 1362 BC. The name probably means 'Pleasing to the Aton' (the latter being the sun-disc). Ikhnaton's changes in religion did not last and the cult of the former gods came back in full vigour.

ILBERT, HILBERT, HIBERT
O.G. *hildeberht* = battle glorious.

ILLES
M.E. *ille* = bad.

ILLUMINATI
a term applied to the Rosicrucians (q.v.) and the Alumbrados (q.v.), but in present-day usage referring to a German, Adam Weishaupt, a professor and former Jesuit in 1776 in Bavaria. The movement was banned by the Bavarian government in 1785 but is strongly suspected of living now under various names. The Illuminati were also known as Perfectibilists. For full

details, see Nesta Webster, *Secret Societies and Subversive Movements*, London, Britons Publishing Society, 1955, and Douglas Reed, *The Controversy of Zion*, Sudbury, Bloomfield, 1978. The Illuminati were republican freethinkers.

ILLUMINATOR, The

St Gregory (c. 240–332), the Apostle of Armenia. He converted King Tiridates and with him the country. St Gregory was consecrated Catholicos (Bishop) of the Armenians and the episcopal office was held by his family for some generations.

ILLUSTRIOUS, The

Albert V, Duke of Austria (1398–1439) and successor of Sigismund as Emperor in 1438.

Ch'ien Lung, fourth Emperor of the Manchu dynasty of China, reigned 1736–96.

Jam-shid, fifth king of the Paisdadian dynasty of Persia (c. 840–800 BC)

'They say the Lion and the Lizard keep The courts where Jamshyd gloried and drank deep'. (E. Fitzgerald, *Rubayyat of Omar Khayyam*, 17).

Nicomedes of Bithynia (died 89 BC).

Ptolemy V of Egypt, see Epiphanes.

IMMORTAL, The

the Chinese Emperor Yong Tching (reigned 1723–36), the third of the Manchu dynasty. He assumed the title.

IMMORTAL DREAMER

John Bunyan (1628–88), because his great work *The Pilgrim's Progress* is described under 'the similitude of a dream'. Bunyan is often represented in illustrations as though asleep.

IMMORTAL TINKER

John Bunyan; see also the Inspired Tinker.

IMMORTALS, The

ἀθανατοι, of the Byzantine army were a select body of soldiers so named in imitation of the ancient Persians. They were embodied by the Emperor Michael Ducas (see Scott, *Count Robert of Paris*, ch. 4). The Persian Immortals mentioned above were a select corps of some 10,000 men, the elite troops of the Persian emperors. The term is also applied to the 40 members of the French Academy.

IMPERIAL MACHIAVELLI

Tiberius the Roman emperor, reigned AD 14–37. Niccolo Machiavelli (1469–1527), in his work *Il Principe*, set out principles of statecraft guided only by expediency.

INCHBALD

O.G. *Engelbald*, Ingilbald = Angle-bold.

INDEPENDENTS

the name formerly borne by Congregationalists (q.v.). Also known as Brownists (q.v.).

INGLEBRIGHT, ENGELBERT

O.G. Engelbert, Ingelbert = angle glorious.

INGRAM(S)

O.G. Engelrammus, Ingelramnus = angle-raven.

INOPPORTUNISTS

bishops at the 1st Vatican Council in 1870 who thought that the moment for defining papal infallibility was inopportune.

INSPIRED IDIOT — Walpole's term for Oliver Goldsmith (1728–74) 'who wrote like an angel and talked like poor Poll'.

INSPIRED TINKER — John Bunyan (1628–88), by trade a tinker, author of 60 books among which is the immortal *Pilgrim's Progress*.

IRISH INVINCIBLES — a secret Fenian Society in Dublin (1881) to get rid of the British; responsible for Phoenix Park murders (1882).

IRISH REPUBLICAN BROTHERHOOD — The Fenians (q.v.).

IRON ARM or FERREUS — Baldwin I, the Count of Flanders, married in 862 Judith, daughter of King Charles the Bald of France.
 François de la Noire (1531–91), a Huguenot soldier.

IRON DUKE — The Duke of Wellington, victor of Waterloo.

IRON GUARD — a violent nationalist organization in Rumania, founded c. 1930 by Corneliu Zelea-Codreanu. The latter was shot with 13 of his followers in 1938 by order of King Carol, who was himself forced to abdicate in 1944.

IRON LADY, The — Margaret Thatcher, first woman Prime Minister of the United Kingdom; the sobriquet derives from her intransigent attitude towards the USSR.

IRON TOOTH — Frederick II, elector of Brandenburg (1440–70).

IRONSIDE — O.E. *iren* and *sid* = ironside, warrior.

IRONSIDE — Edmund II (1016), son of Ethelred II the Unready; so named for his courage and determination in fighting against Canute. Died in mysterious circumstances. In the plural applied to the original cavalry regiments in Cromwell's forces.

IROQUOIS — name given by the French to the Confederation of Six Nations in Canada, the term being derived from a war cry. The Six were, Cayuga, Mohawk, Oneida, Onondaga, Seneca, also Tuscarora (joined in 1715).

IRVINGITES — a sect founded by Edward Irving (1792–1834), a Scottish Presbyterian minister but expelled from Church of Scotland when he took up millenarian ideas, and founded a sect which died out when the dates of Christ's visible return were unfulfilled. The Irvingites had a huge Church in Gordon Square, London.

ISAAC(S), ISAACSON — Hebrew *Isaac* = laugh. (See Genesis xviii, where Sarah laughed at promise of Isaac's birth when she is old, hence the child's name.) The surname in medieval times was not by any means confined to Jews. There is a full account of the Scottish Isaacs in Dr Black's *Surnames of Scotland* and there was also a Highland clan the MacIsaacs.

ISAAC THE MONK — hardly deserves a historical mention, except for his standing as an example of a class of lunatic Christians who were determined to be martyrs under the mild rule of the Moorish Moslems in Cordova. The Moorish regime allowed great toleration to the Christians but naturally did not allow interruptions to the services in the mosques or remarks about Mohammed the Prophet which to Moslems were blasphemous. There is a deeply interesting account of the Christian fanatics in S. Lane-Poole's *The Moors in Spain*, 1897, ch. V. Isaac cursed Mohammed and asked to be put to death. 'The Kady was sorry for the man and begged the Sultan to overlook his crime, but in vain. Isaac was decapitated, and thereupon became a saint, and it was proved conclusively that he had worked many miracles, not only ever since his childhood, but even before he came into the world' (Lane-Poole *op. cit.*). An ironical commentary on the above is provided because under Moslem rule, a particular cult of the Mass, etc. flourished. This was the Mozarabic from Mustarre, Arabic word for Christians. 'La liturgie en usage dans l'Espagne visigothique se maintent sous la domination Musulmane; c'est seulement après la reconquête de Toledo (1085) qu'elle entra en conflit avec l'usage romain, importe par les moines de Cluny. Elle disparut peu après' (Mgr L. Duchesne, *Origins du Culte Chrétien*, 1926, p. 169). The date 1085 was that of the Christian liberation.

ISAURIAN, The Leo III, Byzantine emperor, see Iconoclast.

ISHBOSHETH a Scriptural name used by transference to describe an ineffective sovereign. The original is mentioned in II Samuel iv as a son of Saul, and as being set up as King of Israel after Saul's death in battle, while David was King in Hebron over Judah. Ishbosheth, whose name is said to mean 'man of shame', owed his two years' reign to his general, Abner, and when the latter decided to go over to David, Ishbosheth was murdered by two of his subjects. Richard Cromwell, Queen Dick (q.v.), is meant under the name of Ishbosheth in John Dryden's poem, *Absalom and Achitophel* Pt i. 57, 58. The name is also used by Lord Macaulay in his Essay on *Hallam's Constitutional History*. 'But for the weakness of that foolish Ishbosheth . . . we might now be writing under the government of his Highness Oliver the Fifth or Richard the Fourth, Protector by the grace of God of the Commonwealth of England, Scotland and Ireland etc.', and much more in the same vein.

ISSARD, ISSETT, IZZET O.G. *iskild* = ice battle.

IT GIRL US film star, Clara Bow.

IVOR, IVERSON O. Sw. Ivar = yew army.

J

JACK AMEND-ALL
a name given to Jack Cade who was killed in England in 1450. He had led a rebellion in which he had promised to amend all grievances.

JACK-A-NAPES
applied to William de la Pole, Duke of Suffolk, who was banished but captured at sea by his political enemies and beheaded in 1450. The name came from his badge of the clog and chain of an ape.

JACK KETCH
synonymous for a hangman, the original having been an executioner who died in 1686 and who had delighted in his work.

JACK OF NEWBURY
an early capitalist who was reputed to have 500 work-people. John Winchcombe (died 1520), a wealthy clothier.

JACK STRAW
nickname of one of the leaders in the Peasants' Revolt of 1381 in England.

JACK THE RIPPER
the murderer of half a dozen prostitutes in London in 1888. The bodies of the victims were revoltingly mutilated. The perpetrator was never found.

JACOB(S)
Hebrew, supplanter, as in the well known story in Genesis of Jacob's dealing with his brother Esau, but in medieval England the surname was borne by Gentiles. Impossible to say if it had originally a pejorative meaning.

JACOBINS
the name given to the chief political club in the French Revolution. The name was derived from the meeting place of the club in a convent of the Dominicans or Jacobins in the Rue St Honoré in Paris.

JACOBITES
the followers of James II (1685–8) of England after his deposition in 1688; later of his son, James (Old Pretender (q.v.)) and grandson, Charles Edward (Young Pretender (q.v.)). The name derived from Jacobus, Latin for James.

JACOBITES, SYRIAN
so called after their leader Jacob Baradaeus (c. 500–78), consecrated Bishop of Edessa in c. 542. A leader of the Monophysites (q.v.) in Syria.

JACQUES BONHOMME
the contemptuous term used by the French upper classes to describe any French peasant. When the nobles had lost prestige as a result of defeats by the English in the Hundred Years War, the peasants revolted in the Jacquerie. In 1358 the peasants began to massacre their lords and burn their castles. They were, however, put down with many massacres.

JAHANSUZ
World Burner, the name given to Ala-ud-Din of Ghor who sacked Ghazni and drove out its ruler in 1152.

JANIZARY

new troops, hence Janizaries, the core of the Turkish forces for several hundred years from the late 14th century until their dissolution in 1826. The corps was formed in the first instance from prisoners and by a tribute of Christian children who were then trained in the Turkish language and the Islamic religion. The rule of life of the Janizaries was most strict, involving religious observance and celibacy. The corps eventually numbered 100,000 and became as dangerous to its masters as to the enemies of Turkey. Several Sultans died as the result of Janizary risings. Mohamud II destroyed the Janizaries. Most were killed and those taken prisoner were executed.

JANSENISM

a profoundly involved theological teaching, from the works of Cornelius Otto Jansen (1585–1638) and especially his *Augustinus*, which was published in 1640, i.e. after his death. Jansen became Bishop of Ypres in 1636. His teaching involved a supernatural determinism and was condemned by Pope Innocent X (1653). Among his adherents were Etienne Pascal and Jean Racine; inseparably connected with Port Royal (Auguste Saint Beuve, *Port Royal*, 3 vols, 1964 edition).

JAY(S), JEYES

O.Fr. *jay*, *gai* = jay, hence a chatterer.

JEALOUS

M.E. and O.Fr. *gelos* = wrathful.

JEHOVAH'S WITNESSES

see Pastor Russell.

JENNIFER, JUNIPER

Welsh Gwenhwyvar = *gwen* (fair) and *gwyf* (smooth or yielding).

JERSEY LILY, The

Lily Langtry (1853–1929), English actress, daughter of the Very Rev. W. C. Le Breton, Dean of Jersey, member of the Le Breton family of Loders Court, Jersey (see *BLG*, 1952). She married Edward Langtry and was later a mistress of King Edward VII. She married in 1899 Sir Hugo de Bathe, 5th Baronet (see *Burke's Peerage*, c. 1906). The nickname is from her birthplace and her physical beauty.

JERUSALEM-FARER

Sigurd I, King of Norway (1103–30).

JESTER

O.Fr. *geste* = exploit; M.E. *gester* = a jester or buffoon.

JESUITS

the name commonly given to the Society of Jesus, the famous Roman Catholic Order founded in 1540 by St Ignatius Loyola. The Order was the principal force in the Catholic Counter-Reformation and inevitably became involved in politics. Consequently, the term Jesuit and the adjective Jesuitical were used for a long time in a pejorative sense.

JEUNE, LE JEUNE

Fr. *jeune* = young. Cf. Jevon (q.v.).

JEVON

O.Fr. *jovene*, Latin *juvenis* = young.

JEW

sometimes used as a nickname from Jull (Julian(a)). Cf. Jewson.

JINGO, JINGOISM

comes from a popular song which had the refrain,
We don't want to fight, but by jingo if we do
We've got the ships, we've got the men,
We've got the money too.
This was sung in the period of the Russo-Turkish war
1877–8 when the British Mediterranean fleet was
ordered to Gallipoli to restrain Russia. Another line of
the song declared 'The Russians shall not have
Constantinople'. On one occasion Gladstone's
windows were broken by a jingo mob, as he was not
thought to be upholding British interests. Jingoism is
in fact the British equivalent of Chauvinism (q.v.).

JOB, JOBB, JUPE, JUPP

in some cases a nickname from O.Fr. *jobe* = a fool; in
others, from Job as a character in mystery plays. Or
again as a nickname for someone who could carry a
quantity of liquor, from M.E. *jubbe, jobbe*, a vessel
holding 4 gallons. Cf. Joblin, Jopling, diminutive of
Job, O.Fr. beggar, hence in English = fool.

JOBAR

from East Anglian, to job = to peck with the beak or
with a mattock.

JOCKEY OF NORFOLK

John Howard, 1st Duke of Norfolk, an adherent of
King Richard III of England. The morning of Bosworth
Field (1485) in which he was killed, he found the
following verse pinned on his tent;
Jockey of Norfolk, be not too bold
For Dickon thy master is bought and sold.

JOHN BARLEYCORN

whisky, extolled by Burns by this name in *Tam
O'Shanter*.

JOHN BULL

the conventional representation of the Englishman, a
stout, powerful figure, often shown with a Union Jack
waistcoat and accompanied by a bulldog. The original
is found in satires by John Arbuthnot in 1712 previous
to the Treaty of Utrecht. When used again in 1727 in
The History of John Bull the figure is that of an honest
clothier who has to bring an action against dishonest
Lewis Baboon (Louis XIV).

JOHN COMPANY

the Honourable East India Co. (H. E. I. C.), founded
1600, abolished 1858 after the Indian Mutiny.

JOHN OF NEPUMUK, St

(1340–93) 'born at Pomuk'; drowned by order of
Wenceslas IV of Bohemia.

JOHN OF THE CROSS, St

(1542–91), the Spanish founder of the Discalced
Carmelites. He worked closely with St Teresa.
Canonized 1726.

**JOHN RHETOR or
SCHOLASTICUS**

John Malalas, later 6th century, thought to be the same
as John Scholasticus, Patriarch of Constantinople
(died 577) (q.v.).

**JOHN WITH THE LEADEN
SWORD**

the nickname given by Earl Douglas to the Duke of
Bedford, 3rd son of Henry IV, who was Regent of
France 1427–9.

JOHNNY APPLESEED

American John Chapman, who in late 18th century
planted orchards all over America.

JOLLIFF, JOLLEY

M.E. and O.Fr. *jolif, joli* = gay.

JUDGE RUTHERFORD

Joseph Franklin Rutherford (1869–1941), head of the Jehovah's Witnesses (q.v.) after Pastor Russell (q.v.). He was not a judge.

JUDICIOUS

the adjective applied to Richard Hooker (c. 1554–1600), the author of *The Laws of Ecclesiastical Polity*, the first great post-Reformation theological work of the Anglican Church. It was said of Hooker that he not only knew more than other men but he knew it better.

JUMPERS

a name given to Welsh Calvinistic Methodists because they jumped for joy at their meetings.

JUNIUS

the anonymous name used by the writer of 70 letters which appeared in an English newspaper, the *Public Advertiser*, between 21 January 1769 and 21 January 1772. They were later published in book form. They were Whig in politics and violently opposed to the government of George III in the administrations of the Duke of Grafton and Lord North. The authorship is even now not known, and the anonymity is one of the best preserved secrets of literature. Even the prosecution of the publisher, Woodfall, and the punishment of the bookseller, Almoner, did not penetrate the secret. Lord Macaulay (*Essay on Warren Hastings*) thought Sir Philip Francis was the author. John Taylor, De Quincey and Stanhope held this view, but much disagreement exists among scholars. The name was assumed from that of Lucius Junius Brutus who in Roman history expelled the Tarquins from Rome c. 500 BC.

JUST, The

Aristides (late 6th century BC) an Athenian statesman and general. Plutarch tells the story that an ignorant countryman asked Aristides to write his own name on a shell, thus demanding his ostracism by the state. Aristides complied and asked the man what he had against Aristides. 'Nothing but I am tired of hearing him called the Just.' (The term ostracism comes from the shell on which the name of the person ostracized was written.)

JUSTINUS FEBRONIUS

the pen name of J. N. von Houtheim (1701–90), Suffragan Bishop of Trier in Germany, who wrote a book against the more extreme of the Papal claims, especially as regards the temporal power. Hence Febronianism. This German movement corresponded to the French Gallicanism (q.v.) but ended with the French Revolution.

K

KAFIRISTAN	land of the infidels, name given by Afghans to people of Nuristan (land of light) who were forcibly converted to Islam by the army of the King of Afghanistan, Abdurrahman Chan, in 1895.
KARAITES	from Hebrew word, 'to read', a sect among the Jews, dating from the 8th century AD, which is based on the Scriptures alone, thus rejecting the 'traditions of the Elders'.
KATIN	diminutive of cat.
KAY, KEYES	O.N. *ka* = jackdaw in north country, origin of some surnames. In Lancashire and Cheshire, M.E. *kei* = left, i.e. lefthanded or awkward. Also found in East Anglia.
KEAT(S), KEYTE	from O.E. *cyta*, M.E. *kete* = kite or greedy man.
KE(E)BLE	from O.E. *cybbel*, possibly cudgel, i.e. of a person as heavy as a cudgel.
KEDGE	in East Anglian dialect = brisk or lively.
KEECH, KEITCH	M.E. *keech* = a lump of congealed fat or rolled into a lump, used occasionally to denote a butcher.
KEEN(ES)	O.E. *cene*, M.E. *kene* = wise or brave.
KEMBLE, KIMBELL	O.E. *cynebeald* = kin bold.
KEMP(E)	O.E. *cempa* = warrior. Cf. frequent use in old ballads of 'kemperyman'.
KEN(N)	O.Fr. *ken*, Fr. *chien* = dog.
KENNEDY	Irish Ceinneidigh = ugly head.
KENRICK, KENWRIGHT	from Welsh *cynwrig* = chief man.
KENWARD, KENNARD	O.E. *cenweard* = bold guardian.
KENWAY, KENNAWAY	O.E. *cenwig* = bold war.
KERRICK, KENRICK	O.E. *cyneric* = family ruler.
KEWISH	Manx Mac Uais = the noble's son.
KID(D), KYD	M.E. *kide* = kid.
KING	O.E. *cyning*, *cyng* = king. 'A nickname from the possession of kingly qualities or appearance. Also a pageant name, one who had acted as king in a play or pageant, or had been King of Misrule, or king of a tournament' (Reaney, *Dict. of British Surnames*). Cf. Kingett, diminutive of King and Kingson.
KING, The	Clark Gable, famous US film actor.

KING ACROSS or OVER THE WATER the form of toasting used by Jacobites; when in general company, the glass being passed across a bowl or jug of water.

KING BELOVED OF THE GODS Asoka, Emperor of India (c. 274–232 BC). He was converted from the usual 'time when kings go out to war' to a peaceful life as a Buddhist. His record is that of one who endeavoured in every department of life to promote the good of his people. He sent out Buddhist missionaries to bring other rulers to adopt his benevolent practices. The lions of Asoka form one of the most notable emblems of the Republic of India.

KING BOMBA nickname of Ferdinand II, King of Naples, for his bombardment of Messina in 1848.

KING OF BATH Richard Nash (Beau Nash (q.v.)) (1674–1761), who undertook to manage the ceremonies of the baths at Bath, holding this position for many years.

KING OF DULLNESS thus Alexander Pope called Colley Cibber (1671–1757), Poet Laureate. See *Dunciad* Bk 1.

KING OF ROME the son of Napoleon, the Duke of Reichstadt (1811–32), who is Napoleon II in the Napoleonic legend.

KINGFISH, The Henry Pierce Long, Louisiana politician.

KINGMAKER Richard Neville, Earl of Warwick (1420–71), because he set up Henry VI and Edward IV alternately as Kings of England. At one time he had both the kings in his custody. He was the Last of the Barons (q.v.) and was killed at the Battle of Barnet.

KINSMAN M.E. *kinnes*, genitive case of kin, and man = kinsman.

KIPPING O.E. *cypping*, from Germanic root *kupp* = to swell with reference to persons of fat appearance. Cf. also Kipps.

KNATCHBULL M.E. *knatch* = to knock on the head, nickname for a butcher.

KNIGHT(S) O.E. *cniht* = servant, lad, boy. Applied by the English to the Norman bullies who ruled the land after 1066–72; much the same usage as in modern England where ghastly hooligans are referred to as 'boys'.

KNIGHT OF THE CLOAK Sir Walter Raleigh, from the famous story that he laid his cloak before Elizabeth I to prevent her walking through a puddle. The story is charmingly told in Scott's novel, *Kenilworth*.

KNOOP O.E. *cnoppa* = small round protuberance.

KNOTT O.E. *cnotta*, i.e. of a thickset man.

K OF K Earl Kitchener of Khartoum, from his great victory in 1898 over the Mahdi's forces.

KUMAN, The Laszlo IV (1272–60), King of Hungary. In the reign of his father Stephen V, the Kumans, a wild, pagan people entered Hungary in order to escape the Mongols. In the hope of uniting the Kumans with the Hungarians, Stephen V was married to a Kuman princess, but the son of the union, Laszlo IV, was a

wild youth who died without issue leaving Hungary
in a turmoil.

KUYUJU   pitman; name of Murad Pasha, Turkish general c. 1611,
because he threw the bodies of rebels into pits.

L

LABADISTS	an extreme Pietist Protestant sect founded by an ex-Jesuit, Jean de Labadie (1610–74), in Westphalia.
LACKLAND	or Sans-terre (q.v.), applied to King John (1199–1216) of England. He was the youngest son of Henry II (first of the Plantaganets (q.v.)) and was intended by his father to be Lord of Ireland, but his youthful levity made this impossible. Eventually John succeeded to the entire Angevin empire, though Maine, Touraine and Anjou declared for Arthur, the son of John's elder brother Geoffrey. The nickname acquired fresh significance when in 1204 Normandy was conquered by the French.
LADD(S)	O.E. *lad* = of lowly origin.
LADYBIRD	the nickname of Mrs Lynda Johnson, the wife of Lyndon Johnson, Vice-President of USA, who automatically succeeded President John Kennedy when the latter was assassinated at Dallas, Texas on 20 November 1963. Johnson was President until 1968. His wife's name was Lynda Bird Johnson and this by some weird slurring was turned into Ladybird. To the majority of non-Americans the nickname was thought to be really Mrs Johnson's name, there were also those who thought that it was a kind of title, such as the title-hungry Americans occasionally use. Even in an authoritative work such as *The Death of a President* by William Manchester, London, World Books, 1967, Mrs Johnson is from time to time called Ladybird.
LADY OF CHRIST'S, The	'the nickname given him [i.e. John Milton] in derision by his fellow-students as an attestation of virtuous conduct' (Mark Pattison, *Milton*, London, Macmillan, 1906, p.7).
LADY OF ENGLAND, The	Matilda, the daughter and heiress of King Henry I of England. Her first husband was the Emperor Henry V, who was old enough to be her grandfather. Later she married Geoffrey, Count of Anjou, a boy of 15, by whom she was mother of Henry II, King of England. Her contest with King Stephen for the English Crown lasted 19 years. The Council of Winchester in 1141 gave her the title of *Domina Anglorum*. She was generally referred to as 'the Empress' even after she became Countess of Anjou, thus anticipating the modern practice of widowed or divorced women, by which they use the higher title, after the second or third marriage to a man of lower rank than the first husband.
LADY WITH THE LAMP	Florence Nightingale (1830–1910), originator of modern nursing by her work in the hospitals of the Crimean

War. Her name was earned by her nightly visits to the hospital wards.

LAKE SCHOOL, The   the *Edinburgh Review* gave the title to Wordsworth, Coleridge and Southey, because they lived in the Lake District, not because of any close similarity in their work, except that they were all of the Romantic Revival.

LAKER   in some cases from O.N. *lakari* = player.

LAMB   from the name of the animal with reference to disposition. Cf. Lambkin and Lampen, Lamming.

LAMBARD   O.G. Lambert = land bright.

LAME, The   Albert II, Duke of Austria (1330–58), also called the Wise.
Charles II (c. 1256–1309) King of Naples and titular King of Sicily.
Timur i Leng (or Timur the Lame), frequently known as Tamerlane (1336–1405) supposed very doubtfully to be a collateral descendant of Genghis Khan. They did, however, share Mongol blood and were both conquerors who dealt in appalling cruelty. From Russia to China, from Persia to Egypt, Timur conquered with utter ruthlessness, his favourite memorial being a pyramid of skulls. He is buried at Samarkand, the city which he beautified but did not inhabit. 'His empire, never a cohesive entity even while he was alive, did not survive his death. He is remembered not as the founder of a dynasty, but as perhaps the most comprehensively destructive monarch in history' (Peter Brent, *The Mongol Empire*, London, Book Club Associates, 1976, p.239).

LAME KING, The   Agesilaus, King of Sparta. 'When he claimed the throne an objection was raised on the ground of his deformity; for an oracle had once solemnly warned Lacedaemon to beware of a halt reign' (J. B. Bury, *A History of Greece*, London, Macmillan, – 1906, p.534). The same writer said of Agesilaus, 'he had seen the triumph of Sparta, and had conducted her policy during the great part of thirty years of supremacy, and then, as an old man, he shared in her humiliation' (p. 628).

LANG, LONG   O.E. *lang* = long or tall.

LANGBAIN   O.N. *langabein* = long bone or leg.

LAODICEAN   a term describing a person luke-warm in adherence to any cause. It is derived from the verse in Revelation iii. 15 (to the church in Laodicea in the Roman province of Asia Minor): 'I know thy works; thou art neither cold nor hot. . . . So because thou art lukewarm and neither cold nor hot, I will spew thee out of my mouth.' Thomas Hardy's novel, *A Laodicean* (1880–1), has a character of this type. Among Apocryphal New Testament works is the alleged Epistle to the

Laodiceans, a spurious work derived from St Paul's reference in Colossians iv. 16.

LAPPIN(G)   O.Fr. *lapin* = rabbit.

LARGE   O.Fr. *large* = generous.

LARK, LAVERICK   M.E. *larke* = lark.

LASS, LESS   O.E. *laessa* = less, M.E. *lesse* = smaller, younger.

LAST KNIGHT   Maximilian I, Holy Roman Emperor (1493–1519), famous as a leader of the mercenary Landsknechte, as a hunter and as a patron of the arts.

LAST OF THE BARONS   Richard Neville, the Earl of Warwick, the famous Kingmaker (q.v.). Lord Lytton's novel, *The Last of the Barons*, gives a good account of his power and of his fall in utter defeat.

LAST OF THE ENGLISH   Hereward the Wake (q.v.) (the subtitle of Charles Kingsley's romance of that name); also applied by Tennyson to the Duke of Wellington, 'the last great Englishman is dead'.

LAST OF THE FATHERS   St Anselm, Archbishop of Canterbury, who lived c. 1033–1109. Author of the important work on the Atonement, *Cur Deus Homo*, he is sometimes called The First of the Schoolmen (q.v.). Sometimes the term is applied to St Bernard of Clairvaux (1091–1153).

LAST OF THE GOTHS   Roderick, the last of the Visigothic Kings of Spain who disappeared in 711 in the battle by which the Moors gained their domination in Spain. Both Sir Walter Scott and Robert Southey wrote poems on the subject.

LAST OF THE ROMANS   *Ultimus Romanorum*, the famous philosopher Anicius Manlius Severinus Boethius, a minister of Theodoric the Great, the Ostrogothic King of Italy. Boethius was accused by Theodoric of treason, was tortured and put to death. Whilst in prison he wrote one of the most influential books of the Middle Ages, *De Consolatione Philosophiae*. Boethius lived 480–524.

LAST OF THE TRIBUNES   Cola di Rienzo (or Rienzi) (1313–54), a Roman politician who tried unsuccessfully to humanize Roman politics. Lord Lytton's novel *Rienzi* is about his career.

LAST OF THE VIKINGS   see Hardraade.

LATHYRUS   pulse or vetching. Ptolemy IX Soter II reigned 116–108 BC in Egypt.

LATIMER, LATTIMORE   O.Fr. *latimer* = speaker of Latin, probably applied to one in one of the minor orders.

LATITUDINARIANISM   an opprobrious term for members of the C. of E. who were indifferent to exact dogma or church practices. It appeared in the 17th century in England and combined with the depreciation of Enthusiasm (q.v.) did much to produce what Gibbon called 'the fat slumbers of the church' in the 18th century.

LAUGHING PHILOSOPHER   Democritus of Abdera (5th century BC), said to have been the most learned of the Greeks before Aristotle.

He elaborated the Atomic theory of antiquity. In ethics he taught that happiness is most important and is derived from serenity of mind and control of the appetites. The nickname is not easy to understand.

LAUNCELOT LANGSTAFF the pseudonym under which was published the *Salgamundi Papers* (1807), the object of which was 'to reform the age', a work in which Washington Irving, J. K. Paulding and others collaborated.

LAWLESS M.E. *laweless* = uncontrolled by law; as in lawless man = outlaw.

LAWMENDER Lagaboeter, Magnus V, King of Norway, who ceded the Hebrides and Man to the Scots and replaced the old regional laws by a national code. He reigned 1263–80.

LAWTEY, LEWTY O.Fr. *leauté* = loyalty.

LAX O.N. *lax*, 'a nickname from the salmon, otherwise unrecorded in England' (Reaney, *Dict. of British Surnames*).

LAZAR M.E. *lazare* = leper.

LAZARISTS a body of secular priests founded by St Vincent de Paul in 1625 and taking their name from the priory of St Lazare where the founder lived in Paris. They were devoted to missions and to charitable works.

LEAF(E), LEIF, LIEF O.E. *leof* = dear.

LEAL, LEALMAN M.E. *lele*, O.Fr. *leial* = loyal.

LEAN O.E. *klaene* = lean.

LEAPER O.E. *kleapere* = leaper.

LEATHERSTOCKING NOVELS five novels by James Fenimore Cooper (1789–1851), dealing with the wild west of America and featuring Natty Bumpo, whose nickname was Leatherstocking; also Chingachgook, his Red Indian friend.

LEAVOLD, LEVELL O.E. Leofweald = beloved power or ruler.

LEAVY, LEVEY, LEVY, LEUY O.E. Loefwig = beloved warrior.

LECTOR, Theodore the a Church historian of the 6th century at Constantinople.

LEGARD O.G. Leudgard = people protection.

LEGAT(T) O.Fr. *legat* = ambassador or deputy, a pageant name.

LEGG(E) M.E. *legg*, O.N. *leggr* = leg.

LEGISLATOR OF PARNASSUS term applied by Voltaire to Nicolas Boileau (1636–1711), because of his *Art poétique* (1674) 'at one time regarded as the embodiment of the 17th century classical ideal, it is now seen to be on the whole a work of surprisingly little originality' (*Chambers Encyclopedia*, sub Boileau).

LEMMER	O.E. Leomaer = people-famous.
LEMPIERE	L'Empereur = pageant or play name.
LENG	O.E. *lang* = tall.
LEO SAPIENS	Leo VI, the Philosopher (q.v.).
LEOPARD, LIPPARD	from the name of the animal.
LERINS, St Vincent of	(died *ante* 450) a monk, he wrote the Commonitorium which contains the famous Vincentian Canon or rule of faith: *quod ubique quod semper, quod ab omnibus creditum est*, to determine the catholicity of doctrine or tradition.
LETTICE	from Latin *laetitia* = joy.
LEVELLERS	a body of men in 17th century headed by John Lilburne, who believed in equality, some ages before their time, and were severely repressed by Cromwell.
LEVERETT	in part from O. Fr. *leveret* = young hare.
LEVESON, LOWSON	O.E. Leof = dear son.
LEVIATHAN OF LITERATURE	Dr Samuel Johnson (1709–84), the reference is to the huge creature mentioned in Job in the Old Testament.
LIBERALISM	a term which was first used in the early 19th century to mean the holding of liberal views in politics or theology; an extremely wide description.
LIBERATOR, The	Simon Bolivar (1783–1830), the soldier-statesman who did more than anyone else to liberate the Spanish colonies in America. Six Latin American republics were freed by him and Bolivia is named after him. Daniel O'Connell (1775–1847), because he led the movement for the repeal of the penal laws in Ireland and to gain Catholic emancipation.
LIGHT OF THE AGE	Maimonides (Rabbi Moses ben Maimon) of Cordova, (1135–1204), a very great Jewish teacher, sometimes regarded as second only to Moses.
LIGHTBAND, LIGHTBOUND	coming from O.E. *lyt* = little, hence could be 'little husbandman'; or from O.E. *leoht* = light, meaning active or gay. Cf. Lightbody.
LIGHTBURN	from O.E. *lithe* = gentle, hence small child.
LIGHTFOOT	O.E. *leoht* = light and *fot* = foot, of a swift runner or messenger, e.g. the famous character Martin Lightfoot in Kingsley's novel *Hereward the Wake*.
LIGHTLAD	O.E. *lithe* = active, hence little lad.
LIGURIAN SAGE, The	Aulus Persius Flaccus (AD 34–62), born in Etruria (regarded as part of the ancient Liguria or Northern Italy). Persius was the author of the Satires which bear his name.
LILLAYMAN, LYTEMAN	from O.E. *lytlemann* = little man.
LIMA, St Rose of	(1586–1617), canonized 1671; the Patroness of South America, being the first American saint to be canonized.

LINNETT, LINNITT	sometimes nickname from the bird, M.E. *linet*.
LION, The	Henry Duke of Saxony (1142–80) lived 1129–95, a very quarrelsome ruler who led the Welfs against the Hohenstaufen. William I of Scotland (1165–1214), so called because he was the first Scots king to use the lion rampant on his heraldic shield. Having been captured by the English, he was compelled to do homage for Scotland to Henry II of England in 1274 at Falaise in Normandy.
LION HEART	see Coeur-de-lion.
LION OF GOD	Ali Ibn Talib (c. 600–61), the 4th Moslem Caliph, from whom the Shi'ites derive their origin, so called for his courage. He was son-in-law of Mohammed.
LION OF JANINA	Ali, a Turkish brigand (1741–1822), who became Pasha of Janina.
LION OF THE NORTH	Gustavus Adolphus, King of Sweden, born 1594, reigned 1611–32, killed at the battle of Lützen.
LIPP	O.E. from *lippa* = lip, used as a nickname pre-Conquest, could be the source of the modern surname.
LISIEUX, St Theresa of	Carmelite nun (1873–97). Canonized in 1925, she wrote the world-famous *History of a Soul*. Born and died in France.
LITTLE, LYTTLE	O.E. *lytel* = little. Cf. Littleboy and Littlechild.
LITTLE APOTHECARY	the name given in childhood to Baron von Humboldt, Friedrich Heinrich Alexander Humboldt (1769–1859), because of his large collection of plants and fossils.
LITTLE BROTHERS OF JESUS	see Hermit of the Sahara.
LITTLE CORPORAL, The	Napoleon, the name being given by his soldiers after the battle of Lodi in 1796 when he led the attack. 'The French soldiers had a mode at that time of amusing themselves by conferring an imaginary rank upon their generals, when they had done some remarkable exploit. They showed their sense of the bravery displayed by Bonaparte at the battle of Lodi by creating him a Corporal: and by this phrase of the Little Corporal he was distinguished' (Sir Walter Scott, *Life of Napoleon Buonaparte*, 1827, ch.IV).
LITTLE DAUPHIN	or Second Dauphin, Louis (1682–1712), son of the Grand Dauphin (q.v.). Both the Grand and the Little Dauphin predeceased their father (and grandfather) Louis XIV.
LITTLE ENGLANDERS	those persons who in the time of the British Empire thought that the British should be concerned with Britain only. The term was used at the time of the Boer War (1899–1902) for those who were opposed to imperial policy.

LITTLE FLOWER St Theresa of Lisieux (q.v.). Also used of Fiorello H. La Guardia, Mayor of New York, from his name.

LITTLE GENTLEMAN IN VELVET i.e. a mole, as William III's horse stumbled over a molehill, an accident which led to the king's death in 1702. A favourite Jacobite (q.v.) toast.

LITTLE MAGICIAN Martin Vann Bure (1782–1862), 8th President of the USA, because of his cunning and skill as a politician.

LITTLE SURE SHOT Wild west show star and crackshot, Annie Oakley (Mrs Frank E. Butter).

LITTLE TRAMP, The Charles Spencer Chaplin, star of silent films.

LITTLEFAIR M.E. *fere* = companion, hence little companion. The word *fere* in this sense often occurs in Spenser's *Faerie Queene*.

LITTLEJOHN used of a very big man, e.g. the famous character in the Robin Hood cycle.

LITTLEPAGE from two obvious words.

LITTLEPROUD O.E. *lytel*, O.Fr. *prud* = little value.

LITTLEY in some cases meaning little eye.

LIVY OF FRANCE Juan de Mariana (1537–1624), historian.

LIVY OF PORTUGAL João de Barros (1496–1570), historian.

LLEWELYN FAWR the Great (q.v.).

LLOYD Welsh Llwyd = grey.

LOB(B) O.E. *lobbe* = spider.

LOCK(E) is sometimes from O.E. *loc(c)* = lock, i.e. someone with fine hair.

LOCKLESS O.E. *loc* = lock of hair and *leas* = free from, for someone with straight hair.

LOGOTHETES see Metaphrastes.

LOLLARDS Originally the followers of the reformer John Wycliffe in 14th century England. 'The original meaning of the term would appear to be a "chanter" and so a "mumbler of prayers" (Cf. Middle Dutch *lollen* or *lullen*, "to sing", but possibly it comes from the Latin *lolia* = tares)' (*Oxford Dictionary of the Christian Church*).

LOLLER possibly from M.E. *lolle* = to droop, to lean idly.

LONE STAR STATE Texas, which at first was completely independent.

LONGFELLOW tall fellow. Cf. Longman.

LONGHAND Greek Macrocheir, Latin Longimanus. Artaxerxes I, Persian Emperor, reigned 465–24 BC; having the right hand longer than the left.

LONGSHANKS Edward I (1272–1307) King of England, so called from his great stature; like King Saul he stood head and shoulders above most of his subjects. When his tomb in Westminster Abbey was opened in 1774, his body was found to be 6ft 2ins in length. Also known as Malleus Scotorum (q.v.).

LONGSWORD, William
2nd patrician or Duke of Normandy, son of Rollo the Ganger (q.v.). He was murdered in 942.

William Longsword, Earl of Salisbury, bastard son of Henry II of England (1154–89), by the Fair Rosamund (q.v.).

LORD
O.E. *hlaford* = lord; 'often, no doubt, a nickname for one who aped the lord, or for a lord's servant' (Reaney, *Dict. of British Surnames*).

LORD CUPID
Lord Palmerston; see also Pam.

LORD FANNY
nickname in Alexander Pope's poem *Satires of Horace*, for Lord Hervey (1696–1743) because of his effeminate manners.

LORDING
O.E. *hlafording* = son or follower of the lord.

LOTHARIO
name for a gay philanderer. A character so named in Rowe's play *The Fair Penitent*.

LOUD, LOWDE
O.E. *hlud* = loud, a nickname for a loud-voiced person.

LOVEDAY, LOWDAY
from O.E. *leefdaeg* = dear day, but used as Christian name 'given to children born on a loveday, that is, a day appointed for a meeting between enemies, litigants, etc. with a view to an amicable settlement of disputes' (*Oxford Dictionary of English Christian Names*, 1945). Found in 1830s in Somerset, e.g. Loveday Darby in the will of William Pine.

LOVELACE, LOWLESS
O.E. *lufa* and *leas* = without. Hence = loveless, not inapplicable to the seducer so named in Richardson's *Clarissa*.

LOVELADY
a nickname for a seducer.

LOVELL, LOWELL
from O.Fr. *lovel* = wolf-cub; by the 18th and early 19th centuries had become commonly used in romantic novels for aristocratic heroes.

LOVELOCK
'a nickname for a dandy, a wearer of pendant locks of hair falling over the ears and cut in a variety of fashions' (Reaney, *Dict. of British Surnames*).

LOVELY
M.E. *Lovelick* = lovely.

LOVEMAN, LOWMAN, LEMON
O.E. *leofmann* = beloved man.

LOVER
M.E. *lovere* = lover.

LOVETT
O.Fr. *lovet* = wolfcub.

LOW(E)
O.Fr. *lou* = wolf, or can be from O.N. *lagr* = short, when used as a nickname.

LOW CHURCHMEN
those persons in the C. of E. who have a relatively low view of the claims of the episcopate, priesthood and sacraments and thus approximate to the position of the

Nonconformists. The term was first used in the 18th century.

LUCKY LEAKEY

Louis Leakey – palaeontologist and anthropologist – *à propos* of his extraordinary luck in discovering fossils in East Africa, though the ascription of enormous age to these fossils is very much in doubt.

LUCY

the fossilized remains of a female hominid discovered by Don Johanson in Ethiopia. The name is from a popular song of the time.

LUDDITES

name given to organized bands of English workers who went round destroying machinery because they believed that its introduction would deprive them of work. This movement began in 1811 in the Nottingham area of England. It was well organized with the supposed King Ludd or Ned Ludd as leader. The government reacted strongly with a mass trial in 1813 followed by hangings and deportations. The Luddites struck again in 1815, were again repressed and it was only reviving prosperity which ended the movement.

LUFF

O.E. *leof* = beloved.

LUPUS

Latin for wolf, the name (posthumously) borne by Hugh of Avranches the Fat (q.v.), Earl of Chester *temp.* William the Conqueror. Some families in the area which Hugh had ruled bore the wolf as the principal charge in their arms, and it was supposed that he had borne the same. The charge of the wolf was derived from the name, Hugh Lupus, though it was an anachronism as heraldic devices did not appear until after his time.

LUTHERANS and LUTHERANISM

the followers and beliefs of Martin Luther, the German monk who in 1517 began the movement known as Protestantism. The main tenet is justification by faith. The word was early adopted as the official title and continues in use to this day.

M

MACCABEES
see Hasmoneans and Judas Maccabeus.

MACCABEUS, JUDAS
the Hammerer, from a Hebrew word *maggabi*. Judas was the son of a Jewish priest who in the 2nd century BC raised the standard of revolt in Palestine against the Hellenizing tendencies of the Syrian Kings. The name was later applied in the plural to the whole family to which Judas belonged, though their correct name was Hasmonean, from their ancestor called Hasmon. Another explanation of Maccabeus is from Hebrew verb *magab* to appoint, referring to Judas as one appointed by God. The history of Judas, of his brothers and their ultimate triumph is given in the two books of Maccabees in the Apocrypha.

MACEDONIAN, The
Basil I, Byzantine emperor and founder of the Macedonian dynasty. He was of Macedonian descent, though his family had settled in Armenia. He murdered his benefactor Michael III and was sole emperor in 867. He died in 886.

MACEDONIANS
a heretical sect named after Macedonius, Patriarch of Constantinople in 4th century. This sect denied the Deity of the Holy Ghost but it is doubtful how far Macedonius shared their views.

MAD, The
Juana La Loca, Joan (1479–1555), nominally Queen of Castile (1504–55), and of Aragon (1516–55), was the second daughter of Ferdinand and Isabella, the Catholic kings (q.v.). She appears to have inherited her mental troubles from her grandmother, Isabella of Portugal. She was married to Philip the Handsome (q.v.) of Habsburg. Joan died in retirement, having given birth to two sons (the elder, the Emperor Charles V) and four daughters, who were married into the royal houses of Portugal, France, Denmark and Hungary. 'It seems likely that Joan transmitted her mental instability to her great grandson Don Carlos and through the many Habsburg intermarriages in an attenuated form to Charles II of Spain' (*Encyclopedia Britannica*).

MAD CAVALIER
Prince Rupert (1619–82), famous cavalry leader in the English Civil War; 'the furious German' of Macaulay's verses on the Naseby fight.

MAD POET
Nathaniel Lee (c. 1653–92) confined in Bedlam for 4 years.

MADMAN OF THE NORTH
Charles XII of Sweden (1682–1718), referred to by Pope in *Essay on Man*, iv, 'From Macedonia's madman to the Swede.'

MAGNANIMOUS

Alfonso V, King of Aragon (c. 1394–1458); succeeded in 1415, mainly concerned with Italian affairs and even transferred his capital to Naples. He was a typically brilliant Renaissance prince.

Chosroes, 21st King of Persia (531–79), of Sassanid dynasty called Noushirwan (Magnanimous).

Philip (1504–67) Landgrave of Hesse from 1509, thus known as *der Grossmütige* by his contemporaries because of his efforts to promote the well being of Hesse and the unity of Protestants.

MAGNIFICENT, The

applied to Edmund I (940–6), King of England, by Florence of Worcester, *magnificus*, probably because of wealth at his court and his generosity.

Sobriquet given to Lorenzo de Medici, *Il Magnifico* (1449–92), who succeeded in making himself in effect despot of Florence. A munificent patron of the arts. Father of Pope Leo X (1475–1521), who excommunicated Luther in 1520, without having the least apprehension of Luther's importance.

Also applied to US General Douglas MacArthur, also known as Beau Brummell of the army and Disraeli of Chiefs of Staff, supposedly because of his appearance. Effectively removed by President Truman.

Suleiman I (1520–66), Sultan of Turkey, a great warrior whose empire extended to Algeria and from the borders of Germany to those of Persia. He had a gifted architect who built for him two masterpieces, the Mosque in Istanbul (built 1550–55) and the Selimiye Mosque at Adrianople (now Edirne). (See Wilfred Blunt, *Splendours of Islam*, Abingdon, Purnells, 1976.) Known also as the Lawgiver.

MAGNUS, St Albertus

Albert the Great or Albert of Cologne (c. 1200–80). A scholastic philosopher, scientist and theologian, whose works embraced all the knowledge of his time. 'A pre-eminent place in the history of science must be accorded to him forever' (*Encyclopedia Britannica*). His most distinguished pupil was St Thomas Aquinas, the Angelic Doctor (q.v.).

MAGUS, Simon

the Magician, mentioned in Acts viii, 9–24, a magician in Samaria who offered money to St Peter to enable him to receive the Holy Ghost, hence the derivation of simony, buying and selling holy things. Nothing authentic is known further of Simon Magus but a considerable literature grew up, confusing him with a 2nd century figure, Simon of Gitta in Samaria.

MAHATMA

Sanskrit 'great soul', applied to Gandhi.

MAHDI or AL-MAHDI

in Arabic means the divinely guided one, a species of Messiah in widespread Islamic belief, though not mentioned in the Koran. From time to time people claiming to be the Mahdi have appeared in Islamic countries. The most distinguished was Mohammed Ahmed, the Mahdi of Sudan, who died in 1885 after having killed General Gordon at Khartoum.

MAHOUN, MAHOUND

a term of contempt for a Moslem, used in the period of the Crusades.

MAID OF ATHENS   Theresa Macri, of whom Lord Byron wrote. She died in poverty.

MAID OF KENT   Elizabeth Barton (c. 1506–34), a nun who was reported to have trances and utter prophecies. When the latter became highly critical of Henry VIII and his divorce from Catherine of Aragon, Barton was prosecuted under the Bill of Attainder and executed.

MAID OF NORWAY   Margaret, born c. 1283 and died in 1290. She was grand-daughter and heiress of King Alexander III and was to have succeeded to the Scottish throne. Arrangements were made for Margaret to marry King Edward I of England's young son, later Edward II of England. On Margaret's death there were 12 competitors for the throne of Scotland. They appealed to Edward I to decide between them. He agreed on condition that they accepted him as Lord Paramount which they did, a fact noted by British Rail on Berwick Railway Station. Edward chose Edward Balliol as sub-king of Scotland thus precipitating 300 years of war between England and Scotland until at last James VI of Scotland became James I of England. As Andrew Lang remarked, 'Edward's aim, to unite the whole island was excellent. The end did not justify the means' (*History of Scotland*, Edinburgh, Blackwoods, 1907, vol.1, p.176).

MAID OF SARAGOSSA   Augustina Zaragoza, a heroine in the sieges of Saragossa 1808, 1809, mentioned by Byron in *Childe Harold* 1.54–6. She manned a gun against the French.

MAIDEN   used in derogatory sense of effeminate man; the nickname given to King Malcolm IV of Scotland, born in 1141 and died in 1165. William Anderson describes him as succeeding his grandfather David I in 1153, 'being then only 12 years of age. The same year he was crowned at Scone. He acquired the name of Malcolm the Maiden, either from the effeminate expression of his features or from the softness of his disposition' (*Antiquity of the Scottish Nation*, Edinburgh, Fullarton, 1863). Cf. also Maides.

MAINE, MAYNE   O.G. *maine, meine* = strength. Cf. the Spanish Main.

MAITLAND   O.Fr. *maltalent*, meaning discourteous or rude manners, at least in England; in Scotland said by Reaney to be from a place, but Dr Black says, 'perhaps a nickname but explained without proof or much probability as little or bad wit' (*Surnames of Scotland*.)

MAKEPEACE   obvious meaning: 'Joan Makepeace was the name given to the sister of Edward III of England when the war with the Bruces was partly pacified by her marriage with David II in 1328.'

MAKIN, MEAKIN(S)   from maidekin = little maid.

MALBROOK   name derived from 1st Duke of Marlborough, the great general and statesman, John Churchill. Malbrook being used by the French, as in a popular verse '*Malbrook s'en va-t-en guerre*'.

MALE   O.Fr. *male* = male, masculine.

MALET, MALLETT

originally a nickname from the iron mace, O.Fr. *maillet* (from *mal*, Latin *malleus*, a hammer). For the history of the family, see *Burke's Peerage*, Malet, Bts and *Burke's Landed Gentry* 1952, Malet, formerly of Ash. William Malet held land in England in the reign of Edward the Confessor. Cf. Malleus Scotorum = Hammer of the Scots, applied to Edward I of England.

MALIPHANT

O.Fr. *mal enfant* = naughty child.

MALLARD

O.Fr. *malard* = wild duck.

MALLEUS HERETICORUM

Hammer of heretics. John Faber (1478–1541), from the title of one of his books.

MALLEUS SCOTORUM

the Hammer of the Scots, Edward I of England; he had taken over Scotland, captured Sir William Wallace and had him executed. At the time of his death in 1307, Edward was marching to put down a Scottish rebellion by Edward Bruce. See Longshanks.

MALLORY

O.Fr. *maloret* = the unlucky.

MALMESBURY, William of

(c. 1090–c. 1143) a principal English medieval historian.

MALTRAVERS, MATRAVERS

O.Fr. *mal travers* = bad or hard passage. 'If a nickname, it probably denotes a man difficult to pass, one who can look after himself, a stout soldier' (Reaney, *op. cit.*).

MAMELUKE

Arabic *mamluk*, meaning 'owned'. The Mamelukes were white male slaves from the Caucasus and Russia and were formed into a *corps d'élite* by the Caliphs of Baghdad. They gradually became a very powerful body which ruled several lands, Egypt particularly. Mohammed Ali Pasha, who became ruler of Egypt under the Sultan of Turkey, massacred the remaining Mamelukes in 1811.

MAMERTINES

'children of Mars'; some Campanian mercenaries who were besieged in Messana by Hiero of Syracuse, appealed to Rome for help. This brought the Romans into Sicily and began the 1st Punic War (264–241 BC).

MAMZER

a slang expression for a bastard; said to be used in the Liverpool area; found in Charles Kingsley's novel *Hereward the Wake* as applied surreptitiously to William the Conqueror (q.v.).

MAN IN THE IRON MASK

perhaps the best kept secret in history, a person held prisoner for 40 years by Louis XIV and who remains to this day unknown. Perhaps the best conjecture is that of Alexandre Dumas in the novel of that title; the prisoner there being the twin brother of Louis XIV.

MAN OF A THOUSAND FACES

Lon Chaney, American film star, because of his numerous changes in make-up.

MAN OF BLOOD

Roundhead name for Charles I with not very clear significance. Cf. Macaulay's poem on Naseby.

MAN OF BLOOD AND IRON

Bismarck (1815–98) so called because his policy of securing supremacy for Prussia was pursued whether in peace or in war.

MAN OF CHIOS

Homer, who is supposed to have lived at Chios, near

the Aegean Sea.

MAN OF DECEMBER   Napoleon III (1808–73); the most important events in his progress from President to emperor of France occurred in December, 1848–52.

MAN OF DESTINY   Napoleon Bonaparte, evidently self-called.

MAN OF ROSS   John Kyrie (1637–1724), born in Whitehouse, in Gloucestershire, who lived for most of his life in Ross, in Herefordshire, and was a very charitable benefactor of churches.

MAN OF SEDAN   Napoleon III, as at Sedan he surrendered to William I, King of Prussia, in 1870.

MAN OF SILENCE   Napoleon III, from his (supposed) taciturnity.

MANCHESTER MASSACRE Peterloo (q.v.).

MANCHESTER SCHOOL   Cobden and Bright School of Free Traders, so dubbed by Disraeli in 1845.

MANCLARK, MOCKLER   O.Fr. *mal + clerc* = bad cleric.

MANDEANS   a Gnostic sect still in existence near Baghdad, holding a farrago of semi-Christian beliefs connected with a variety of other ideas.

MANICHAEANISM   the teaching generally held to be derived from Manes or Mani (c. 216–76) who lived in the Persian empire. By his opposition to the Zoroastrian doctrines, he fell foul with the Persian King, Bahram I, and was put to death by being flayed alive. His teaching corresponded to Gnosticism (q.v.) in inculcating a system of dualism, i.e. two powers, Good and Evil, in conflict. There was in Manichaeanism an emphasis on ultra-puritanism to avoid the impurity of the body.

MANKIN   diminutive of man = little man.

MANTEL   O.Fr. *mantel* = cloak.

MANTUAN, The   called also Swan or Bard of Mantua, the birthplace of the greatest Latin poet, Publius Virgilius Maro, author of the *Aeneid*.

MARCIONITES   the followers of Marcion, a man from Pontus who died c. 160. Tertullian called him the Pontic mouse, because he nibbled at the Scriptures. Marcion accepted only the Epistles of St Paul (excluding the three Pastorals) and the Gospel of St Luke. He believed in two gods, the Demiurge or Creator, a God of Law, and the God of Jesus Christ, a God of Love.

MARCOSIANS   a Gnostic sect of the 2nd century, one of the many mentioned by St Irenaeus in his *Adversus omnes haeresos*, as founded by a charlatan called Marcus, and living in the Rhône valley.

MARGA, Thomas of   a 9th century Nestorian historian, Bishop of Marga in Mesopotamia.

MARIAVITES   a Polish sect which originated in 1906 having much in common with the Old Catholics (q.v.). The founders were a Polish priest, J. Kowalski and a Tertiary sister,

F. Kozowska. The name came from the words, *qui Mariae vitam imitatantur*, because of the great devotion of the sect of the Blessed Virgin.

MARIOLATRY
(the second part of the word from Greek δατρεία = worship) – an abusive term used by Protestants to describe Catholic devotions to the Blessed Virgin Mary; abusive because no Christian can worship a creature, however exalted.

MARISTS
a term for the Society of Mary, founded in France in 1824 by the Venerable Jean Claud Marie Colin (1790–1875).

MARK RUTHERFORD
writing name of William Hale White (1831–1913), author of religious works.

MARK TWAIN
renowned American author, real name Samuel Langhorne Clemens (1835–1910).

MARONITES
a body of Uniat Christians (i.e. in communion with Rome but having their own liturgy) in the Lebanon. They were originally Monothelites (q.v.), although they themselves derive their name from St Maron (*tempore* St Chrysostom), Syriac for 'my lord'.

MAROSIANS
a Gnostic sect of 2nd century named after Marcus, an Egyptian.

MARROW(S)
M.E. *marwe* = mate or lover.

MARS OF PORTUGAL
Alfonso de Albuquerque (1452–1515), Viceroy of the Indies, so called from Mars, the god of war.

MARSHAL FORWARDS
Marschall Vorwarts, the name earned by Blücher (1742–1819) because of his constant exhortations to his soldiers.

MARSHALL OF THE ARMY OF GOD AND OF HOLY CHURCH
the grandiloquent title of Baron Robert Fitzwalter, leader of the English Barons against King John, 1215.

MARTEAU DES HÉRÉTIQUES
Hammer of the heretics, Pierre d'Ailly (1350–1425), President of the Council of Constance, which condemned and burnt John Huss.

MARTEL
the Hammer, the name of Charles, illegitimate son of Pepin the Younger (q.v.) of France. Charles Martel is famous for his great victory in 732 at Tours over the Saracens who had carried all before them from their invasion of Spain in 711. The battle is listed as one of the *Fifteen Decisive Battles of the World* by Sir Edward Creasy. Charles died in 741, his position being then that of Mayor of the Palace to the Merovingian nominal kings (rois fainéants (q.v.)).

MARTEL(L)
as a surname is often a nickname from O.Fr. *martel* = hammer, the *martel de fer* or mace used in medieval battles. The most famous use of the nickname was that borne by Charles Martel (q.v.).

MARTER, MARTYR
O.Fr. *martre* = weasel, applied to a crafty, nasty individual.

MARTIN MARPRELATE

the assumed name of a group of writers in 1589 who
attacked the Elizabethan Church of England,
especially on the subject of episcopacy. The identity of
some of the writers was suspected, so two of them,
Perry and Barrow, were executed in 1593 and Udall
died a prisoner.

MARTINET

a very strict observer of military discipline, derived
from the French Colonel, the Marquis de Martinet,
who reformed the infantry in the reign of Louis XIV.

MARTYR, The

St Edmund, King and Martyr (c. 840–69) King of East
Anglia, killed by the heathen Danes; his shrine at
Bury St Edmunds in Suffolk was one of the most
magnificent in England as its present ruins testify. For
a full account, see Rev. Bryan Houghton's *Saint
Edmund King and Martyr*, Lavenham, Terence Dalton,
1970.

Edward II (pre-Norman Conquest 975–78), murdered
at Corfe Castle in Dorset by orders of his stepmother,
Elfrida, who schemed to get the throne for her own
son. 'No worse deed than this for the English people
was committed since first they came to Britain. . . . His
earthly kinsmen would not avenge him, but his
Heavenly Father has greatly avenged' (*Anglo-Saxon
Chronicle*, year 978, D Version). There Edward is
mentioned as a saint and martyr.

MARTYR OF YORK

Margaret Clitherow (c. 1536–86). She was charged with
harbouring Roman Catholic priests. In order to save
her children from being forced to witness against her
and to save their inheritance she refused to plead.
She was subjected to the *peine forte et dure,* i.e. was
crushed to death. One of 40 martyrs canonized by
Pope Paul VI in 1970.

MARTYR, St Justin

(c. AD 100–65) an early Christian apologist, converted
after studying all the Greek philosophers; wrote
works in support of Christianity (*First and Second
Apology* and *Dialogue with the Jew Trypho*). Was
martyed in 165.

MARTYR PRESIDENT

James Abrah Garfield (1831–81), American president
who was assassinated. Also known as Canal Boy and
Preacher President.

MARVAL, MARVELL

O.Fr. *merveille* = the marvel, though many of the
surnames come from place names in France or in
England.

MASSILIENSIS

i.e. of Massillia or Marseilles, the name given to the
Christian writer, Salvian (c. 400–c. 480).

MASSORETES

from a Hebrew word meaning tradition, a school of
Jewish grammarians who established between 6th
and 10th centuries AD what they regarded as the
correct text of the Old Testament.

**MASTER OF THE
SENTENCES**

Magister Sententiarum, Peter Lombard (c. 1100–60), a
medieval theologian, born in Lombardy, whose book,
Sententiarum libri quatuor, became the standard text-
book of Catholic theology in the Middle Ages.

MAUDUIT, MUDDITT	O.Fr. *mal duit*, Latin *male dictus*, ill-educated.
MAULEVERER	O.Fr. *mal leverier* = poor harrier.
MAURISTS	a Congregation of Benedictine monks taking its name from St Maurus (6th century disciple of St Benedict), and founded in 1621.
MAW(E)	in some cases from O.E. *maew* = sea-mew.
MAY, MAYES, LE MAY	M.E. *may* = young boy or girl.
MAYER, MEYER	O.Fr. *maire*. 'It may have been sometimes a nickname for one who aped the mayor, a much more exalted person in England than in France.'
MEAGER	O.Fr. *megre* = thin.
MEEK(S)	M.E. *meke* = meek.
MEIKLE, MICKEL	'a name descriptive perhaps of its first bearer, Middle Scots meikill, meikle, mekill = big, large' (Dr Black, *Surnames of Scotland*.) Cf. Meiklejohn.
MELANCHTHON	Philip (1497–1560), whose real name was Schwarzerd. German theologian and Protestant Reformer, he took Melanchthon as the Greek form of Schwarzerd, 'black earth'.
MELCHIORITES	an Anabaptist sect named from Melchior Hoffman who died in 1543; still firmly convinced of the Second coming of Christ which he confidently expected in his lifetime.
MELCHITES, MELKITES	a word derived from the Greek form of a Syriac word which meant 'imperial'. The term was and is applied to Christians in Syria and Egypt, who refused Monophysitism and adhered to the orthodox Christology of the Council of Chalcedon (451). Some of them adhere to the Orthodox Church, others form one of the Uniat branches of the Roman Church.
MELODUS	from Greek ὁ μελωδός, the name of St Romanos (lived c. 540), a Greek religious poet.
MELUN, Robert of	a scholastic theologian (died 1167); an Englishman who studied in France and lived in Melun.
MEMORY WOODFALL	William Woodfall (1746–1803), who could memorize a meeting without taking a single note.
MEN OF HAN	designation (self-applied) of the Chinese. It shows the enormous impression made upon the Chinese mind by the great dynasty of Han which ruled the Chinese empire from 202 BC to AD 221. Han is a territory in western Shansi. The first Han Emperor was Liu Pang, known after his death as Kao-tsu. See Shih Huang Ti.
MENNONITES	derive their name from their founder, originally a Catholic priest, Menno Simons (1496–1561), in Holland. They were similar to the Anabaptists (q.v.). With very wide diversity of faith and practice, they exist in several countries, including the USA.
MENSHEVIKS	the members of the Russian revolutionary party from which the Bolsheviks split after the failure of the 1905

Revolution in Russia. For full analysis, see C. Hill, *Lenin and the Russian Revolution*, English University Press, 1947 and Marcel Liebman, *The Russian Revolution*, London, History Book Club, 1970.

MERCATOR, Isadore name taken by the author of the Forged Decretals, purporting to be letters from Popes to various churches setting out papal authority; they appeared in the 9th century in France. Their invalidity was established by Lorenzo Valla (c. 1406–57).

MERCEDARIANS a religious order taking its name from *Orden de Nuestra Señora de la Merced*, Our Lady of Mercy. Founded c. 1220 by St Peter Nolasco, the members, in addition to the threefold vows of chastity, poverty and obedience, took a fourth vow, to offer themselves as hostages for the redemption of Christians captured by the Moors.

MEROVINGIANS see Rois Fainéants.

MERRIMAN literally, the merry man. Cf. merry, M.E. *merrie*.

MERRY MONARCH Charles II. Described in an epitaph (in his lifetime):
Here lies our sovereign lord the king.
Whose word no man relies on,
Who never said a foolish thing
Nor ever did a wise one.

MERRYWEATHER from O.E. *myrige* = merry, and *weder* = weather; a nickname for a gay fellow.

METAPHRASTES, St Simeon (lived c. 960), also known as Logothetes, a Byzantine who wrote saints' lives; he had worked over, or metaphrased, older accounts.

METAPHYSICAL POETS a term first used by Dr Samuel Johnson in a derogatory sense, of some seventeenth-century poets, Crashaw, Donne, Herbert, Traherne and Vaughan. Since then the term is used appreciatively.

METCALF possibly from O.E. *mete-cealf* = a calf to be fattened for eating, hence 'fat as a prize-calf'.

METHODISTS a term now used officially to denote the many Methodist churches throughout the world, but originally bestowed in derision on the religious habits of the members of the 'Holy Club'. These were John and Charles Wesley, and George Whitefield, who sought to live the Christian life through methodical study and devotion. The origin of the movement may be dated from 24 May 1738 when John Wesley's 'heart was strangely warmed' as Luther's preface to the Epistle to the Romans was being read.

METHUSELAH a term often applied to very elderly people. The original was a patriarch in Genesis v. 27 who is recorded as dying aged 969, the greatest age found in records.

MIDDLE in some cases a nickname for someone neither big nor small.

MIDDLETON, Richard of (born c. 1249), a Franciscan philosopher and theologian.

MIDNIGHT	from birth at that time. Cf. also Midwinter, i.e. born at Christmas.
MIGNOT, MINETT, MYNOTT	O.Fr. *mignot* = dainty.
MILD The	Frederick II (1411–64) Elector of Saxony. John Count of Holstein, who helped to dominate Denmark during the period 1332–40.
MILDMAY	gentle maiden; or, by contrast, wild lad.
MILK	O.E. *meole* = milk, used pejoratively for one who was without much spirit, a milk-drinker. Cf. milksop, also Milsopp, Melsopp.
MILLENARIANS	those Christians who believe in a reign of 1000 years by Christ, the belief being based on a passage in Revelation, xx, 4–7. Millenarianism is also called Chiliasm, (q.v.).
MILLICAN, MILLIGAN, MULLIGAN	O. Ir. Maelican, double diminutive, meaning the little bold one.
MINCHIN	O.E. *mynecen* = nun.
MING	meant 'bright' and was the name taken by the founder of the Chinese dynasty, Chu Yuan-chang, known as Emperor Hung Wu. This dynasty lasted from 1368 to 1644.
MINGAY, MINGEY	a Breton name meaning stone dog.
MINIMS	from *minimi*, the least; applied to an order of friars founded in 1435 by St Francis of Paolo in Italy, their chief object being the practice of humility, regarding themselves as the least of all monks.
MINORITES	the Franciscan Friars Minor.
MNEMON	'the mindful'. Artaxerxes II, Persian emperor, reigned 404–359(358) BC. It was against him that his brother, Cyrus the Younger, rebelled (*Xenophon, Anabasis*).
MODERN BABYLON	London.
MODERN MESSALINA	Catherine II of Russia (1729–96), called after the first wife of the Emperor Claudius who was renowned for her licentious behaviour and was executed in 48.
MODERNISTS	those who wished to bring the Christian Faith completely into line with modern science and scholarship, mainly by altering the doctrines of the faith. While the phenomenon of Modernism has appeared among the clerics of all the main Christian denominations, it was in the Roman Church that the theory and practice of Modernism appeared in the present century. Modernism was condemned by Pope Pius X in 1907 in the decree *Lamentabili* and the Encyclical *Pascendi Gregis*. Modernism is no longer mentioned in theological circles but the methods and attitudes of the modernists have, since the Second Vatican Council (1962–5), gained control in the Church of Rome; also in the C. of E.
MOERBEKE, William of	(c. 1215–86), a Dominican who translated many Greek

works into Latin.

MOHAMMEDAN the name given by very many persons to the followers and the religion of Mohammed (c. 570–629), but often resented by adherents of Islam. They prefer the name of Moslem, because to them, Mohammedan implies that they worship Mohammed, as Christians worship Christ, whereas to the Moslems, Mohammed, however great, is still only a prophet and a man.

MOIR Gaelic *mor* = big.

MOLLY MAGUIRES a secret society in Ireland which began in 1843, consisted of young men who dressed as women and who gave a rough handling to those who sought to enforce the payment of rent.

MONDAY O.E. *mondanaeg* = monday, given perhaps to a person born on that day.

MONEYPENNY many pennies; a rich man but ironically for a poor man.

MONGO from Greek μογγός, hoarse, the name of Peter, Monophysite Patriarch of Alexandria (died 490).

MONK, MONCK O.E. *Munuc* = monk.

MONK LEWIS the name given to Matthew Gregory Lewis (1775–1818), a writer of somewhat gruesome stories including one called *The Monk* (1795).

MONKEY MEN name used by the Chinese to describe the Japanese.

MONOPHTHALMUS one-eyed, Antigonus I (382–301 BC), Macedonian general and after the death of Alexander the Great the ruler of a good part of his empire. Eventually Antigonus was restricted to Europe and made himself King of Macedonia. Also called Cyclops after the one-eyed tyrannical giant blinded by Odysseus in the *Odyssey*.

MONOPHYSITES followers of Eutyches (q.v.). Some African and Asiatic churches still adhere to Monophysitism, though probably in a nominal sense only. (Greek μόνος one and φίοίς nature.)

MONOTHELITES from Greek μόνος, one, and θέλειν, to will; Monothelitism (more correctly Monotheletism) teaches that in the Person of Christ there is but one Will. The Council of Constantinople in 680 proclaimed the existence of two wills in Christ, Divine and Human, as the Orthodox Faith.

MONTANISTS a sect of Christians in the 2nd century in Phrygia, derived from a man called Montanus. He believed that the Holy Spirit was not yet given, but was about to come, also that the New Jerusalem was about to descend from heaven. Montanism was thus an apocalyptic sect. The great African theologian Tertullian embraced these views towards the end of his life.

MOON A. Fr. *moun mun* = monk. Cf. modern, moine.

MOOR — from swarthy appearance, as a Moor. Cf. Morel, O.Fr. *more* = brown.

MOORCOCK — a nickname from the bird.

MOORSLAYER — i.e. Mata Moros, the name given to St James the Great, brother of St John and an apostle. His martyrdom is recorded in Acts xii.21. His name was used in Spain because of the belief that he appeared as a mounted cavalier in battles against the Moslems. He is St Iago de Compostella, which was long regarded as his place of burial. 'St James and forward Spain' was a popular Spanish battle cry, e.g. given by Pizarro as signal to his men when attacking the Inca of Peru.

MOPSUESTIA, Theodore of — (c. 350–428), Bishop of Mopsuestia, a learned theologian and biblical interpreter.

MORAL GOWER, The — John Gower (died 1408), whose tomb is in Southwark Cathedral, a poet thus named by Chaucer in his *Troilus and Cressyde* (v.1856).

MORAVIAN BRETHREN — successors to the Bohemian Brethren who arose in the 15th century. The Moravians date from 1722, having adopted a simple and unworldly form of Christianity.

MORFEY, MORPHY, MAFFEY — O.Fr. *malfe, malfeu* (Latin *malefactus*), evil omened; a term of abuse applied to Saracens and the devil; a demon or devil.

MORLEY, Mrs — the name used by Queen Anne in her correspondence with Mrs Freeman (q.v.).

MORMONS — the name popularly given to the Church of Jesus Christ of the Latter Day Saints. The word Mormon comes from the Book of Mormon, a revelation given to Joseph Smith, the founder of the sect. According to its doctrines, Mormon was one of the later prophets of the period 600 BC to about AD 420 when a colony of Israelitish origin was thought to have settled in North America. The Mormons settled in Salt Lake City, Utah in 1848 and after.

MORNING STAR OF THE REFORMATION — John Wycliffe (c. 1330–84), a popular usage in the 19th century to describe the powerful personality and teachings of the 14th century priest. For views equally prejudiced on Wycliffe's career, see Hilaire Belloc, *History of England Vol III*, and G. M. Trevelyan's. *England in the Age of Wycliffe*. For sound appreciation, *English Historical Documents*, vol. IV.

MORO, IL — The Moor, Ludovico Sforza, Duke of Milan (1451–1508), but died in the castle of Lochges as a prisoner of the French.

MOSES OF MESOPOTAMIA — St Jacob of Nisibis, early 4th century; very little is known of him for certain.

MOST CHRISTIAN DOCTOR — John Charlier de Gerson (1363–1429).

MOST CHRISTIAN KING	style borne by King of France from 1469 when conferred by Pope Paul II on Louis XI.
MOST FAITHFUL KING	title given to the Kings of Portugal by the Pope.
MOST PROFOUND DOCTOR	Aegidius de Columna (died 1316), a Sicilian schoolman.
MOST SERENE	the Doge of Venice. The term 'Serene Highness' was used after the Council of Constance (1417) to denote respect for a prince who was not in the same class as monarchs of France, Germany, etc.
MOTHER OF BELIEVERS	Ayesha, the youngest wife of Mohammed.
MOTHERS	O.N. *mothur*.
MOTHERSOLE	O.E. *modig* and *sawol* = brave or proud soul.
MOWSE	O.E. *mus* = mouse.
MOYLE	Gaelic *maol* = bald.
MUCKLE, MUTCHELL	O.E. *mycel* = big.
MUDDIMAN	O.E. brave man.
MUGGLETONIANS	a very small sect founded in 1651 which existed until 1868. The founders, Ludowiche Muggleton (1609–98) and his cousin John Reeve (1608–58) believed themselves to be the two heavenly witnesses of Revelation xi. 3–6. Muggleton, who was a tailor, was sentenced to stand in the pillory and to pay a fine of £500.
MULE, MOULE(S)	O.E. *mul*, M.E. *moul*, O.Fr. *mule* = mule.
MULLINGS, MOWLING	O.E. *mulling* = darling.
MURCH	dwarf.
MURCHIE, MURCHISON	son of sea-warrior.
MURPHY	Ir. meaning sea-warrior.
MURVABHIDUN	the Moslem name for the Wahhabis (q.v.).
MUSCULAR CHRISTIAN (ITY)	a term applied to Charles Kingsley and his teachings.
MUSSARD	O.Fr. *musard* = absent-minded or stupid.
MUSTARD	O.Fr. *mustarde* = mustard in some cases of someone with a sharp tongue.
MUSTELL, MUZZEL	O.Fr. *mustelle* = weasel.
MUTCH, MUCH	M.E. *moche*, *muche* = big.
MY ANGEL	Queen Victoria's description of her late husband, Prince Albert the Good (q.v.).

N

NAMBY PAMBY

anything insipid or weakly sentimental; the nickname of Ambrose Philips (1671–1749).

NAPOLEON II

not a nickname, but a title never granted or recognized; used by the Bonapartists after the death of Napoleon I to denote his son, Napoleon François Joseph Charles (1811–32) created Duke of Reichstadt by the Emperor of Austria in 1818. The myth of his title as Napoleon II was perpetuated by his cousin when in 1852 he made himself emperor of the French as Napoleon III. Reichstadt was also styled by his father King of Rome, reminiscent of the Holy Roman Emperors' usage as King of the Romans. When Napoleon I abdicated at his earlier exile in 1814 he did so for himself and his son.

NARES

A. Fr. *neir* = black.

NAVIGATOR, The

Henry (1394–1460), 3rd son of King John I of Portugal by Philippa, daughter of John of Gaunt (son of Edward III of England). He had a very great interest in voyages of discovery. He established himself in a castle near Cape St Vincent, with the port of Sagres close by, whence the Prince organized the Portuguese voyages of discovery (Winwood Reade, *The Martyrdom of Man*, London, Trübner, 1872, 26 edn, pp.325 *et seq.*).

NAZARENE

a term applied to Jesus Christ by unbelieving Jews, possibly from His residence at Nazareth, also applied to the earliest Christians and to a 4th century group of Jewish Christians who observed part of the Jewish law. The saying in St Matthew ii. 23: 'He shall be called a Nazarene', which is ascribed to the prophets, is of unknown origin. It is not in the Old Testament.

NAZARITES

Jews who undertook certain vows, for example, to abstain from wine and not to cut their hair. Reference is made to Numbers vi.

NAZISM

the practical creed of the Nationalsozialistische Deutsche Arbeiters Partei (National Socialist German Workers' Party), existed 1920–45. The terms Nazism and Nazis have become synonyms for downright evil.

NEANDER

was the name taken by David Mendel, a Jew who became a Christian. His full name was Johann August Wilhelm Neander (= new man). He became a distinguished church historian, lived 1789–1850.

NEAP, NEEP

O.E. *naep* = turnip.

NEAT(E)

O.E. *neat* = ox, cow; in some cases applied to personal characteristic.

NEAVE(S)

O.E. *nefa*, M.E. *neve* = nephew, 'also a nickname for a prodigal or parasite' (Reaney, *Dict. of British Surnames*).

NECK

a nickname for one with some peculiarity of the neck.

NECK-ENTHRONED

Ruler; the meaning of the name of the Tibetan King Gnya-khri-Btsan-po, said to be the first monarch of the country. The name alludes to the belief that his followers carried him on the napes of their necks.

NEOPLATONISTS

i.e. the new Platonists, a group of philosophers, started by Proclus (c. 205–70) who had a religious aim. They were very much opposed to Christianity.

NERO OF THE NORTH

Christian II of Denmark (1480, reigned 1534–50) massacred the Swedish nobility at Stockholm in 1520. Also called the Cruel. Nero was the tyrannical emperor of Rome who reigned AD 54–68 and was the first to persecute the Christians.

NESTORIANS, NESTORIANISM

the followers and teaching of Nestorius, who in 428 became Patriarch of Constantinople. He taught that in Jesus Christ there were two persons – the Son of God and a man. This was contrary to the Orthodox teaching of One Person, at once God and Man. One of Nestorius' greatest objections was to the term Theotokos, Mother of God. He said that he could not call a child, three days old, God. He was condemned by the General Council of Ephesus, deposed and died in exile.

NEW

O.E. *nirve*, M.E. *nerve* = new, newcomer. Cf. Newcombe.

NEW CYRUS, The

Charles VIII, King of France (1470–98), so styled by the great Dominican preacher, Fra Giralamo Savonarola who prophesied that, like Cyrus, the French King would accomplish great things. Charles did indeed penetrate as far as Naples, but was forced to retreat to France having accomplished nothing.

NEW THEOLOGIAN, The

St Simeon (949–1022) a Byzantine spiritual writer. His appellation implies a comparison with St Gregory the Theologian (q.v.).

NEWMAN, NIMAN, NYMAN

the new man or newcomer.

NICATOR

Seleucus I, King of Syria (c. 358–280 BC) one of the generals of Alexander the Great, though not one of the most important. In the turmoil following Alexander's death Seleucus gained control of the eastern portion of the empire and founded the Seleucid dynasty. The name Nicator, or conqueror, was given by later generations.

NICOLAITANS

a sect mentioned twice in the Book of Revelations ii.6 and ii.14 with a suggestion of a return to pagan worship.

NIGHTINGALE

O.E. *nihtegale* = night singer, a nightingale = sweet singer.

NIGHTMARE OF EUROPE

Napoleon I.

NIHILISM

a Russian movement in the middle of the 19th century, aiming at the overthrow of all law and order to produce anarchy, Latin *nihil*, nothing.

NIKATORES

name of the soldiers of the royal Macedonian bodyguard. Livy xliii.19 *cohors regia quos Nicatores appellant*.

NIKER

O.E. *nicor* = water monster.

NINE DAYS QUEEN

Lady Jane Grey, 1553. An interesting story giving most of the necessary details is W. H. Ainsworth's *Tower of London*.

NINEVEH, Isaac of

(died c. 700) inclined to Nestorianism (q.v.) and wrote extensively on ascetic subjects all in Syriac. Also known as Isaac Syrus.

NIVEN, NEVEN

Ir. Gaelic, *naomkin* = little saint.

NOBLE

Fr. *noble* = well known, noble.

NOBLE, The

Charles III (1361–1425), King of Navarre, son and successor of Charles II, the Bad.
    Soliman Tchelibi, a Turkish prince at Adrianople who died 1410.

NODDER

explained by Bardsley (*English Surnames*) as denoting someone of sleepy or nodding habits, but considered by Reaney (*Dict. of British Surnames*) as coming from O.E. *naedre* = an adder; in either case a nickname.

NOETICS

from Greek νοητικός pertaining to the mind; term applied to some early 19th century thinkers in Oxford who were critics of orthodoxy.

NONCONFORMERS

see Dissenters.

NON-JURORS

were nine bishops (including Archbishop Sancroft of Canterbury) some 400 clergy and some lay people who left the C. of E. in 1689 after the accession of William III. The non-jurors did not feel that they could take the oath to William as they were already bound by oath to James II. The schism did not end until 1805 and did much to weaken the C. of E. in the 18th century.

NORRISON

O.Fr. *norriscun* = nursling.

NORWICH, St William of

(1132–44), supposed to have been murdered by the Jews; his body, with marks of violence, was found in a wood.

NOSEY or NOSEY PARKER

very inquisitive. There is no apparent connection with Matthew Parker, chosen by Queen Elizabeth I as her first Archbishop of Canterbury. The character of the man was retiring and gave no impression of desire to pry into other people's affairs, nor is there reference to it in John Strype's extensive *Life of Matthew Parker*.

NOTHOS

the bastard, Darius II Ochus, Persian Emperor from 423–404 BC. He was the son of Artaxexes I by a Babylonian concubine. His younger son was Cyrus the Younger (q.v.).

NOTT	O.E. *knott* = bald-headed. Cf. Notting, bald-headed one.
NOTTAGE, NOTTIDGE	from the name of the bird, the nuthatch.
NOURMAHAL	the light of the harem, one of the members of the harem of the Caliph Haroun-al-Raschid.
NOVELIST OF WESSEX, The	Thomas Hardy (1840–1928).
NOY, NOYCE, NOISE	from Hebrew proper name, Noah, from part in the mystery plays.
NUNN(S)	applied to a man as meek and demure as a nun.
NURISTAN	see Kafiristan.
NURSE, NURRISH	O.Fr. *nurice* = nurse.
NUTBROWN	nickname from the complexion.

OAKMAN — O.E. Acmann = oakman.

OBADIAH — occasional rude term for a Quaker.

OBSERVANTINES — the strict observers of the rule of St Francis of Assisi in the Franciscan Order. Separated from the Conventuals (q.v.) in 1517 and all incorporated into the single Order of Friars Minor by Leo XIII in 1897.

OCCAM or OCKHAM, William of — (c. 1285–1349), a celebrated English medieval philosopher. Famous for Occam's razor: *entia non sunt multiplicanda*.

ODAM, ODHAMS — O.E. *athus*, M.E. *odam* = son-in-law.

ODART — O.G. *authard, othard* = riches-hard.

ODGEAR, ODGERS — O.G. *odger* = wealth-spear.

OECOLAMPADIUS, John — (1482–1531), a German humanistic scholar and reformer whose real name was Huszgen.

OLD, The — Mircea, a kinsman of Petri Nuset, Prince of Moldavia (1374–92).

OLD ACE OF SPADES — General Robert Edward Lee, who commanded Southern armies in Civil War, so called because of trenches which he had dug.

OLD BAGS — John Scott, Lord Chancellor Eldon (1751–1838); name derived from the bags in which he carried home with him the cases which still required his judgments. He was extremely slow in settling cases and is satirized in Dickens's *Bleak House* where the case of Jarndyce against Jarndyce drags on for years.

OLD BELIEVERS — a body of people who left the Russian Orthodox Church because they did not agree with the reforms of the Patriarch Nikon (died 1681). Their separate existence was recognized by the State in 1881. Also called Raskolniki (schismatics) and Popovtsy.

OLD BLUE EYES — Frank Sinatra, American singer.

OLD BRUIN — Commodore Matthew Perry, the commander of the American naval squadron which in July 1853 entered Japanese waters at Uraga near Yeddo, thus making the first breach in the two-centuries-old seclusion of Japan.

OLD CATHOLICS — the term generally applied to those Catholics who refused to accept the dogma of the infallibility of the Pope as promulgated by the first Vatican Council of 1870. Dr Dollinger, the celebrated historian, was one of the principal leaders. But the name of Old Catholics is also used by the Church of Utrecht which seceded from Rome in 1724 (and from which the Old Catholics of 1870 received their episcopate), and also some small bodies in the Slav nations in Poland and Yugoslavia. The Dutch Old Catholic Church originated in the Jansenist controversy. All the Old Catholic Churches recognize the validity of Anglican orders and are in communion with the C. of E.

OLD CONTEMPTIBLES, The — the name given by themselves to themselves by members of the British Expeditionary Force of 160,000 men, being the bulk of the British Army which went to France in 1914. The term contemptible is supposed to have been used in an order issued by Kaiser Wilhelm II.

OLD COPPER NOSE — Henry VIII, for using copper in alloy with silver in coins and in which the king's nose in particular showed the colour of copper.

OLD DOMINION — Virginia; being called a dominion in Acts of the British Parliament.

OLD FELLOW, The — the nickname of the Emperor Tiberius, the successor of Augustus, ὁ πρεσβύτης: S. Baring Gould (*The Tragedy of the Caesars*, (1923, p. 233) states that the name was bestowed because of the future ruler's precocious gravity from his boyhood.

OLD FRITZ — Frederick the Great of Prussia (q.v.).

OLD GLORY — the flag of the USA, the stars and stripes, often called the Star Spangled Banner.

OLD GROANER — Bing Crosby (Harry Lillis Crosby) (1904–77), American singer and film star.

OLD GROVER — US President Grover Cleveland (1837–1908), also called the People's President and Sage of Princeton.

OLD HICKORY — General Jackson, President of the USA (1820–37), supposed to have been originator of OK which he wrote as 'ol krett' Also called Hero of New Orleans because of his defeat of British in 1812.

OLD HOOKEY — applied to Arthur Wellesley, 1st Duke of Wellington (1769–1852), because of his pronounced Roman nose. Napoleon once said that in choosing between two men for important work, he would, other things being equal, select the one with the big nose. Napoleon was right, though he did not, of course, select Wellington for his *coup de grâce*. This selection was made by Providence.

OLD JEW, The — Bismarck's term for the British Prime Minister, Benjamin Disraeli, at the Congress of Berlin in 1878. 'The old Jew, he is the man', was Bismarck's tribute to Disraeli's diplomatic skill.

OLDKNOW — O.E. *eald*, *genoh* = old enough.

OLD LADY OF THREADNEEDLE STREET — the Bank of England.

OLDMAN — O.E. *eald* = old and man.

OLD MAN ELOQUENT, The	Isocrates (436–338 BC), Greek orator, so named by John Milton in his sonnet to Lady Margaret Ley.
OLD MAN OF THE MOUNTAINS	see Hassan-Ben-Sabah.
OLD NOLL	Oliver Cromwell (1599–1658), Lord Protector of England, around whose character and conduct controversy is still active, the nickname being pejorative.
OLD PRETENDER, The	James, only legitimate son of James II of England. Styled by his Jacobite (q.v.) followers, James VIII of Scotland and III of England. James was born in 1688 and died in 1766. He had two sons, Charles Edward, the Young Pretender, (q.v.) and Henry, Cardinal of York, the last male of the House of Stuart. On the death of Charles Edward, the Cardinal had a medal struck with the inscription *Henricus nonus, Dei voluntate, non hominum.*
OLD Q	William Douglas, 4th Duke of Queensberry (1724–1810), notorious for his dissolute ways. The present Marquess of Queensberry is his collateral descendant, the Dukedom having devolved upon the Duke of Buccleuch.
OLD QUEEN, The	Queen Victoria, known also as the Grandmother of Europe as most of the crowned heads of Europe were related to her.
OLD ROWLEY	euphemism for Satan, often applied to Charles II (1660–85) of England.
OLD TROUPER	Marie Dressler, American film star, also called Queen Marie of Hollywood.
OLIVETAN, OLIVETANUS	from burning the midnight oil, nickname of French Protestant reformer named Pierre Robert (c. 1506–38).
OLIVETANS	the Order of Our Lady of Mount Olivet, a branch of the Benedictines founded in 1319 at Monte Oliveto near Siena by St Bernard Ptolomei.
OLYMPIAN, The	the name given by the comic poets to Pericles (c. 490–429 BC), the great Athenian democratic statesman who was leader of Athens for 30 years. He was of great intellectual ability and during his tenure of power Athens became the most beautiful city in the world.
ONE EYED, The	Bogdan III, Prince of Moldavia (1504–17).
ONRAET	O.E. *unraed* = evil counsel.
OPIUM-EATER, The	Thomas de Quincey (1783–1859), celebrated English prose writer, whose works include *The Confessions of an English Opium Eater* (1821). He had a long struggle against the taking of opium but eventually emerged into serene old age.
ORACLE OF THE CHURCH, The	St Bernard of Clairvaux (1091–1153).
ORANGE PEEL	nickname of Sir Robert Peel, who was Chief Secretary for Ireland (1812–18) because he was strongly anti-Catholic.

ORANGEMEN
members of the movement who uphold the cause of Protestantism in Northern Ireland. Hence Orange Order. Name is derived from William of Orange, King William III of England who established Protestant supremacy in Ireland at the battle of the Boyne, 1689. Orange is in the south of France and was the scene of many important events in ancient times (See *The House of Orange*, Marion E. Grew, London, Methuen, 1947).

ORATORIANS
members of the Oratory of St Philip Neri which was derived from the latter c. 1564, and took its name from the oratory of St Girolamo at Rome where the members gathered. The Order spread into various countries and by the work of Cardinal Newman the Brompton Oratory was established in 1854 at Kensington, London.

ORDER OF PREACHERS
the Dominicans.

ORGEL, ORGILL
O.Fr. *orgueil* = pride.

ORIGENISTS, ORIGENISM
supposed to be the followers and the teaching of the very great Alexandrian scholar, Origen (c. 185–254). He was a profound scholar, knowing Hebrew as well as Greek, and inspired many outstanding Christians. Origen's teachings were condemned by the Second Council of Constantinople, but as many of his works have perished and the surviving volumes are mostly in translations, we do not know how many of the charges of heresy against him could be substantiated. That he remains an inspiration to Christian thinkers is a fact, particularly to the great bishop B. F. Westcott and his not undistinguished disciple T. H. Passmore. Some of Origen's views were unorthodox – e.g. universal salvation (even for the devil) and pre-existence of the human soul. But had his methods of Scriptural interpretation been more generally adopted, the Church would not have experienced the immense difficulties of Darwinism versus literal Biblical inspiration in the 19th century.

ORNAMENT OF THE PALACE
Mumtaz Mahal, the wife of the Mogul Emperor Shah Jahan (1592–1666), for whom he built the Taj Mahal at Agra.

ORPET(T)
O.E. *orped* = stout, bold.

OTTOMAN
a term with a curious history. It has no ethnic significance but is a dynastic term derived from the name of Osman I (died 1326) who is regarded as the founder of the Turkish Ottoman state. The use of the word to describe furniture came much later from the dais-type seat of the Turkish magnates.

OUGHTRED, UGHTRED
O.E. *uhtraed*, from *uhte* = twilight dusk, and *raed* = advice.

OUR LADY OF THE SNOWS
Canada, in Kipling's poem, *The Five Nations* (1903).

OUTLAW
M.E. *outlawe*, from O.N. *utlagi* = outlaw.

OWLES
O.E. *ule* = owl. Cf. Owlett = little owl.

OXFORD GROUP
a term given in South Africa to the followers of F. N. D. Buchman, an American evangelist (1878–1961). The form which the movement assumed was given the name of Moral Rearmament. The 'Oxford' of the nickname came from Buchman's success after 1926 in attracting undergraduates at Oxford.

OXFORD MOVEMENT
see High Church, Puseyites and Tractarianism.

P

PACIFIC, The

Amadeus VIII, Duke of Savoy 1391–1439, became an anti-Pope in 1440 until 1449 when he gave up and was given a place in the College of Cardinals. He died in 1451, 'undisputably an earnest minded and pious nobleman, specially ordained and consecrated for his dubious honour' (John Farrow, *Pageant of the Popes*, New York, Sheed & Ward, 1950, p.182).

Frederick III, Holy Roman Emperor (reigned 1440–93).

Olaf III of Norway (1030–93).

PADDOCK

O.E. *padduc* = frog.

PAGAN

literally a country person. Its use for heathens thus arose: 'Whereas therefore religion did first take place in cities, and in that respect was a cause why the name of Pagans which properly signifieth country people came to be used in common speech for the same that infidels and unbelievers were' (Hooker, *Ecclesiastical Polity*, Oxford, Clarendon Press, 1874, V, ch. LXXX).

PAGE

O.Fr. *page*. Cf. Paget, Padgett.

PALLOTTINE FATHERS

founded in 1835 by Blessed Vincent Pallotti (1795–1850) in Italy, a society of Catholic priests, lay brothers, sisters and associates to carry on social work.

PAM

Lord Palmerston (1784–1865). Henry John Temple, 3rd Viscount in the peerage of Ireland, British statesman, twice Prime Minister, a great patriot and upholder of the rights of Britons in foreign countries. He had no legitimate issue and the title became extinct.

PANORMITANUS

name given to a Sicilian monk Niccolo de Tudeschi (1386–1445) from his being Archbishop of Palermo (i.e. Panormitan). Also known as Abbas Modernus. A notable canonist.

PAPE

O.E. *papa* = pope, whence M.E. *pope*. 'A nickname for one of an austere, ascetic appearance, or a pageant name' (Reaney, *Dict. of British Surnames*).

PAPIGAY, POBJOY, POPEJOY,

M.E. *papejai, popingay*, O.Fr. *papegai* = parrot.

PAPILLON

O.Fr. *papillon* = butterfly, used of inconstant person.

PAPIST

an adherent of the Pope, the Bishop of Rome. Used in previous centuries as a term of contempt, it is now sometimes used by Roman Catholics themselves.

PARABOLANI

from Greek παραβολανοι, those who disregard; men who were devoted to looking after the sick. Found in Alexandria and later Constantinople in 4th and 5th centuries; operative passage is in Philippians ii.30. Some account of them is given in C. Kingsley's *Hypatia*.

PARAMOR, PARRAMORE
M.E. O.Fr. *paramour* = lover.

PARDEW, PARDY, PARDOE
from the oath *'Par Dieu'*.

PARFAIT, PARFITT, PARFECT
O.Fr. *parfeit*, Latin *perfectus* = perfect.

PARLABEAN, PARLBY
Fr. *parle bien* = speak well.

PARODY, FATHER OF
Hipponox of Ephesus (6th century BC); supposed to have been the first to produce parodies of epic poetry, but principally noted for his bitter iambic verses. Only a few fragments of his work remain.

PARROT, PERROTT
in some cases used as a nickname from the bird.

PARTHENIAS
Greek παρθένος virgin, was a name applied to Publius Vergilius Maro (70–19 BC). This led to the spelling of his name being altered to Virgil. He lived at Parthenope near Naples and wrote the Fourth or Messianic Eclogue, hence the change of spelling from e to i. The 4th Eclogue is thought to be prophetic of the birth of Christ.

PARTICULAR BAPTISTS
founded in 1633 in England, extremely strict Calvinistic sect, possibly the same as the Ebenezer Baptists.

PARTRICK, PARTRIDGE
M.E. *pertriche*, O.Fr. *perdrin* = partridge, often but not always a nickname.

PASSENGER
O.Fr. *passager* = wayfarer.

PASSIONISTS
founded in Italy in 1720 by St Paul of the Cross (q.v.); full title Congregation of Discalced Clerks of the Most Holy Cross and Passion of our Lord Jesus Christ.

PASTOR RUSSELL
Charles Taze Russell (1852–1916), founder of International Bible Students Association, known as Jehovah's Witnesses and *Watch Tower*. He assumed the title of Pastor.

PATARINI or PATARENES
a term of uncertain derivation but supposed to be from the name of the rag-pickers' quarter in Milan. It was used for a sect which originated in Milan in the 1050s. The first objects of the sect were clerical celibacy and the extirpation of simony but the sect was soon numbered with the Cathari and the Bogomils (q.v.).

PATE(S)
M.E. *pate* = head.

PATHFINDER
another name for Leatherstocking (q.v.). Also name given to the American Major General John Charles Fremont (1813–90), for his work in surveying and mapping the west of the USA.

PATRIPASSIANS
people in the 3rd century who believed that God the Father suffered on the Cross. Also called Monarchianism and Sabellianism.

PAUL OF THE CROSS, St
(1694–1775), founder of the Passionists (q.v.).

PAULICIANS
a sect of the Byzantine empire. They were called either after St Paul whom they particularly venerated, or

after an entirely different character, Paul of Samosata, a bishop who held heretical opinions and with whom the Paulicians had affinities. They were persecuted from the 7th century and later amalgamated with the Bogomils (q.v.).

PAULISTS

popular name of The Missionary Society of St Paul the Apostle in the State of New York, founded in 1858 by J. T. Hecker.

PAUNCEFOOT, PONSFORD

O.Fr. *pance* + *volt* = face, i.e. paunch-face; M.E. *pauche* = stomach, referring to a corpulent person.

PAW, PEA, POE, POWE

O.E. *pawa* = pea, M.E. *po* = peacock.

PEACEFUL, The

Edgar, King of England (959–75). During his reign England was at peace as Edgar was acknowledged as overlord by all other rulers in Britain, hence the famous account of his being rowed on the Dee at Chester by eight regal vassals.

PEACEMAKER, The

Edward VII (1901–10) of Great Britain, so called because of his influence in helping to bring about the Entente Cordiale in 1904 between Britain and France, which secured the disastrous bloodbath of British troops in France 1914–18. King Edward's sarcastic treatment of his nephew, Kaiser William II did much to aggravate the latter's essential weakness of character and propel him towards war.

PEACOCK

O.E. *peacocc*, M.E. *pecok* = peacock.

PEAR

O.Fr. *peer* = peer or paragon.

PECULIAR PEOPLE

small sect of people founded in London in 1838, who avoid medical treatment and rely on faith healing. The name comes from St Peter's First Epistle, ii.9 which uses the expression, a peculiar people, of the early Christians. By transference, Cromwell applied it to the Puritans.

PEELER

a policeman; used first of the Irish Constabulary instituted by Sir Robert Peel, Chief Secretary for Ireland (1812–18) and then for the Metropolitan Police also begun by Peel in 1829.

PEEPO'DAY BOYS

a secret society composed of Protestants in 18th century northern Ireland engaged in acts of hostility against Catholics. Also known as Protestant boys and Wreckers.

PELAGIANISM

the teaching ascribed to the British monk Pelagius (late 4th and early 5th centuries), which held that man can advance to salvation by his own efforts without the aid of divine grace.

PELLEAN CONQUEROR

Alexander the Great because born at Pella in Macedonia; also called the great Emathian conqueror by Milton.

PELLEW, PELLOW

O.Fr. *pel de lo* = wolf skin.

PELLY

Fr. *pele* = bald.

PELVIS, The

Elvis Presley, American pop singer (1935–77).

PENDEREL PENDRELL — Fr. *pendre* = to hang and *oreille* = ear, thus 'hang-ear'.

PENNEY, PENNY, PENNINGS — a nickname from the coin, O.E. *pening, penig*.

PENNYFATHER, PENNEFATHER — O.E. *penig* and *faeder* = penny father, a term for a miser, a niggard.

PENTECOSTALS — name of a movement which began in America in the early years of the 20th century and experiencing phenomena such as speaking with tongues which occurred on the day of Pentecost (Acts ii).

PEPPERDAY — described as an oath name O.Fr. *Pape-Dieu*, the Pope God, a particularly unpleasant usage which marked a speaker.

PERDITA — a character in Shakespeare's *Winter's Tale*, and name given to an actress, Mrs Robinson, who took the part and was mistress of George IV.

PEREBOURNE — O.E. *pere* = pear and *brun* = brown, pear brown for a person of swarthy complexion.

PERFECT, The — King John II (reigned 1481–95) of Portugal, because of his skill in dealing with Castile and with his nobles.

PERFECTIBILISTS — see Illuminati.

PERFECTIONISTS — name of a communist sect founded in America in 1834 by J. H. Noyes (1811–86), dissolved in 1881.

PERIPATETICS — following of Aristotle, so called from his habit of walking while teaching in a covered walk (περίπατος) at Athens.

PETCH, PECHEY, PEACH, PEACHEY — from O.Fr. *peche*, Latin *peccatum* = sin; 'a curious name for Robert Peche, Bishop of Coventry'.

PETER MARTYR — (1500–62) named by his father after St Peter Martyr (q.v.). His name is the Anglicized form of Pietro Martire Vermigli. He was an Italian monk who became a Protestant reformer and had to leave Italy. He came to England and eventually settled in Zürich.

PETER MARTYR, St — (c. 1200–52), worked to convert the Cathari (q.v.) to Catholicism. He was murdered by an assassin while journeying from Como to Milan. Patron of Inquisitors.

PETERLOO — or the Manchester massacre on 16 August 1819. A large crowd estimated at 60,000 including many women and children gathered in St Peter's Fields, Manchester. They were demonstrating because of great economic discontent. There had been other gatherings and the magistrates were nervous and ordered the Manchester Yeomanry to arrest the speakers, but they charged the crowd and attacked with their swords. Thereupon the chairman of the magistrates ordered the 15th Hussars and the Cheshire Yeomanry to charge the crowds. In 10 minutes the ground was cleared with 11 dead and some 500 injured.

PETROBRUSIANS — a medieval sect getting its name from Peter Bruys in 1105, a Provençal priest who was opposed to most of the Church's practices.

PETTIFER, PUDDIFER — O.Fr. *pedifer*, *pied de fer*, iron foot, possible reference to an old soldier, even, in London, a centurion.

PETTIGREE, PETTIGREW — O.Fr. *cru* = growth + *petit*, little growth, reference to a man of stunted growth.

PETTIT, PITTET — O.Fr. *petit* = little. The name of an Essex family for many centuries.

PEVERALE, PEPPRELL — from O.Fr. roots meaning pepper. It has been suggested that 'the ref. may have been to one of small, rounded shape "peppercorn-sized" or a man with a darkish complexion or hair. But it may well have been applied to a small man with a fiery, peppery temper' (Reaney, *Dict. of British Surnames*).

PHARISEES — from Hebrew word meaning 'departed ones', recorded by Josephus as existing c. 145 BC. They disappeared after the fall of Jerusalem, AD 70.

PHEASANT — M.E. *fesaunt*, a nickname from the bird.

PHILADELPHIANS — a 17th century religious sect in England which reflected the views of J. Boehme.

PHILADELPHUS — brother-loving; title borne by Ptolemy II of the Macedonian dynasty of Egypt. Born in 308 BC, he reigned 285–246 BC, held a most brilliant court, and was a patron of the arts, sciences, and founded the great library at Alexandria. The Ptolemies soon adopted the Egyptian custom of brother and sister marriage. Ptolemy II married as his 2nd wife, his full sister Arsinoe. The name Philadelphus really belonged to her but the king used it of himself. He deified his parents as 'saviour gods' and he and Arsinoe were deified as 'brother gods'.

PHILHELLENE — Lover of Hellenes (Greeks). Alexander I (before 492–c. 450) King of Macedonia. His name shows his desire to win Greek sympathies, to the extent that he spread a legend of his descent from the Temenids of Argos. He entertained Pindar at his court.

PHILIPPISTS — followers of Philip Melancthon (q.v.).

PHILOMETOR — loving one's mother. Ptolemy VI, King of Egypt (181–145 BC) succeeded as an infant under the rule of his mother, Cleopatra, wife of Ptolemy V Epiphanes (q.v.).

PHILOPATOR — lover of one's father. Seleucus IV (c. 218–175 BC), King of the Seleucid dynasty of Syria.
    Ptolemy IV (born c. 238 BC, reigned 221–c. 205), King of Egypt.
    Ptolemy VII, styled Philopator Neos, the new. Several of the later Ptolemies bore the title of Philopator. See also Physon.

PHILOPATOR, PHILADELPHUS — loving one's father, loving one's brother. Mithridates IV, King of Pontus; he reigned conjointly for some while with his brother, and then acted as regent (c. 170–150 BC) for his nephew; singularly unusual in Oriental monarchies, when an Amurath an Amurath succeeds.

PHILOSOPHER, The

Aristotle (384–322 BC) known in medieval western Europe simply as the Philosopher. This is how he is referred to in St Thomas Aquinas's *Summa Theologia*. In Dante's *Inferno*, Aristotle is named only as 'the master of those who know' (Canto IV.131) and all the other thinkers, including Socrates and Plato do him reverence.

Leo VI (866–912) Byzantine Emperor and a considerable writer on religious themes, also called Leo Sapiens.

PHILOSOPHER OF FERNEY

Voltaire (1694–1778), from his living for the last 20 years of his life at Ferney, near Geneva.

PHILOSOPHER OF MALMESBURY

Thomas Hobbes (1588–1679), Malmesbury being his birthplace.

PHILOSOPHER OF SANS-SOUCIS

Frederick the Great (q.v.), King of Prussia, who built a palace so named ('without care') near Potsdam in 1747.

PHILOSOPHIC PARTY

see the Encyclopedists.

PHILOSOPHUS TEUTONICUS

Jakob Boehme (1575–1624), German Lutheran theosophical writer, whose mystical writings are obscure and often unorthodox but have had considerable influence.

PHOEBUS

Gaston III, Comte de Foix (1331–91) was so called after Phoebus Apollo because of his good looks. He was a great hunter, but also fond of art and literature. He wrote *Deduits de la chasse des bestes sauvages et des oiseaux deproye*, preserved in 40 mss with many beautiful illustrations. (For a full account see L. G. Pine, *The History of Hunting*, London, League Against Cruel Sports, 1973, p.110.)

PHYSCON

fat paunch, nickname of Ptolemy VII of Egypt because of his corpulence. See also Philopator.

PIARISTS

order of secular priests founded 1597 in Rome by St Joseph Calasanctius with the object of better education for the middle and upper classes. Their popular name comes from the last word of their title in Latin, *Regulares pauperes Matris Dei scholarum piarium*.

PICKERELL, PICKRILL

M.E. *pykerel* = a young pike.

PIDGEON, PIGEON

from Fr. *pigeon*, perhaps of a person easy to pluck.

PIE, PYE

a nickname from the magpie which in M.E. was *pie*.

PIETISM

name of a movement in the 17th century in the German Lutheran Church, begun by P. J. Spencer with the aim of putting life into the official Lutheranism of the age.

PIGACHE

O.Fr. *pic* = pick axe, applied to a workman.

PIGG

from the animal (O.E. *picga*).

PIKE, PYKE, PICK

sometimes nicknames from Norse *pik* = tall thin man, or from O.Fr. *pic* = woodpecker; or again M.E. *pike*, the fish.

PILCH

M.E. *pilche* = a fur garment.

PILGRIM FATHERS, The   a fairly modern title for a band of English Puritans who sailed from Holland and England in 1620 in the *Mayflower* to found the colony of Plymouth, Massachusetts.

PILL   O.Fr. *pile* = little ball.

PILLAR SAINTS   Stylites, see St Simeon Stylites.

PILTDOWN MAN   name given to some remains found in 1912 on Piltdown Common near Lewes, Sussex, England. These remains were doctored into a forgery which for 40 years deceived the entire scientific world. For example, Sir Arthur Keith, one of the great missionaries of Darwinism (q.v.), in his 2 volume work *The Antiquity of Man* gives up 80 pages (out of 800) to the Piltdown Man and even had an engraving of the Piltdown fragments on the cover of each volume. By 1959 the remains were shown up as an elaborate forgery. The village of Piltdown is attractive but its only claim to fame lies in this 'phoney' which did, however, provide an inn sign that is unique.

PINCHEN, PINSON   O.Fr. *pincon*, Norman-Picard *pinchon* = finch, used as a symbol of gaiety.

PINNELL   O.Fr. *pin* = pinetree, applied to a tall thin man.

PINNOCK   M.E. *pinnock* = hedge-sparrow.

PIO NONO   frequently used of Pope Pius IX, the Pope of Vatican Council I, and the only Pope to exceed the 25 years traditionally ascribed to St Peter. Pius IX reigned 1846–78; his firm policy held the Church together in a difficult age.

PIOUS, The   Ernest I of the House of Gotha (1601–74).
     Eric IX of Sweden (died 1161).
     Frederick III (1515–76), Elector Palatine of the Rhine, converted to Protestantism in 1546.
     Henry II, the Pious, of Silesia (1238–41).
     Louis I, King of France, only surviving son of Charlemagne, who succeeded his father in 814 and died in 840. He was, as his name implies, very deeply concerned with Christian and ecclesiastical ideas. Also styled Le Débonnaire.
     Robert II, King of France, 970–1031, called le Pieux, probably because of his support for the Cluniac monks and for the Truce of God movement.
     William, Duke of Aquitaine, founded Cluny in 909.

PIOUS SOCIETY OF MISSIONS   popular name of the Pallottine Fathers (q.v.).

PLANTAGENET   surname given in modern times to the English sovereigns from Henry II (1154–89) to Richard III (1483–5). The name is a later bestowal as the first official use of it was in 1460 when Richard, Duke of York claimed the throne and is entered in the Parliament Roll as Richard Plantagenet. The name originated with Geoffrey, Count of Anjou (died 1151) the father of Henry II, and may have come from

Geoffrey's use of a sprig of broom (*genista*) in his helmet, or perhaps from his habit of planting broom to improve his hunting covers.

PLATIFOT   O.Fr. *plat* = flat foot.

PLAYBOY OF NEW YORK   James J. Walker, New York Mayor in 1890s.

PLAYFAIR   probably 'play fairly'.

PLAYFOOT   thought to mean 'splay-foot'.

PLEIAD   a name given to seven French poets of the 16th century, Ronsard and DuBellay being the chief – the term comes from the name of the seven daughters of Atlas and Pleione, and was given to a group of stars in the constellation of Taurus.

PLON-PLON or PLOMB-PLOMB   sometimes Crait-plomb = fear-led, nickname given by soldiers in the Crimean War to Prince Napoleon, Joseph Charles Paul (1822–91) a son of Jerome Bonaparte who was brother of Napoleon I and King of Westphalia.

PLOUGHPENNY, PLOYPENNING   Eric IV, King of Denmark, 1241, murdered by order of his brother, 1250.

PLYMOUTH BRETHREN   a small sect set up at Plymouth in 1830 by J. N. Darby, a former Anglican priest. Extremely strict Puritanic Calvinism describes this outlook. Some parts call themselves Open Brethren; other Exclusive Brethren. They administer baptism in the sea.

POAD (PODD)   M.E. *pode* = toad.

POCKET   A.Fr. *pogue* = a small pouch.

POGONATUS   bearded; Constantine IV, Byzantine emperor, succeeded 668.

POINTEL   O.Fr. *pointel* = point, i.e. a sharp pointed instrument, applied to a tall thin man.

POINTS, POYNTZ   from M.E. *poynte*, a lace or cord of twisted material used to fasten hose and doublet; used sometimes as nickname for a fop. Cf. Shakespeare's *Henry VI*, Pt 1 'their points being pierced, down fell their hose'.

POLIORCETES   a taker of cities; Demetrius I (336–283 BC) King of Macedonia 294–88, but died in captivity in Syria.

POLISH BAYARD   Prince Joseph Poniatowski (1762–1813), served with Napoleon who made him a Marshal of France.

POLISH BYRON, The   Adam Mickiewicz (1798–1855), author of *Pan Tadeusz the last foray in Lithuania*, English translation, by G. R. Noyes, 1930, Everyman edition.

POLLARD   derived from Paul, pronounced Poll in 12th century, but sometimes used as a nickname from M.E. *poll* = to clip and *poll* = the head. Used of someone with close-cropped hair.

POOK, POUCK   O.E. *puca* = elf, sprite, goblin. Cf. *Puck of Pook's Hill*, by Kipling.

POOR CLARES	the Second Order (for women) founded by St Francis of Assisi and St Clare, c. 1212–14.
POOR LITTLE RICH GIRL	Gloria Vanderbilt, from a child custody case in late 1920s.
POOR MEN OF LYONS, The	the order which Pope Lucius III condemned in 1184, the Waldenses (q.v.).
POOR RICHARD	the assumed name of Benjamin Franklin, who wrote a series of almanacks (1732–57) under that title.
POP	Adolph Zuchor, founded the motion picture industry.
POPE OF GENEVA, The	John Calvin (1509–64).
POPERY	a contemptuous term used by Anglicans and Protestants to describe the Roman Catholic Church. It is used even by Judicious Hooker (q.v.).
POPPY	so nicknamed from the flower.
PORCH, The	name given to the Stoics (q.v.) from the porch, Greek στὄα, where their founder, Zeno, taught.
PORPHYROGENITUS	born in the purple, title of Constantine VII (905–59), Byzantine emperor who succeeded his father, Leo VI, in 912. He wrote various works both on the administration of the empire, and on the ceremonies of the court. His nickname may have been given because of his great interest in ceremonial and protocol but the term Porphyrogenitus was applied to members of the imperial family because the royal ladies occupied for their childbirth a chamber hung with purple curtains.
PORTUGUESE ILIAD	*Os Lusíadas, The Lusiads* by Luis Vaz de Camões (c. 1524–80), an epic principally devoted to the great achievements of Vasco da Gama. Camões had himself served in the Portuguese forces in Africa and Asia. His life was poverty-stricken and unhappy; he died of the plague and was buried in a common grave, so that the elaborate tomb in Lisbon is a cenotaph. Naturally he was lauded after his death, 36 editions of his great poem being published between 1580 and 1640 thus keeping alive Portuguese national spirit during the Spanish captivity.
POSITIVISM	name originally given to the system of thought of Auguste Comte (1798–1857), but applied later to any system of thought which discarded philosophy and theology, and confined itself to physical science.
POSTHUMOUS, The	Ladislas or Laszlo V of Hungary, born 22 February 1440, son of Albert V, German king, by his widow. He died in 1457. King of Bohemia.
POSTLE(S)	O.E. *apostol*, O.Fr. *apostle* = apostle, nickname or pageant name.
POYNER	from O.Fr. *poigneor* = fighter.
PRATT, PRETT, PRITT	O.E. *praett* = cunning or astute.
PREACHER	O.Fr. *precheor* = preacher.

PRECISIAN

a name used of the Puritans in the 16th and 17th centuries, because of their behaviour in using external religious forms and particular language e.g. referring to themselves as the godly.

PRENTICE, PRENTISS

sometimes a nickname as in case cited from 1350, perhaps meaning tradesman who has never learnt more than an apprentice's skill.

PRESBYTERIANISM

form of Church government by presbyters, first appeared after the Protestant Reformation.

PRESTER, PRESSER

O.Fr. *prestre* = priest. Cf. the famous medieval legend of Prester John (q.v.). See also Priest.

PRESTER JOHN

i.e. John the Priest or Elder (Presbyter), the name given in the latter Middle Ages to a Christian King and priest who was supposed to have a powerful kingdom in central Asia. The basis of the legend may have been in the widespread Nestorian Christianity of medieval Asia, of which much is said in Marco Polo's *Travels*, for example. But with the Portuguese discoveries in Africa in the sixteenth century Prester John was identified with the Negus or Emperor of Ethiopia where Christianity had persisted from early times although Ethiopia was surrounded by Moslem powers.

PRETTY, PRITTY

O.E. *praettig* = crafty, cunning. Cf. Prettyman.

PRETTY BOY FLOYD

an American gangster, Charles Floyd, member of Dillinger gang.

PREW, PROW, PRUE

M.E. = valiant.

PRIDE

a name from character in medieval moralities and mysteries.

PRIDHAM, PRODHAM

O.Fr. *prudhomme* = upright, honest man.

PRIEST, PRESS

O.E. *preost* = priest, 'in early examples denoting office but later usually a nickname for a man of "priestly" appearance or behaviour, or, no doubt, often for one of a most unpriestly character' (Reaney, *Dict. of British Surnames*). Cf. Prester (q.v.).

PRIME

O.Fr. *prime* = fine, delicate.

PRIMITIVE METHODISTS

a form of Methodism (q.v.), originating in 1811 but united with other bodies in 1832.

PRIN, PRYNNE

O.Fr. *prin* = first, also small, slender.

PRINCE OF ARTISTS

Albrecht Dürer (1471–1528), one of the greatest German artists.

PRINCE OF DESTRUCTION

Timur the Lame (q.v.), the cruel Mongol conqueror (1336–1405).

PRINCE OF HUMBUG

the circus owner, Phineas Taylor Barnum.

PRINCE OF HYPOCRITES

Tiberius Caesar (born 42 BC, reigned 14–37 AD), adopted son and successor of Augustus, Emperor of Rome. Tiberius was hated by those who chronicled his reign. They represented him as indulging in the most horrible vices (on the Isle of Capri, where he had retired) while pretending to care for decency.

PRINCE OF PHYSICIANS	Avicenna, the Persian philospher and physician (980–1037); his full name was Abu-Ali-Husain ibn Adbullah ibu Sina.
PRINCE OF THE APOSTLES	St Peter.
PRINNEY	the Prince Regent, later George IV.
PRIOR, PRYOR	O.Fr. *prior*, said to be at times a nickname.
PRISCUS	the old name for one of the Etruscan Kings of Rome, Lucius Tarquinius, who reigned 616–578 BC. His son was Lucius Tarquinius Superbus (q.v.).
PRISONER OF CHILLON	one François de Bonnivard (died c. 1570), imprisoned for political reasons in the Castle of Chillon on the Lake of Geneva, the title being taken by Lord Byron for his poem.
PRITILOVE, PRETLOVE	M.E. *prikke* and O.Fr. *love* = wolf. Thus prick wolf, a hunter and killer of wolves.
PRODIGAL, The	Albert VI, Duke of Austria (1418–63).
PRODIGY OF LEARNING, The	(Christian Friedrich) Samuel Hahnemann (1755–1843), a German physician and founder of homeopathy, thus denominated by H. F. Richter.
PROFOUND DOCTOR, The	a title applied to some of the 14th century schoolmen, e.g. Thomas Bradwardine.
PROPHET, PROFIT	O.Fr. *prophete* = prophet.
PROSELYTE	used loosely of a convert but originally meaning a convert in New Testament times to Judaism. The name comes from the Greek προσήλωτος, a stranger.
PROSPERITY ROBINSON	Cobbett thus ridiculed Viscount Goderich, Earl of Ripon (1782–1859), Chancellor of the Exchequer, who boasted of national prosperity on the verge of the financial crash of 1825.
PROTESTANT	the term applied to Western Christian communions separated from the Church of Rome. The term is nowhere found in the formularies or Prayer Book of the Church of England. The historical origin of the word comes from the imperial Diet of Speyer (1529) in which a minority of 6 princes and 14 cities issued a formal *Protestation* which stated that 'in matters which concern God's honour and salvation and the eternal life of our souls, everyone must stand and give account before God for himself'. At one time in certain quarters it was held that Protestant was derived from *Pro Te stant Jesu*, completely ridiculous.
PROTO-MARTYR	St Stephen, Acts vi and vii.
PROTO-MARTYR OF ENGLAND	or rather of Britain, St Alban, whose shrine was at St Albans in Hertfordshire. His martyrdrom is put either in the Diocletian persecution c. 305 or in that of Septimius Severus, c. 209.
PROTO-MARTYRESS	St Thecla, said to have been converted by St Paul.
PROUD(E)	O.E. *prut, prud* = proud. Cf. Prout.

PROUD, The

Henry (c. 1100–39) Duke of Bavaria and Saxony, 2nd son of Henry, The Black, Duke of Bavaria (q.v.).

Earl Hugh of Chester, killed in 1098 by King Magnus Barfoot (q.v.).

Otho IV, Holy Roman Emperor (born 1175, reigned 1209–18).

Semen (reigned 1341–53), Grand Prince of Moscow.

Tarquin II of Rome, *Superbus*, the father of false Sextus (q.v.), reigned 534–510 BC.

PROUD DUKE, The

Charles Seymour, Duke of Somerset (1662–1750). 'His pride of birth and rank was nothing short of a mania. He had an almost overwhelming sense of his own dignity and aping the seclusion observed by oriental monarchs, shunned to expose himself to the profanation of vulgar eyes. When he took the air in his state coach, running footmen preceded him to warn everyone off the road. His daughters never sat down in his presence' (The Duchess of Cleveland, *The Battle Abbey Roll*, pp.378–9). He built the great House at Petworth, Sussex, later called princely Petworth. 'The monument to the Duke in the chapel is apt to make one wonder to what deity it is dedicated. One enters a fairly plain and simple chapel of a great house, and then turning around beholds a vast canopy setting forth the heraldic magnificence of the 6th Duke' (L. G. Pine, *Sons of the Conqueror*, Charles Tuttle Inc., 1973, p.188).

PROUDFOOT

O.E. *prud* (*prut*) and *fot* = foot, one who walks with a proud foot. Ekwall is cited as saying that the first known bearer of the name was one who was likely to have walked proudly, he being Sheriff of London, c. 1140 (Reaney, *Dict. of British Surnames*). Cf. Proudlove and Proudmant.

PROWSE, PROUSE, PRUCE

M.E. and O.Fr. *prous* = valiant.

PSEUDO-AREOPAGITE

a mystical theologian of c. 500, Dionysius, possibly a Syrian. See the Areopagite.

PUBLICAN

in its original meaning, had no connection of any sort with the modern publican, the keeper of a tavern or public house. The term is used in the English New Testament as a translation of the Greek τελώνς, Latin *publicanus*, meaning a person to whom the Roman Government gave the farming of the taxation. The system was obviously and inevitably open to great abuses.

PUCELLE, La

The Virgin; one of the names given to St Joan of Arc, usually in a sarcastic sense, as in Shakespeare's *Henry VI*. Joan lived c. 1412–31, was burnt alive at Rouen as a heretic but was canonized as a saint on 9 May 1920.

PUDDIFOOT, PUTTIFOOT

German root, *Pud(d)* = to swell, applied to person with prominent belly. Much the same origin and use for Pudding.

PUDE

round and stout, as in Puddifoot.

PUNNETT possibly from O.Fr. *poignier*, to strike with the fist, hence the fighter.

PURCELL O.Fr. *pourcel* = little pig.

PURDY an oath name, Fr. *pour Dieu*. Cf. Purefoy from *par foi*.

PURITAN a term coined as an epithet of contempt during the 1560s in England. It was applied to persons within the Church of England who wished to have it more thoroughly reformed on Continental lines. The word is now used in two senses (a) of the historical body of persons prominent in England in the 17th century and (b) pejoratively as in the adjective puritanic.

PUSCAT, PUSSYCAT clearly pejorative.

PUSEYITES, PUSEYISM a term used always in a derogatory sense for members of the Tractarian or Oxford Movement which began in 1833. The term was derived from the name of Dr Edward Bouverie Pusey (1800–82), a very learned scholar and the principal leader of the Tractarians.

PUTTERILL Med. Latin *pultrellus* = a colt; meaning someone of a lively character.

PUTTOCK O.E. *puttoc* = kite, denoting someone ravenous.

PYATT O.Fr. *pye* = magpie.

PYRRHONISM originally a system propounded by Pyrrho of Elis, the Greek philosopher of c. 300 BC, which taught that certainty in knowledge was unattainable. The word has come to apply to any sceptical system of thought, e.g. it was said of Michel de Montaigne that he even doubted his doubts.

Q

QUAKERS

the name by which members of the Religious Society of Friends are often mentioned. George Fox, the founder of the Society, recorded that in 1650 Justice Bennet of Derby 'first called us Quakers because we bid them tremble at the Word of God'. There are, however, earlier instances of the use of the term before the advent of the Quakers, to describe some religious enthusiasts, possibly because of emotion shown in their meetings.

QUANT

M.E. *cointe, quante* = wise or clever, but also in bad sense of cunning, crafty.

QUANTRELL

O.Fr. *cointerel* = a fop.

QUARRELSOME, The

Henry, Duke of Bavaria.

QUARRIE

O.Fr. *quarre*, M.E. *quarre* = squarely built.

QUARTERMAIN, QUATERMAINE

A.Fr. *quatremayns* = four hands, supposed to denote mailed fists, i.e. hardness.

QUARTODECIMANS

those Christians who observed Easter, the Christian Passover as the Jews observed their Passover, i.e. on the 14th day of the month Nisan. The practice was found in Asia Minor and lasted until the 5th century.

QUAYLE

O.Fr. *quaile*, a bird supposed to be amorous and timid, in the bestiaries and unnatural natural history of older times.

QUEEN ANNE'S BOUNTY

money allowed by Queen Anne (1702–14) of Great Britain to augment poor livings. The money came from sums which before the Reformation went to the Pope but which Henry VIII had annexed to the Crown.

QUEEN DICK

nickname for Richard Cromwell (1626–1712), who succeeded his father as Protector of England in 1658 but soon resigned the office.

QUEEN OF HEARTS

Elizabeth, the daughter of James I of Great Britain, who married Frederick V, the Winter King (q.v.) King of Bohemia. Elizabeth was so called in the Netherlands owing to her nice character and pleasant manners.

QUEEN'S MARYS or THE FOUR MARYS

four young ladies, companions of Mary Queen of Scots (executed 1587). They were surnamed Beaton, Livingstone, Fleming and Seaton. See the novel, *The Queen's Maries*, by G. J. Whyte-Melville.

QUEEN SQUARE HERMIT

Jeremy Bentham (1748–1832), as he lived in 1 Queen Square, London. Bentham was the English utilitarian philosopher and writer on law reform whose works had great influence in the 19th century in England

and abroad. In George Borrow's *The Bible in Spain* there is an amusing account of Borrow's interview with a Spanish official who was an enthusiast for the 'grand Baintham'.

QUICKLY   = nimbly.

QUIET, The   (*Kyrri*), Olaf III, King of Norway (1066–93).

QUIETISM   a term for a spiritual state by which the soul simply rests in the presence of God in pure faith. No outward acts of religion are required. The teaching was founded by M. de Molinos and condemned by Pope Innocent XI in 1687.

QUINE   Irish *conn* = counsel.

QUINNEY   Manx = the crafty.

QUIRINUS   a pen name of the great German church historian J. J. I. von Dollinger. In 69 letters Quirinus contributed his views on Vatican Council I to the *Augsburger Allgemeine Zeitung* 1869–70. Dollinger was one of the originators of the Old Catholics (q.v.), so the letters are opposed to Papal Infallibility. Name derived from Quirinus, the name of Romulus after he was deified. Hence the name of the Quirinal Hill as the seat of Italian Civil Government.

QUISLING   full name Vidkun Abraham Lauritz Jonson Quisling, a Norwegian fascist whose name became synonymous with traitor. He set up a species of government in Norway during the German occupation 1940–5. He was found guilty after the liberation of Norway in May 1945, and was executed on 24 October 1945.

QUIXOTE OF THE NORTH Charles XII of Sweden (born 1682, reigned 1697–1718).

R

RADICALS
a term originally applied in 1818 to politicians who desired radical reform (from Latin *radix*, root) usually with a republican flavour. The term has long lost a distinctive application and is now used generally not as a noun, but as an adjective.

RAGMAN ROLL
an important term in Scottish history, derived from the seals of Scots nobles hanging from a document in which they gave their fealty to King Edward I of England in 1291.

RAIL SPLITTER
President Abraham Lincoln, because he worked in this way in youth.

RAILWAY KING
Sydney Smith thus described George Hudson (1800–71), the Yorkshireman who for a few years dominated the expansion of railways in England. He died in penury.

RAIN(E), RAYNE
Fr. *reine* = queen, used in derogatory sense.

RAINHA-SANTA
Queen Saint, the name popularly given to Isabella the Queen of King Diniz (1279–1325) of Portugal. She was the daughter of Peter III of Aragon and was the mother of King Alfonso IV of Portugal. She was canonized as St Elizabeth of Portugal. She died in 1336.

RAITHU, Theodore of
a monk of the monastery of Raithu on the Gulf of Suez. He lived c. 550 and was author of several theological works.

RAL-PA-CAN
Long Hair, the nickname of a King of Tibet who ruled from 815 to 836. He was a zealot for Buddhism and persecuted non-Buddhists which caused his assassination.

RAMAGE, RAMADGE
O.Fr. *ramage* = wild.

RANK
O.E. *ranc*, M.E. *rank* = strong.

RANTERS
a pejorative term applied in 19th century to nonconformist preachers, especially to the Primitive Methodists. Originally the name was given to a 17th century sect which rejected all religious authority.

RANTIPOLE
one of the nicknames of Napoleon III, meaning harum-scarum. See also Badinguet, Man of December, Man of Sedan, Man of Silence.

RAPPAREE
an Irishman armed with a rapaire or half pike, and engaged in robbery.

RASKOLNIKI
see Old Believers.

RAT, CAT AND DOG
used in the rhyme by William Collingbourne (1483), the full text being:

The catte, the ratte and Lovell our dogge
Rule all England under a hogge.

Ratcliffe or (Radcliffe) a proper name of a noble, Cat,
Sir William Catesby, Lovell, Viscount Lovell known
as the King's Spaniel. Hog = Richard III (see Boar).
Collingbourne's wit cost him his life.

RATTER — O.Fr. *raton* (the form used in *Piers Plowman*) = rat.

RAVEN — O.E. *hraefn* = raven. Cf. Ravening.

RAWBONE — O.N. *ra-bein* = roe-bone, used of one as swift as a roe.

RAY, REY — O.Fr. *rei* = king, given because bearer had pride, or
the bearing of a king, or was champion in a sporting
competition.

READ(E), REID — O.E. *read* = red, applied to hair or complexion.

READMAN, REDMAN — in some cases from 'red man'. Cf. the reddleman in
Hardy's *Return of the Native*.

READY — M.E. *raedi* = prompt or quick.

REBECCAITES — from Rebecca in Genesis xxiv.60, part of whose
blessing was that her descendants should possess the
gates of those that hate them; so applied to some
Welshmen in 1843 led by a man dressed as a woman
who demolished turnpike gates.

RECHABITES — a term used by a small section in ancient Israel which
abstained completely from the use of wine (Jeremiah
xxxv.6) hence applied in modern times to total
abstainers.

RECUSANTS — the term applied to those who refused to conform to
the C. of E. after 1570 when Pope (St) Pius V
excommunicated Queen Elizabeth I.

RED, The — Eric, (c. 950–1003) a Norse explorer, banished from
Norway for manslaughter, he settled in Iceland and
in 986 colonized Greenland with settlers from Iceland.
His son, Leif, discovered North America. A saga, *Eric
the Red*, describes his exploits.

Gilbert de Clare, Earl of Gloucester, son-in-law of
King Edward I of England.

RED COMYN or DOUGLAS — This term was used to distinguish one part of the
Comyn and Douglas families from the other line, the
Black Comyn and Douglas. The origin of the term is
not clear; it could refer to the colour of hair or
complexion of the original members or to sanguinary
or brutal dispositions. In neither case is the origin of
the family known. The Douglas name derives from the
Douglas stream, the dark water. The Comyn, or more
usually Cumming, surname was anciently given the
ludicrous explanation that the original ancestor was a
janitor who said 'come in' to visitors to the king's
chamber. This gem of nonsense was too much for the
author of *Antiquity of the Scottish Nation*, but the
scholarly Dr A. C. Black in his *Scottish Surnames* found
it too good to resist.

REDEMPTORISTS

a congregation under the title of the Most Holy Redeemer founded by St Alphonsus Ligouri in 1732 and designed for mission work among the poor.

REDHEAD

O.E. *read, heafod* = red head.

REPUBLICAN QUEEN

Sophia Charlotte (1668–1705), wife of Frederick I of Prussia.

RESHID

name of Mohammed V (1844–1918), Ottoman Sultan of Turkey from 1909 to 1918, kind and weak.

RESOLUTE DOCTOR

John Baconthorp, who died in 1346, a Carmelite and commentator on Aristotle.

REVEL, REVILLE

O.Fr. *revel* = pride, rebellion, from *reveler* = to rebel.

REVERE

in some cases from M.E. *revere* = reiver, robber.

RHYMER, Thomas the

a Scots poet who lived at the end of the 13th century and who made many prophecies in verse. He was Thomas of Erceldonne and also named Thomas Learmont.

RHYS, REESE, RICE

O. Welsh *ris*, Welsh *rhys* = ardour.

RICH, The

Jakob II (1459–1525), one of the most successful of the Fugger family of merchant bankers of Germany.

RICHARD YEA AND NAY

nickname of Richard I of England, Coeur-de-Lion (q.v.), Lion Heart. The title of a romance about King Richard by the novelist Maurice Hewlett in 1900.

RIDEOUT

meaning a rider.

RIDER, RYDER

O.E. *ridere* = rider; reference to a knight or mounted warrior.

RIGHTEOUS HARMONY, BANDS OF or FISTS OF

see Boxers.

ROB ROY

i.e. Red Robert, the nickname of Robert Macgregor (1671–1734), a noted Highland freebooter who had red hair. He took the name of Campbell because the name of Macgregor was proscribed by Scots Law. A romantic account of his doings is in Sir Walter Scott's novel *Rob Roy*.

ROBERT DES RUINES

name given to the French painter Hubert Robert (1733–1808) because of his paintings of Roman remains.

ROEBUCK

O.E. *ra* and *bucc* = roebuck.

ROI PANADE

i.e. King of Slops, applied to the restored Bourbon King Louis XVIII of France; born 1755, reigned 1814–24.

ROI SOLEIL, Le

The Sun King (q.v.).

ROINECKS

term used by the Boers in the South African War of 1899–1902 to describe British troops; 'red necks' because of their rosy complexions.

ROIS FAINÉANTS, Les

the do-nothing kings; name applied to the Merovingian Kings of France, termed the first race of that kingdom (the Carolingian and Capetians being the second and third). The Merovingian kings derived from one Merovech, and his grandson Clovis I became the first king in 481–2. Over the centuries the kings of this line became mere ciphers, the power being in the hands of the mayors of the palace. The last Merovingian, Childeric II, was deposed 751–2 by Pepin the Short (q.v.), the first Carolingian.

ROMANIST

a term used pejoratively of Roman Catholics and commonly found in use up to at least the middle of the 19th century.

ROMISH

a term applied with offensive meaning to the Roman Catholic Church e.g. in John Henry Newman's writings before 1845, the year in which he became a Roman Catholic. Not now employed save by the more obscure Protestant sects.

ROOK(S), RUCK

O.E. *hroc* = rook.

ROSCIUS

a very distinguished Roman actor (c. 62 BC), hence a nickname for a notable actor.

ROSICRUCIANS

a secret society which arose in Germany in 17th century, using the Rose and the Cross as symbols of Christ's Resurrection and Redemption. In modern masonry what are called the Christian degrees go under the name of Rose Croix.

ROSMINIANS

a congregation founded in 1828 by Antonio Rosmini-Serbati in Italy, and having for its object the performance of charitable works. Known as Fathers of Charity.

ROTERODAMMENSIS or ROTERODAMUS

Desiderius Erasmus (1466–1536) (q.v.), the great European scholar, born in Rotterdam. He produced a Greek text of the New Testament in 1516 with a translation into classical Latin.

ROUGH AND READY

name given to General Zachary Taylor (1784–1850), 12th President of the USA.

ROUGH RIDERS

the soldiers whom Theodore Roosevelt (1858–1919) led into Cuba in the Spanish-American War of 1898. Theodore Roosevelt, kinsman of the later President Franklin Delano Roosevelt, was Vice President of the USA, but when President McKinley was assassinated in 1901 he became President and was elected for a second term in 1905. He had many other nicknames.

ROUGHHEAD, ROWED, RUFFHEAD

O.E. *ruh* and *heafod* = rough head (of hair).

ROUND(S), ROUNCE

O.Fr. *roond* = round, fat.

ROUNDHEADS

the name given to the supporters of Parliament against King Charles I in the great Civil War in England 1642–5. It is usually stated that the Puritans wore their hair short, but Antonia Fraser in *Cromwell, Our Chief of Men*, St Albans, Panther, 1975, pp.85–6, points out that the Parliamentary leaders, Cromwell *par excellence*, wore their hair very long. She gives as the origin of Roundhead 'the short lived fashion of the apprentices who deliberately cropped their hair in scorn of the "unloveliness of love locks" (the title incidentally of an early pamphlet by William Prynne)' But as the New Model Army was the foundation of the British Regular Army could the short hair have been, for the rank and file, the original of 'short back and sides'?

ROUS(E), RUSS M.E. and A.Fr. *rous(e)* = red.

ROY O.Fr. *roi* = king.

ROYAL MARTYR, The Charles I (1625–49) of England, executed on 30 January 1649 by order of Cromwell and the Puritan minority. Described himself as 'a martyr of the people'. When buried a week later at Windsor, a snowfall was held to be a pall of innocence. He was almost at once described as having died for the liberties of the Church of England. A book was written possibly by an Anglican clergyman, John Gauden, the *Eikon Basilike*, purporting to be the spiritual autobiography of Charles. After the Restoration in 1660 a special service was put into the Book of Common Prayer for King Charles. In the alternative Service Book, 1981, his commemoration falls on 30 January.

ROYALIST BUTCHER, The Blaise de Montluc (1502–77), Marshal of France, very cruel to Protestants.

RUDD O.E. *ridig* = ruddy. Cf. Ruddick, O.E. *ridoc* = robin.

RUDGE A.Fr. *rug(g)e*, Fr. *rouge* = red.

RUFFETT O.E. *ruh* = rough, and *fot* = foot, rough foot.

RUFUS 'the red', the name given to William II (1086–1100) of England, owing to his having red hair.

RUMP from a dialectal word meaning an ugly rawboned creature.

RUNCIE M.E. *runcy* = rouncy, a nag.

RUPERT OF DEBATE, The name given by Lord Lytton to Edward Geoffrey Stanley, 14th Earl of Derby (1799–1869), when he was Mr Stanley and a member of the House of Commons.

RUSSELL, ROUSEL O.Fr. *rousel*, diminutive of *rous* = red.

RUSSIAN BYRON Alexander Sergeivich Pushkin (1799–1837), a very great all-round Russian writer, a friend of Mickiewicz, the Polish Byron (q.v.).

RUST O.E. *rust* = rust; i.e. in reference to reddish hair or complexion.

S

SABBATARIANISM

an excessive and extremely rigorous observance of the Sabbath, as the Jewish day of rest. Unknown on the European continent, it was peculiar to the English and Scottish Reformation.

SABELLIARISM

an ancient heresy which failed to distinguish the three Persons of the Holy Trinity. Named from one Sabellius, of whom very little is known.

SABREUR, LE BEAU

handsome swordsman, Joachim Murat (1767–1815) distinguished as a general of cavalry. One of Napoleon's marshals and king of Naples, tried to conquer Italy for Napoleon in the Hundred Days but was captured and shot (13 October 1815).

SACCHARISSA

the name given by the poet Edmund Waller to Lady Dorothy Sidney, eldest daughter of the Earl of Leicester and who in 1639 married the future Earl of Sunderland.

SADD

M.E. *sad(de)* = serious, firm.

SADDUCEES

the name given to a Jewish sect in New Testament times which represented the rich and the priestly aristocrats. They did not believe in the Resurrection or in angels or spirit. Not found after the fall of Jerusalem in AD 70.

SAFFER

O.Fr. *saffre* = glutton.

SAGE OF CHELSEA

Thomas Carlyle (1795–1881), Scottish historian and essayist, so named because he lived for many years in Chelsea, London.

SAGE OF CROTONA

Pythagoras, because he established his school of philosophy there c. 530 BC.

SAGER

O.Fr. *sage* = wise.

SAILOR KING

William IV of Britain (1765, reigned 1830–7) was a midshipman, 1779, and Lord High Admiral, 1827.

SAINT, SANT, SAUNT

O.Fr. *sant* = saint.

SAINT, The

King David I (1124–53) of Scotland, because of his character and his endowment of the Church; known in Scots tradition as 'a sair saint for the Crown' which was impoverished by his benefactions.

Ferdinand III (1201–52), King of Castile 1217–52 and of Leon 1230–54, was canonized in 1671, because of the crusading spirit which he brought into Spanish-Moorish relations. As a result of his efforts only Granada remained under Moslem rule in Spain, and that was under tribute to Castile. He also began the policy of expelling the Moors from their homes in the conquered territory which was to have a had economic effect on the life of Spain.

Henry II (973–1024), German King from 1002, Holy Roman Emperor, pious benefactor of the Church, canonized 1146.

Olaf II, died 1030 in battle, King of Norway, set about converting Norway to Christianity having himself been converted in England. Reputed a saint at once after his death, his body was enshrined in 1031.

ST GEORGE'S CAVALRY   term used in France to denominate the erstwhile financial power of Britain.

SAINT SAVA (SABAS)   lived c. 1174–1236, the first Archbishop of the Independent Serbian Church, was 3rd and youngest son of Stephen Nemanya, the Grand Zhupan of Serbia. Saint Sava lived for many years as a monk on Mount Athos, and emerged to crown Stephen the First Crowned (q.v.) King of Serbia. He secured the adherence of the Serbian Church to Constantinople instead of to Rome. His feast day is 14 January.

ST THIERRY, William of   (c. 1085–1148) a theologian and mystical writer.

ST VICTOR, Richard of   (died 1173), a Scottish mystic and theologian who entered the Abbey of St Victor in Paris.

ST VICTOR, Walter of   (died post 1180) prior of the Augustinian canons of St Victor, Paris, called the Victorines (q.v.); a philosophical writer strongly opposed to Abelard's dialectical method.

SAKYAMUNI   a name for Gautama or Siddhartha, the founder of Buddhism in the 6th century BC, and derived from the tribe of the Sakhyas to which he belonged.

SALESIANS   i.e. the Society of St Francis de Sales founded in Italy in 1859 by St John Bosco to promote Christian education of the poor.

SALLITT   O.E. *saelida* = seafarer or pirate.

SALVATION ARMY   founded by William Booth (General Booth) in 1865, took the present title in 1878. A world-wide organization which dispenses with all sacraments, it is strongly Evangelical and does an immense amount of social work.

SAMIAN SAGE   Pythagoras (6th century BC), who was born on the island of Samos.

SAMOSATA, Paul of   a 3rd century heretic and bishop of Antioch. A full account of this man is given in Gibbon's *Decline and Fall of the Roman Empire*, ch. XVI. Samosata was the important Roman outpost on the right bank of the Euphrates.

SAMOSATIAN PHILOSOPHER   Lucian of Samosata, a Greek famous for his satirical dialogues (2nd century AD).

SAMWAYS   O.E. *samwis* = dull, foolish.

SANGLIER DES ARDENNES, Le   the wild boar of Arden, William de la Marck (1446–85), an account of whose misdeeds is given in Scott's *Quentin Durward*.

SANGUINE, SANGWIN   M.E. and O.Fr. *sanguin* = of a sanguine complexion.

SANS CULOTTES   without knee breeches, the term given by the French aristocrats to the extreme republicans in the French Revolution.

SANS GÊNE, Mme   nickname meaning 'without constraint', given to the wife of one of Napoleon's Marshals, Lefère, Duke of Dantzic (1775–1820), because she always retained the manners of her social origin as a washerwoman.

SANTER   O.Fr. *sanz terre* = without land. Cf. Lackland (q.v.).

SAPPHO   Mlle de Scudéry (1607–1701), French writer, was so called (after the Greek poetess of Lesbos) by her intimates.

SARABAITES   meaning not known but applied in early times of monasticism to some ascetics who lived in small groups but without a definite rule or a superior.

SARACENS   a word from Greek Σαρακηνος, possibly from Arabic, meaning 'Oriental' and applied generally in the Middle Ages to all the Moslem races but not used by the Moslems themselves.

SARAH GAMP   a character in Dickens's *Martin Chuzzlewit* who has become proverbial as a thoroughly disreputable nurse.

SARONG GIRL   American film star, Dorothy Lamour.

SAROV, St Seraphim of   (1759–1833), a Russian monk and anchorite of great sanctity, canonized 1903.

SARSON(S)   O.Fr. *sarrazin* = saracen, i.e. used of one of a swarthy complexion.

SARTIN   O.Fr. *carteyn* = self-assured.

SASSENACH   Gaelic word for an Englishman.

SATANIC SCHOOL   Robert Southey's term for Byron and Shelley, because they were opposed to religion.

SAVAGE, SALVIDGE   O.Fr. *salvage* = savage, wild (from Latin *silvaticus* and thence dog Latin *salvaticus*).

SAWNY or SANDY   a contraction of Alexander, a common Christian name in Scotland, hence used to denote a Scotsman.

SCAFE, SCAIFE, SKAIFE   O.N. *skeifi*, N. Eng. dial *scafe* = crooked, awkward.

SCARF   O.N. *skarfe* = cormorant.

SCARFACE   Al (Alphonso) Capone (1895–1947), probably the most notorious, and successful, gangster in American history. An Italian by birth, he ruled Chicago in the prohibition era and is thought to have been responsible for 500 murders. Opponents were 'bumped off'. Eventually he was tried and sentenced to 11 years imprisonment – for tax evasion!

SCARLET WOMAN   in Revelation xvii,1–6, see Whore of Babylon.

SCATTERGOOD

reference to a spendthrift.

SCAVENGER'S DAUGHTER

an instrument of torture invented by Sir William Skevington, Lieutenant of the Tower, *temp*. Henry VIII.

SCHOLASTICUS

Greek σχολαστυκός, a lawyer, the name given to Socrates the Greek church historian. His *Church History* is in 7 books (c. 380–450).

John III, Patriarch of Constantinople from 565, a celebrated writer on canon law (he had been a lawyer in earlier years). Also the name given to John Chimacus.

Zacharias (died post 536) a Monophysite theologian, also called Mitylene and Rhetor.

SCHOOL-AUTHORS

a reference to the Schoolmen (q.v.), and used in the Thirty-Nine Articles of the Church of England, the authors of which had all been trained in the works of the Schoolmen.

SCHOOLMASTER IN POLITICS

US President Woodrow Wilson (1856–1924), because of his academic background.

SCHOOLMEN

those writers who from the 11th to 15th centuries in western Europe endeavoured to elucidate the mysteries of the Christian faith by the use of the reason and to reconcile reason with revelation. It was mighty philosophical and theological effort, since the knowledge of physical facts (i.e. the sciences as now understood) was very limited. The greatest of the schoolmen was St Thomas Aquinas, the Angelic Doctor, (q.v.), whose greatest works were (1) *Summa contra Gentiles*, where the only authority is reason, and (2) *Summa Theologica*, in which all Christian theology and ethics are handled. The philosophy is based on Aristotle who is constantly referred to as The Philosopher (q.v.)

SCOTCH HOBBEMA

Patrick Nasmyth (1737–1831), landscape painter named from the Dutch painter Meindert Hobbema.

SCOTTER, SCUTTER

O.Fr. *escoute* = spy.

SCOTTISH ADDISON

Henry Mackenzie (1745–1831), whose collected works fill 8 volumes and who held a commanding position in the Scottish literary world. Sir Walter Scott dedicated *Waverley* to him under the above title.

SCOURGE OF GOD

Attila the Hun, who died in 453. He commanded a horde of nomadic warriors whom he led from the region of the Caspian Sea. He invaded and pillaged both the western and eastern Roman Empires. His only defeat was at Chalons, 451. Attila died on the night of his marriage to a girl named Ildico. His burial place remained unknown, those who buried him and his treasures having been put to death.

SCOURGE OF GRAMMAR

a minor poet, Giles Jacob (1686–1744), thus termed by Alexander Pope in the *Dunciad*, iii.149.

SCRIMGEOUR

given by Reaney (*Dict. of British Surnames*) as derived from O.Fr. *escremisseor* = fencing-master. This is, however, completely at variance with the explanations which Dr Black (*Surnames of Scotland*) quotes from the medieval Scots historian Hector Boece, who says that Sir Alexander Carron received from his exploits the name Scrymgeour = sharp fighter. This agrees with the traditional account in *Burke's Peerage* under the Earl of Dundee. The first-mentioned Scrymgeour, Sir Alexander, was appointed Standard Bearer of Scotland in 1298 by Sir William Wallace. The traditional account is that the original Bannerman refused to cross the Spey against the rebels whereupon the Scots king transferred the standard to Sir Alexander Carron. The Earl of Dundee, head of the Scrimgeour Wedderburn family, is hereditary Royal Standard Bearer of Scotland.

SCROPE

'crab'. The head of the great medieval house of Scrope was the plaintiff in the dispute with Grosvenor of 1385. 'Although we cannot trace their actual pedigree link by link to a Norman who figured in the Conquest, there is no doubt that Lord Scrope was right in claiming Norman ancestry. The name Scrope is not English. It is believed that it is derived from an old Norse nickname meaning crab, out of allusion to some peculiarity in the gait of a remote ancestor and from this circumstance many of the family bore a crab as a crest', (L. G. Pine, *They Came with the Conqueror*, 1954, pp.20–1).

SCULLABOGUE MASSACRE

in 1798 Scullabogue House, Wexford, was seized by the Irish rebels and there they slaughtered their prisoners.

SEA-GREEN INCORRUPTIBLE

Maximilien Robespierre. Thomas Carlyle in his *History of the French Revolution* describes Robespierre as having a 'complexion of a multiplex atrabiliac colour, the final shade of which may be the pale sea green. That greenish coloured (verdâtre) individual' (Bk iv, ch.iv).

SEAMAN, SEWMAN, SAAYMAN

O.E. *saemann* = sea man.

SECOND ADVENTISTS

see Adventists.

SECOND EVE, The

The Blessed Virgin Mary, a play being often made on the angelic greeting Ave Maria, Ave being the reverse of Eva.

SECULAR, SECKLER

O.Fr. *seculier* = secular, lay, and ultimately = worldly. Cf. Chaucer's Monk, a prime example of monastic worldliness.

SECULARISTS

persons who ignore or deny any action of the supernatural in the interpretation of the world and life. A term first used by G. J. Holyoake (1877–1906) in an expository system. Later developed into atheism by Charles Bradlaugh.

SECUNDUS, Octavianus

(1549–1600), a member of the great Fugger family of Germany, the merchant bankers.

SEED(S)

O.E. *sidur* = custom, manner, morality, purity.

SEEKERS

some Puritans of the early 17th century who held that no true Church existed and that in His time God would create a new church. One of their members, Bartholomew Legate (c. 1575–1612) was burnt at Smithfield. Legate was one of two men (Wightman was the other) who were the last to be burnt for heresy under the Act *De Heretico Comburendo* (1403). 'Legate was a man of real intelligence whom the King had found a stimulating opponent when closeted with him, he had tried to win him from his Arianism' (G. P. V. Akrigg, *Jacobean Pageant*, London, Hamish Hamilton, 1962, p. 311).

SEELEY, SELLY, SILLY, CEELEY, ZELLEY

O.E. *saelig* = blessed. The phrase 'silly Suffolk' is a complete misunderstanding. Suffolk was blessed because it possessed one of the greatest shrines in England, the Abbey of St Edmundsbury, which contained the body of St Edmund, king and martyr (died 870). The original name of the town Bedricsworth was changed to Bury St Edmunds.

SELF(E)

O.E. *saewulf* = sea-wolf.

SELIMAN, SILMAN

O.E. *saelig* and *mann* = happy or blessed man.

SEMI-ARIANS

those who held a belief about Christ's Sonship which was intermediate between that of the Arians (q.v.) and of the Orthodox. While the Catholic Church in the Nicene Creed held that Christ was of the same substance (ὁμοούδιος), the semi-Arians taught that He was of like substance (ὁμοιούδιος). This is the source of Thomas Carlyle's epigram about the Christian world being divided over a diphthong, but a much more understanding account will be found in Cardinal J. H. Newman's *Arians of the Fourth Century*.

SEMIRAMIS OF THE NORTH

Catherine II of Russia; Semiramis's figure 'comprises a kernel of attested fact with a later accretion of fabulous history' (*Ency.Brit.*, sub Semiramis) where she is equated with Sammuramat, mother of the Assyrian King Adad-nirari III (reigned 810–782 BC). She was the widow of King Shamshi-Adad V and ruled Assyria after his death and during the early years of her son's reign.

Also applied to Margaret of Denmark, Sweden and Norway (1353–1412) in reference to the Union of Kalmar in 1397 which for a time united the three countries.

SEMPLE

in Scotland derived from simple (q.v.).

SENIOR, SENYARD, SINYARD, SYNYER

O.Fr. *seignour* = lord. Latin *senior* = older, though sometimes used as denoting rank, often bestowed on one who gave himself airs.

SEPARATISTS

a term applied to the Brownists (q.v.).

SEPPINGS, SIPPINGS

described as coming from 'seven pence' and used of a poor person.

SEPTEMBER MASSACRES	occurred in the French Revolution. The allied armies had captured Verdun and the revolutionaries led by Danton then murdered 8,000 royalist prisoners.
SERAPHIC DOCTOR	see Doctor Angelicus.
SERAPHIC SAINT	St Francis of Assisi.
SERENDIP	an ancient name of Ceylon as in an old story, *The Three Princes of Serendip*. Hence Horace Walpole coined the word serendipity to denote lucky finds, as the Princes were said to have had.
SERPENT OF OLD NILE	Cleopatra of Egypt, thus mentioned by Mark Antony in Shakespeare's play.
SERVITES	an order founded in 1240 by seven wealthy Florentines who gave up mundane life to devote themselves to the service of the Blessed Virgin Mary, hence their official title. *Ordo Servorum BVM.*
SEVEN SLEEPERS OF EPHESUS	seven Christian young men who were said to have slept in a cave during the Diocletian persecution (c. AD 250) and to have been awakened under Theodosius II (c. 450).
SEVENTH DAY ADVENTISTS	see Adventists.
SFORZA	name given to an Italian condottiero, Nurzio Attendolo (1369–1424), because of his strength. He acquired lands in Italy and from him descended the Sforza Dukes of Milan.
SHACKLOCK, SHATLOCK, SHADLOCK	'a nickname for one with a habit (not unknown today) of shaking back his long hair' (Reaney, *Dict. of British Surnames*).
SHAD	O.E. *scadd* = a shad (a fish).
SHADE, SCHADE	O.E. *sceadu*, M.E. *shade*, possibly used as nickname for a very thin man.
SHAKERS	a name given to an obscure sect, an offshoot of the Quakers, founded in England in 1747 by James and Jane Wardley. Their own name was The United Society of Believers in Christ's Second Appearing; the nickname came from the members' habit of shaking under spiritual exaltation. They are probably now extinct as most members were celibates.
SHAKESBY	from *sakespe* = draw sword, used probably of a quarrelsome person.
SHAKESPEARE	shake-spear, of a spearman. Cf. Shakelance, Shakeshaft. In Garter King of Arms, William Dethick's grant of arms to the poet, there is a reference to the applicant's 'parents and late antecessors who were for their valiant and faithful service advanced and rewarded by the most prudent prince King Henry VII', etc. Tudor heralds were notoriously complacent on the subject of arms grants but the above in the draft (still preserved) of 1596 may well reflect a family tradition of service in the Hundred Years War. In the

draft of 1599 when the arms were granted, 'grandfather' was substituted for 'antecessors'. Sir Sidney Lee (*Life of Shakespeare*, London, Smith, Elder, 1915, p. 281 *et seq.*) gives full details but Dr Reaney's researches confirm that the surname was a nickname, clearly from military sources. The canting coat granted to John and William Shakespeare – the spear on a bend – clearly established the spelling of Shakespeare.

SHANKE(S) O.E. *sceanca* = shank.

SHARP(E), SHAIRP O.E. *scearp* = sharp, quick, smart.

SHE-WOLF OF FRANCE Isabella, *la plus belle dame du monde*, daughter of the King of France, married to Edward II of England. She and her paramour Mortimer caused King Edward to be put to a most awful death. The description, 'the she-wolf that tarest thy mate's bowels', comes from Thomas Gray's poem *The Bard*. Mortimer was eventually hanged. Isabella was removed from politics by her son Edward III and sent to live at Castle Rising in Norfolk where, despite the small size of the castle, she apparently lived in considerable style and was visited twice a year by her son.

SHEEP O.E. *sceap* = sheep, sometimes used as a nickname.

SHEEPSHANKS i.e. with legs like those of a sheep. O.E. *sceanca* = leg.

SHELDRAKE derived from the duck species sheldrake, which has bright and varied colouring.

SHEPHERD LORD Henry Clifford, 10th Lord Clifford and Westmorland, who died in 1523, had been brought up in humble circumstances owing to the Wars of the Roses. On being reinstated in his inheritance he proved to be a man of peace. Wordsworth celebrated him in his poem *Song at the Feast of Brougham Castle*:
The Shepherd-Lord was honoured more and more,
And ages after he was laid in earth,
The good Lord Clifford was the name he bore.

SHEPHERD OF THE OCEAN Sir Walter Raleigh was thus described by Edmund Spenser.

SHERLOCK O.E. *scir* = bright and *loc(e)* = lock of hair, i.e. fair-haired.

SHERRARD, SHERRETT O.E. *scir* = bright.

SHERWEN O.E. *sceran* = to cut + *wind*, i.e. cut wind; used for a swift runner.

SHIH HUANG TI the name self-bestowed on the prince of the Ch'in family and which meant, 'First Emperor'. He organized the whole of China as an empire and although there were afterwards periods of breakdown into feudal disorders, the imperial tradition was always remembered and dynasty after dynasty arose to rule the vast country. The First Emperor reigned 221–210 BC. After his death the empire relapsed in 207 BC but was restored by the great Han dynasty which ruled from 202 BC to AD 221. It was the great Shih Huang

Ti who built the Great Wall of China and ordered the burning of the books, as he thought that any philosophies hostile to his own ideas were dangerous to the state.

SHI'ITES
originally the followers of Ali, the 4th caliph of Islam and son-in-law (also cousin) of the Prophet Mohammed. Ali was murdered in 661. His adherents number possibly one tenth of all Moslems, the remaining nine tenths being known as Sunnis. Persia (Iran) is the principal seat of the Shi'ites.

SHILLING
O.E. *scilling* = shilling, used of a person not worth much financially.

SHIMMING
possible origin O.E. *sciming* = the fair one.

SHORT
O.E. *scevit* = short.

SHORT, The
Pepin, younger son of Charles Martel (q.v.) who deposed (c. 751–2) the last Merovingian monarch and was anointed by the Church as King of France.
Wyladyslaw I, King of Poland 1320.

SHORTHOSE
translated from Curthose = short boot, but more probably, 'short hose'; see Courthose.

SHORTREED
O.E. *sceort* = short and *raed* = counsel; used of limited counsel.

SHOULDERS
O.E. *sculdor* = shoulder, i.e. of a person with broad or some peculiarity of shoulders.

SHOVE
O.E. *scufa*, from *scufan* = push. Cf. Showers in the same sense.

SHUTTLE
M.E. *shytell*, *shuttle* = inconstant, variable, fickle.

SICK MAN OF EUROPE
meaning in the 19th century the weakened and ailing Turkish Empire. Term used by Czar Nicholas I in 1844 when in London. The Czar proposed that Britain and Russia should partition Turkey.

SIDETES
the name of Antiochus VII (c. 159–129 BC), King of Syria, from the fact that he had been brought up in the Greek city of Side in Pamphylia.

SIDETES, Philip
from Side in Pamphylia, Philip was a historian of church affairs but only fragments of his work remain (early 5th century).

SILENT, The
William I (1533–84), Prince of Orange and Count of Nassau, who led the struggle of the Dutch for independence from Spain. His nickname came fron an incident when he was hunting at Vincennes with Henry II of France. The latter opened to William the plan which the French and Spanish kings had made to exterminate Protestantism in their dominions. 'William of Orange earned his name of "silent" from the manner in which he received these communications of Henry without revealing to the monarch by word or look, the enormous blunder which he had committed.' (J. L. Motley, *Rise of the Dutch Republic*, Pt 2 ch 1). Also known as the Taciturn.

SILENT CAL   US President Calvin Coolidge (1872–1933), famous for his remark on allied war debts, 'they hired the money, didn't they'.

SILENTIARY, The   a Christian poet of 6th century named from silentiarius, i.e. an usher whose duty was to maintain silence in the imperial palace at Constantinople.

SILKEN THOMAS   Lord Thomas Fitzgerald (as he was called, though his real title was Lord Offaly), eldest son of the 9th Earl of Kildare. He received his nickname from the gorgeous trappings of himself and his retinue. Having rebelled against Henry VIII, Silken Thomas who had succeeded his father as 10th Earl, was hanged, drawn and quartered at Tyburn in 1537. His descendant is the Duke of Leinster (see *Burke's Peerage*). The ruins of Silken Thomas's principal stronghold are at Maynooth.

SILURIST   the name given to himself by Henry Vaughan (1621–95), because he was born and lived near Brecon in South Wales (the Silures were known to the Romans as a tribe in that region). Vaughan was a distinguished religious poet whose works gained critical acclaim 100 years after his death.

SILVERLOCK   silvery haired.

SIMPLE   O.Fr. *simple* = honest, open, free from guile.

SIMPLE, The   Charles III of France, crowned at Rheims in 893. He was compelled by the Norsemen to allow them to settle in what was to become the province of Normandy in 911. He died a prisoner in 929.

SINGLER   O.Fr. *singler*, *seingler* = singular, possibly living alone.

SIRE, SYER(S)   O.Fr. *sire*, M.E. *sire* = master. Also can mean an elderly person.

SISTERS OF MERCY   applied to any religious community engaged in nursing work. Since the 19th century revival of religious orders in the Anglican Church, the term has been used in this way.

SIX PREACHERS   a number of preachers in Canterbury Cathedral founded by Archbishop Cranmer in 1541 to represent the new learning. Their work was quite considerable but by the 1941 Statutes of Canterbury Cathedral they are now required to preach one sermon a year for five years.

SKANDERBEG   the name of the national hero of Albania. His real name was George Katrioto (1405–68). His father was defeated by the Turks and had to give his sons as hostages. George was converted to Islam and educated at military school at Edirne (Adrianople). The Sultan Murad II gave him the name of Iskander (Alexander), which was made into Skanderbeg by the Albanians. Skanderbeg returned to Christianity and headed Albanian resistance to the Turks on whom he inflicted a long unbroken series of defeats.

SKEAT, SKEET   O.N. *skjat* = swift.

SKILL　　　O.N. *skil*, M.E. *skill* = reason, discernment.

SKILLMAN　　　O.N. *skil amatt* = trustworthy man.

SKOTKONUNG　　　King Olaf of Sweden, died c. 1022; the first Swedish King to be baptized.

SLAVEN, SLAVIN　　　O.Fr. *eslavine* = a pilgrim's mantle, name given to one who on return from pilgrimage wore the distinctive clothing.

SLAY, SLEE, SLEIGH　　　O.N. *slaegr* = clever, cunning, sly.

SLEEMAN, SLEMMINGS, SLIMMING　　　can come from root denoting cunning or sagacity in a man.

SLING　　　O.N. *slengr* = idler.

SLOW　　　sometimes from O.E. *slaw* = slow or sluggish.

SMALE, SMALL　　　O.E. *smael* = small, thin.

SMALLBONE　　　O.E. *smael* and *ban* = small bone.

SMART　　　O.E. *smeart* = quick, active.

SMEATHMAN　　　a smooth, suave man.

SMECTYMNUS　　　a supposed author's name but in fact made up of the initials of the five writers of a book in favour of Presbyterianism and against episcopacy. In 1641 John Milton wrote to defend the work.

SMEWINGS　　　O.N. *smeawine* = sagacious friend.

SMITH OF SMITHS, The　　　Sydney Smith (1771–1845), an English clergyman, renowned for his wit.

SMOLLETT　　　said to mean 'small head'.

SNAIL　　　O.E. *snezel* = snail, hence used of the slow and indolent.

SNEL(LE)　　　O.E. *snell* = smart or active. Cf. Sneller and Snelling.

SNOOK(S)　　　O.E. *snoc* = a projecting piece of land. A reference to a long-nosed person.

SNOW　　　O.E. being used of someone with snow-white hair. Cf. snowball, of a white patch on an otherwise dark head.

SNOW BABY　　　Marie Abnighhito Peary, daughter of the explorer, Commodore Peary, so termed by natives.

SNOW KING, The　　　King Gustavus Adolphus of Sweden (reigned 1611–32) was so termed by the Austrians.

SOAPY SAM　　　nickname of Samuel Wilberforce (1805–73), Bishop of Oxford, because of his unctuous way of speaking.

SOAR(ES)　　　O.Fr. *sor* = reddish brown. Cf. Sorrel.

SOCINIANS　　　more or less equivalent to the Unitarians, the latter having no belief in the distinctive doctrines of the Christian Faith, the Trinity, the Incarnation, Original Sin, the Fall – but the name is derived from the Latinized form of the name Sozini. This was borne by two Italians, Lelio Francesco Maria Sozini (1525–62) and his nephew Fausto Paolo Sozini (1539–1604). Their writings were by no means orthodox, but while Socinianism meaning denial of the Deity of Christ, is named after them, it appears that other writers were the founders of Unitarianism.

SOLE, SOAL(L)   sometimes literal, from O.Fr. *sol* = sole, lonely.

SOLID DOCTOR, The   Richard Middleton, a Franciscan theologian of late 13th century.

SOLLAS, SOLLIS   O.Fr. *solaz* = comfort.

SOLOMON OF FRANCE, The   Charles V (1364–80) le Sage.

SOLON OF PARNASSUS, The   term applied by Voltaire (q.v.) to Nicolas Boileau (Despréaux), with particular reference to the latter's *Ars poétique*. In this he set out in verse the literary principles which governed writing in the 18th century. The term *le legislateur de Parnasse* is in allusion to the celebrated Athenian legislator and reformer in 6th century BC about whom Herodotus tells some very interesting stories particularly of Solon's relations with Croesus, King of Lydia.

SOMASCHI   an order of Clerks regular founded in 1532 by St Jerome Emiliani at Seemasca, northern Italy, to work among the poor.

SONS OF LOYOLA   the Society of Jesus, see Jesuits.

SONS OF THUNDER   Boanerges (q.v.).

SOPHIST   a Greek term originally applied to the sages or wise men of Greece, but around the 4th century BC there arose a number of men who professed to impart knowledge on most subjects, for fees, of course, and who were distinguished from the philosophers or lovers of wisdom. In some of Plato's *Dialogues*, the Sophists are contrasted with Socrates, the truly wise man who professed that he knew nothing.

SORRIE   O.E. *sarig* = sorry, sad.

SOT, The   Selim II (1524–74), Sultan 1566–74, son of Suleiman the Magnificent (q.v.). He was murdered by the Janizaries (q.v.).

SOTER   Saviour, Antiochus I (324–262/1 BC), King of Syria, who took the name of 'Saviour' because of his victory over the Celts in Asia Minor.
   Ptolemy I (367–283 BC), reigned as Pharaoh of Egypt from 323. He had been one of Alexander the Great's successful generals; the name Soter was given to him by the Rhodians because he had saved their city in 304 BC from a siege.
   Possibly 'lucky' as applied to Seleucus III, King of Syria, for conquests in Asia Minor.

SOWDEN, SODEN   O.Fr. *soudan* = sultan, often derived from parts played in mysteries or pageants.

SPARE   O.E. *spaer* = sparing.

SPANISH BRUTUS, The   Alfonso Pérez de Guzmán (1258–1320), supposed to have given the sword with which the enemy could kill his son, rather than yield to treachery. The Brutus of the title was Junius Brutus who c. 509 BC condemned to death his two sons because they had joined in a conspiracy to restore the Tarquin monarchy to Rome.

SPANISH CAPTIVITY   a period of 60 years from 1580 during which Portugal was a conquered territory united to Spain and ruled as a Spanish province from Madrid.

SPANISH ENNIUS   Juan de Mena of Cordova (died 1456), from the Latin epic poet Ennius.

SPANISH LIVY   Juan Mariana (1536–1623), a Spanish Jesuit, one of the leading historians of Spain; also wrote *De Rege et Regis Institutione* (1559) in which he justified the assassination of a ruler hostile to Catholic interests e.g. in the Gunpowder Plot in England (1605).

SPARK(E)   O.N. *sparkr* = lively.

SPARROW   O.E. *speariva* = sparrow.

SPARROWHAWK,   O.E. *speark(e) afoc* = sparrow hawk, found sometimes
SPARHAWK   as a nickname before 1066.

SPARTAN   an adjective originally applied to the inhabitants of the ancient state in the Peloponnese, Greece, who lived under a very frugal regime. They practised (in theory at least) a form of communism. Hence the use of the term to denote someone living an extremely simple life, or who endures pain unflinchingly. For comment on Spartan habits, see Alcibiades; 'he crunched their disgusting coarse bread with relish and smacked his lips over the abominable black broth; it was as if he had never in his life eaten a meal prepared by a decent cook' (E. F. Benson, *The Life of Alcibiades*, 1928, p. 184).

SPEAK, SPEKE   O.Fr. *espeche* = woodpecker.

SPEED   O.E. *sped* = speed, success.

SPEIGHT, SPEAIGHT   O.E. *speoht*, M.E. *speight* = woodpecker.

SPENDLOVE, SPENDLAW   O.E. *spendan* = to spend or be lavish with + *lufu* = love; a philanderer.

SPIER, SPEIRS   M.E. *espyen*, O.Fr. *espier* = to spy.

SPILLMAN   O.E. *spilemann* = a jester (used pejoratively).

SPINK   M.E. *spink* = a finch (chaffinch).

SPIR(E)   O.E. *spir* = spike, used for a tall, thin man. Cf. Spirett, Spirit.

SPIRING   O.E. *spiring* = the tall one.

SPIRITUALISTS,   those who state that they are in communication with
SPIRITISTS   the deceased, by the services of mediums. A seance is recorded in I Samuel xxviii.8.

SPOONER, Rev. W. A.   (1844–1930) Warden of New College, Oxford, whose name is perpetuated in the term Spoonerism, that is a ludicrous transposition of letters. He is supposed to have given out the first line of a well-known hymn as 'Kinkering Kongs their titles take'. Spooner was very absent-minded and is said on one occasion when boarding a train to have kissed a porter and given his wife a tip.

SPOUSE OF JESUS, The   St Teresa of Avila. The English mystical poet, Crashaw thus terms her in a poem of 1632. The Rev. T. H. Passmore (1866–1941) wrote that all men who are saved become brides of Christ.

SPRACKLING,
SPRATLING,
SPRANKLING   O.E. *spraecaling*, from O.N. *sprakaleggr* = man with the creaking legs.

SPRAGG   Wiltshire dialect, *sprack* = lively.

SPREAD-EAGLISM   in the USA much the same violent nationalism as in Jingoism and Chauvinism (q.v.). The eagle with wings raised is the symbol of the USA.

SPRIGG(S)   Lonsdale dialect, *sprig* = a small, slender person.

SPRING   M.E. *spring*, reference to active person. Cf. Springall, sometimes from M.E. *springald* = young, active man. Cf. Springett.

SQUIRREL, SCURRELL   O.Fr. *esquirreu* = squirrel. 'Used contemptuously of men in the 16th century, but as a surname probably a nickname denoting agility or thrift' (Reaney, *Dict. of British Surnames*).

STABLE(S)   in some cases from O.Fr. *stable* = steadfast, resolute.

STAFF   O.E. *staef* = staff, used with reference to thinness.

STAGG   O.E. *stagga* = stag.

STAGIRITE, The   Aristotle the Philosopher (q.v.), he having been born in Stagira in Macedon.

STALKER   O.E. *stealcian*, M.E. *stalke* = to walk stealthily, especially in pursuit of game. A perfect description of the activity of a deer stalker albeit crawling is as necessary as walking in the art.

STALLAN, STALLION   O.Fr. *estalon* = stallion, as applied to a man, denoting one lascivious.

STALLWOOD   O.E. *staelwierlthe* = sturdy, brave.

STAMER   O.E. *stamera* = stammerer.

STAMMERER, The   i.e. le Bègue. Louis II of France, died 879, son of Charles II the Bald (q.v.).
Michael II, Byzantine emperor c. 829. 'Michael's accession was brought about in remarkable circumstances. He was awaiting death in prison on Christmas Eve for high treason; his friends murdered the emperor in Santa Sophia on Christmas Day and he was enthroned while still wearing his fetters' (C. A. Alington, *Europe*, London, Hollis & Carter, 1946, p.43).

STANDALONE, STANDERLINE a nickname for a self-reliant man. Cf. Standfast and Standwell.

STANHOPE an open one-seater carriage made for the Rev. the Hon. Fitzroy Stanhope (1787–1864). Also name given to a lens and to the first iron printing press both having been invented by Charles Stanhope, 3rd Earl of Stanhope (1753–1816). The latter was a 'politician and scientist, F.R.S., author of many inventions, disinherited all his children' (L. G. Pine, *New Extinct Peerage*, London, Heraldry Today, 1972, Chesterfield and Stanhope).

STANNARD, STONARD O.E. *stanheard* = stonehard.

STARK(S) O.E. *stearc* = firm, harsh. Cf. Starkey, 'The king was so very stark, and deprived his underlings of many a mark' (*The Anglo-Saxon Chronicle*, 1087, describing the character of William the Conqueror).

STARKMAN = strong, stern man.

STARLING, STERLING O.E. *staerling* = starling, perhaps with reference to chattering.

STARR M.E. *sterre* = star.

STARS AND STRIPES or STAR-SPANGLED BANNER 'Old Glory', the national flag of the USA.

STARTIFANT, STURTEVANT M.E. *sterten* and A.Fr. *avaunt*, meaning a messenger one who literally 'starts forward'.

STARTUP O.E. *steortan* = to leap or jump. This was the original form of upstart.

STARVATION DUNDAS name applied to Henry Dundas, 1st Lord Melville (1780–1811), by Walpole, because of a Bill to restrain trade with the Thirteen Colonies which might cause suffering to innocent and guilty alike.

STAY M.E. *staye* = support, prop. Cf. the hymn line 'O strength and stay upholding all creation'.

STEADFAST, The John (1468–1532) Elector of Saxony from 1525, a very firm supporter of Martin Luther. At the Diet of Speyer (1529) the Catholic majority gained control, but John was one of those who signed the minority's protest, thus becoming one of the original Protestants (q.v.).

STEADY M.E. *stedye* = steadfast, firm.

STEEL(S) O.E. *style*, *stele* = steel, of one as true as steel.

STEENIE the nickname given by James I of Great Britain to his handsome favourite, George Villiers, 1st Duke of Buckingham. St Stephen (Steenie) was regarded as a handsome saint because it is stated in Acts vi. 15 that his countenance was like that of an angel.

STEFF M.E. *stef* = firm, strong.

STENDHAL assumed pen name of Marie Henri Beyle (1783–1842).

STERN, STEARNE O.E. *styrne* = severe, stern.

STICK   O.E. *sticca* = rod or staff of wood used with reference to a tall thin man.

STICKETS, STICKLES   O.E. *sticol* = steep, rough as of a rough stickle-haired individual.

STINKOMALEE   a witticism much appreciated in 1828 when University College London, the beginning of London University, was erected. The abusive expression, coined by Theodore Hook, later became a name of pride.

STIRK   O.E. *styre* = bullock.

STITTLE, STUTTLE   O.E. *stytell*, to knock against, thus dialectal *stot* = stupid, awkward fellow.

STOCK, St Simon   (c. 1165–1265), a member and general of the Carmelite order (q.v.), an Englishman supposed to have lived as a young man in a tree trunk, hence the name stock.

STOICS   a body of Greek philosophers founded by Zeno of Citium (335–263 BC), the name being derived from the stoa or porch in which Zeno had taught. Stoicism had a philosophy of law, the law of nature and the law of conscience. The term stoicism in modern language does not denote the philosophical system, but an attitude of determined endurance of the difficulties of life. The Roman emperor Marcus Aurelius set forth in his *Meditations* many of the Stoic attitudes. For expositions of Stoic doctrine, see in Latin, Manilius' poem the *Astronomica* and in Greek, Plotinus' *The Enneads* (original texts, with translation, in Loeb Library).

STOLERMAN   a sturdy, courageous man.

STONEWALL JACKSON   nickname of General Thomas J. Jackson (1824–63) a Confederate general in the American Civil War whose men were said to stand in battle, like a stone wall. Also known as Deacon Jackson because of his deep involvement in the Presbyterian Church.

STORK   O.E. *storc* = stork, i.e. with reference to a long-legged man.

STORR   O.N. *storr* = big.

STOTT, STOAT   M.E. *stott* = bullock, with possible allusion to one wild as a young bullock.

STRAD   a violin made by Antonio Stradivarius (1644–1737) of Cremona.

STRAIGHT   M.E. *strezt* = straight, erect.

STRANGMAN, STRONGMAN   O.E. *strangmann* = strong man.

STREAKE, STREEK   O.E. *straec* = strong in a violent sense.

STREIT   M.E. *streit* = narrow, strict.

STRINGFELLOW   M.E. *streng* and O.E. *feolaga* = strong fellow.

STRIPLING, STRIBBLING   M.E. *stryplynge* = a youth.

STRONG, STRANG   O.E. *strang*, M.E. *strong* = strong.

STRONG, The

Augustus II (1670–1733), King of Poland (by electoral bribery) and also Elector of Saxony as Frederick Augustus I. He was not a successful monarch as he brought a great deal of suffering upon Poland. His sobriquet is due to his achievements in begetting illegitimate children, of whom the numbers are hardly credible. He left one legitimate son, Frederick Augustus II of Saxony and Augustus III of Poland. Among his bastards was the Marshal de Saxe, one of France's most celebrated soldiers.

Robert, died 866, was count of various territories near the river Loire, Count of Anjou and Blois, ancestor of the Capetian dynasty of France.

Sancho VII (died 1234) King of Navarre 1194–1234. He was the last Spanish-descended King of his country for 200 years. He fought with the allied Spanish army which won the decisive victory against the Moors at Las Navas de Tolosa in 1212.

STRONGBOW

the name by which Richard de Clare, 2nd Earl of Pembroke, is best known. As Strongbow he was immortalized as the leader of the Anglo-Norman invasion of Ireland in 1169–70. He came to Ireland to restore Dermot McMurrough, King of Leinster, to his kingdom. Strongbow married Eva, the daughter of Dermot. Henry II of England became jealous of Strongbow's success and himself landed in Ireland. Strongbow was then able to hold the conquered lands in Ireland as Henry's vassal. He died in 1176. His name was derived from the size and strength of the bow which he could bend and use, as with Ulysses and William the Conqueror. He inspired his soldiers with great confidence, one of the reasons for the easy victories which he achieved over the Irish with very small forces.

STRONGITHARM

a self-explanatory north of England nickname.

STUBB, STOBBE(S)

O.E. *stybb* = stub, denoting someone of short, stumpy 'height'.

STUBBORN, The

Le Hutin. Louis X (1314–16), King of France.

STUDIOS, St Theodore of

(769–826), so named from the monastery of Studios at Constantinople which he revived as part of his monastic reforms.

STUNT

O.E. *stunt* = foolish.

STUPOR MUNDI, THE WONDER OF THE WORLD

Frederick II (1194–1250), Holy Roman Emperor. The Hohenstaufen dynasty did not long survive. Frederick was more a modern than a medieval man in his outlook and his characteristics. It was Matthew Paris who described him as *stupor mundi et immutator mirabilis* (wonderfully versatile). He wrote a book on falconry which is regarded as being in the critical spirit of modern science (for full details, see L. G. Pine, *The History of Hunting*, London, League Against Cruel Sports, 1973, p.120).

STURDEE

O.Fr. *estordet* = reckless, M.E. impetuously brave.

STURGEON	O.Fr. *esturgeon* = the fish.
STUTTER(S)	M.E. *stutte, stoten* = to stutter.
STYLITES, St Simeon	(c. 390–459) the first of those called the pillar saints, from Greek στῦλος, a pillar. He was a Syrian born in Cilicia and after an austere life on the ground, spent the rest of his life on top of a pillar, some 60 feet high. He exercised great influence on the pilgrims and inquirers who came to him.˙The subject of a fine poem by Lord Tennyson.
SUBLAPSARIAN or INFRALAPSARIAN	one who holds that God devised His scheme of redemption after Adam's lapse or fall.
SUBTLE DOCTOR	Duns Scotus (c. 1265–1308). See Doctor Subtilis.
SUCKER	O.E. *sucan* = to suck, a sucker.
SUCKLING	O.E. *sucan* = to suck; hence a suckling.
SUDBURY, Simon of	Archbishop of Canterbury, also Chancellor and as such initiated unpopular taxation. He also took moderate measures against the Lollards. In the Peasants' Revolt of 1381 he was captured and beheaded by the rebels.
SUFFRAGETTE	a woman who agitated for the right to vote before 1914. One such was killed when she came in front of the horses at a Derby. Suffrage = a vote.
SUGG	O.E. *sucga*, M.E. *sugge* = a bird.
SUN KING, The	Le Roi Soleil, Louis XIV King of France, was 5 years old when he came to the throne in 1643. He reigned until 1715. His reign was distinguished by a great extension of French power and influence; by a brilliant artistic success; and by the building of Versailles, a palace imitated by all the continental sovereigns. Louis's reign closed in the disasters of the War of the Spanish Succession, and the impoverishment of France. See Sir Winston Churchill's *Life of Marlborough*.
SUNG	an ancient feudal state in China, which was taken as the name of his dynasty by the founder Chao K'uang-yin. The dynasty lasted from 960 to 1279.
SUNNIS	followers of the Prophet's way, the orthodox Moslems, distinguished from the main other division of Shi'ites (q.v.).
SUPERBUS	Tarquinius, the Proud, King of Rome 534–510 BC. His son was 'False' Sextus (q.v.).
SUPRALAPSARIAN	contrary to Sublapsarian (q.v.), who holds that God's scheme of redemption was devised from the foundation of the world and therefore before Adam's lapse or fall.
SUTTLE, SUTTELL	A.Fr. *sotil* = subtle, clever, cunning.
SWADDLER	a term of abuse applied to various Protestant bodies originally by a Catholic who was so ignorant of Scripture that he thought the term swaddling in St Luke's Gospel to be ridiculous.
SWALLOW	O.E. *swealwe* = swallow, sometimes as a nickname.

SWAN(N)	sometimes a nickname from O.E. *swan* = swan.
SWAN OF AVON	William Shakespeare, so described by Ben Jonson.
SWART	O.N. *svartr*, O.E. *sweart* = swarthy.
SWEARS	sometimes from O.E. *sweore* = neck.
SWEATMAN, SWEETMAN	O.E. *swetemann* = sweet man.
SWEDENBORGIANISM	a movement of thought among Christians propounded in many volumes by Emanuel Swedenborg (1688–1772), whose name was originally Swedborg. He was a brilliant Swedish scientist and also a mystic.
SWEDISH NIGHTINGALE	Jenny Lind (1820–87), Swedish soprano, operatic singer and after 1849 devoted to concert work and oratorio.
SWEET	O.E. *swera* = sweet. Cf. Sweetapple and Sweetlove.
SWEET SINGER OF THE REFORMATION	sometimes applied to Philip Melanchthon (1497–1560), whose real name was Schwarzerd. He was a follower of Luther but much more reasonable.
SWEETSER, SWITZER	sweet sire.
SWIFT	O.E. *swift* = swift or fleet.
SWORD OF GOD	Khaled Ibn al Waled (died 642), who conquered Syria for Islam.
SWORD OF ROME	Marcellus who fought against Hannibal and was killed in battle against him 216–214 BC.
SYBARITE	a person excessively devoted to luxury, from the people of Sybaris in southern Italy, famed for their self-indulgence.
SYLVESTRINES	an order founded in 1231 by St Sylvester Gozzolini in Italy; akin to the Benedictines.

T

TABORITES	see Moravian Brethren.
TAE PINGS	Chinese rebels 1850–64, the name meaning universal peace; they were led by a man called Hung-sew-tseuen, who conceived the idea of universal peace being achieved by fighting. The rebels were subdued by Chinese Gordon (q.v.).
TAIT, TEYTE	O.N. *teitr* = gay.
TALL, The	Le Long, Philip V (1316–22), King of France.
TALL BROTHERS, The	four monks who upheld the doctrines of Origenism in the 4th century in Alexandria and in Constantinople.
TALMADGE, TOLLEMACHE	O.Fr. *talemache* = knapsack. The original form of the surname Tollemache, was Talmash, and the nickname (knapsack) must go back to a remote period, as this family can be traced to the 11th century. Cf. Scrope.
TANTIVY MEN	High Churchmen of the period after the Restoration of Charles II in 1660. Riding tantivy was to ride at a fast gallop, so these men were supposed to be riding fast to Rome.
TARANTAISE, St Peter of	(died 1175), a Cistercian monk who became Archbishop of Tarantaise in the Savoy. Also the name of Pope Innocent V 1276.
TARDEW, TARDIF	O.Fr. *tardif*, Fr. *tardieu*, sluggish, hence tardy.
TARSUS, St Theodore of	(c. 602–90), an Asiatic Greek who became Archbishop of Canterbury in 668. He had great influence on the nascent English church, and to him is due its parochial organization.
TARSUS, Saul of	better known at St Paul, the Apostle of the Gentiles.
TARTARS	really Tatars, a Turkish speaking people living now along the Volga river in the USSR, but in former times the name was used of various semi-nomadic tribes. Their actions were so brutal and cruel that they were said to have come from Tartarus, the ancient name for hell.
TEAGUE	a contemptuous term in 17th and 18th century for an Irishman, e.g. in the famous song Lillibullero.
TEAL(E)	from M.E. *tele* = water fowl.
TEGART	O.E. *tegga* = young sheep. Cf. also Tegg, Tigg = young sheep.
TELFER, TAILLEFER, TELFORD, TULLIVER	from O.Fr. *taille* = 'cut-iron or iron cleaver, used as a personal name, an original nickname for a man who could cleave clean through the iron armour of his foe' (Reaney, *Dict. of British Surnames*). This was the name

of the famous Norman, Taillefour, who had permission to begin the battle of Hastings and was slain by his third antagonist.

TEMPEST

O.Fr. *tempeste* = a violent storm, i.e. agitation or perturbation.

TEMPLARS, or KNIGHTS TEMPLAR

an order of military monks who added to the three usual vows a fourth, to fight in defence of the Holy Land. Founded in 1118 by Hugh de Payens, a knight of Champagne. The order was suppressed in 1312 by the Pope, after King Philip the Fair of France (q.v.) had treated the Knights with great cruelty.

TENCH

O.Fr. *tenche* = a tench (a fat and sleek fish).

TENTH MUSE

applied to the poetess Sappho. Then subsequently to various women writers, including Hannah More (1745–1833).

TERRIBLE, The

Ivan IV (1530–84). In 1547 he was crowned Czar and Grand Prince of all Russia. His name was gained because of his numerous cruelties and fits of rage, in one of which he killed his own son. It appears, however, that by the bulk of the people he was regarded as a good ruler (see Ian Grey, *Ivan the Terrible*, London, History Book Club, 1966). Another form of the name is John the Dread.

TESTAR, TESTER

O.Fr. *testard*, from *teste* = head, i.e. big head, bumptious.

TEUTONIC ORDER

an order of military monks on the lines of the Templars (q.v.) founded 1190 in Palestine. From c. 1226 the Order turned its crusading activity against the heathen Prussians. In 1525 the Grand Master became a Lutheran. The Order still survives engaged in charitable work.

TEW

Welsh, *Tew* = fat, plump.

THAT MAN IN THE WHITE HOUSE

US President Franklin Delano Roosevelt (1882–1945).

THAUMATURGUS

wonder worker, the name bestowed on St Gregory of Pontus (c. 213–c. 270), a very active bishop whose reputation was so great that the most extraordinary miracles, like the removal of a mountain, were attributed to him. He wrote among other works an *Exposition of the Faith*, which was said to have been given to him by St John at the command of the Blessed Virgin Mary, the first recorded instance of an appearance of the Virgin.

THEATINES

an order founded in Rome in 1524 by St Cajetan and Gian Pietro Caraffa, the latter being Bishop of Chietti or Theate, hence the name popularly given to the Order. The official name is Clerks Regular of the Divine Providence.

THEBAN EAGLE, The

Pindar (c. 522 BC–c. 440 BC) the greatest of Greek lyric poets who was born at Cynoscephalae, near Thebes.

THEBES, St Paul of (died c. 340) the first Christian hermit, in Thebaid in Egypt.

THEEDAM M.E. *theodam* = thriving.

THEODORIC Dietrich of Bern, see under the Great.

THEOLOGIAN OF CHURCH UNITY Johann Adam Möhler (1796–1838), profoundly concerned with unity of all Christians in one (Roman) Church.

THEOS the God, Antiochus II (c. 287–247 BC), King of Syria. His title foreshadows the Roman use of Divine Caesar and the practice of deification of the Roman emperors. 'The designation of Antiochus II as Theos in public documents indicates that the Seleucid Kingdom had by this time adopted the cult of the living ruler' (*Ency. Britannica*).

THEOSOPHY literally God wisdom, a vague term which has been applied to numerous systems which claim intuitive knowledge of the Divine.

THERAPEUTAE literally physicians, see Essenes.

THESSALONICA, Simon of (died 1429), Archbishop of Thessalonica, a considerable writer on Byzantine theology.

THEWLESS O.E. *theawleas* = ill-mannered, from O.E. *theaw* = usage, and *leas* = vicious, immoral.

THICK(S) M.E. *thikke* = thick set.

THIEF OF TUSKINO term applied to a pretender to the Russian throne, the Pseudo-Dimitri (Dimitri being the legal heir of the old Russian line) who caused an uprising in 1608. As a result of Russian disunity, Polish troops occupied Moscow and nearly succeeded in placing a Polish prince on the Russian throne. The Pseudo-Dimitri was killed in 1610. In the end the young Michael Romanov was chosen as Czar in 1613. He was descended from a nephew of the first wife of Ivan IV, the Terrible.

THIN, THYNNE O.E. *thynne* = thin. It is advisable to remember that this surname in the case of the Marquess of Bath's family is derived from 'at-the-inn'. Their original surname was Boteville, but the acquisition of Thynne is described in e.g. *Burke's Peerage*, post 1949 editions.

THOMAS OF CANTERBURY, St see Thomas Becket.

THOMISTS adherents to the teachings of St Thomas Aquinas.

THOROUGH nickname of the Earl of Strafford who was an uncompromising ruler of Ireland. He was executed in 1641.

THREE KINGS OF COLOGNE often simply known as The Three Kings; the three wise men from the East mentioned in St Matthew's Gospel (though no number is given there). By tradition their names were Caspar, Melchior and Balthazar, and their bones were held to be enshrined in Cologne Cathedral where the shrine still exists.

THRESHERS an Irish faction opposed to the Orangemen and the payment of tithes, who signed their minatory letters, 'Capt. Thresher'.

THROSSELL, THRUSTLE O.E. *throstke* = a nickname from the bird, now spelt as throstle = song thrush.

THRUSH, THRESH O.E. *thrysce* = a thrush.

THUM possibly as in 'Tom Thumb' a reference to size, but perhaps from loss of thumb.

THUNDERBOLT, The Ottoman Turkish Sultan Bayazid I (1354–1403), called Yildirim (Thunderbolt). Name often appears as Bajazet. He was successful until engaged in war with Timur the Lame (q.v.), when he was captured and died, perhaps by suicide.

THUNDERER, The the name bestowed on *The Times* newspaper in the mid 19th century.

TIGER, The the French statesman, Georges Benjamin Clemenceau (1841–1929). Also known as Père la Victoire for his energetic prosecution of the First World War.

TINE-MAN, The Archibald Douglas, 4th Earl of Douglas, died 1424. The nickname can be translated as 'the losing man', for although a gallant soldier and leader, Douglas was decisively beaten on three major occasions. He was defeated by Henry Percy at Homildon Hill, 1402 (where Douglas was wounded in five places and lost an eye). He joined Percy and the other English rebels in the battle of Shrewsbury, 1403, where he became the prisoner of Henry IV of England. Finally he took service with the French king to fight the English. He received many honours but at Verneuil in 1424 he lost the battle and his life. He is a character in Shakespeare's *Henry IV* Pt 1.

TIPLADY, TOPLADY all probably names for a libertine. Cf. *Othello*, i. lines 88–9; 'Even now, now, very now, an old black ram, is tupping your white ewe'.

TIRRELL, TERRELL, TYRILL Fr. *tirand* = one who pulls on the reins, i.e. obstinate.

TITI, PRINCE Frederick, Prince of Wales, eldest son of George II but pre-deceased his father. Supposed to have written memoirs under this pseudonym.

TITLER, TYTLER M.E. *title* = a tell-tale.

TITO *nom de guerre* (lit. 'do this, do that') of Josip Broz (1892–1978), the leader of the Yugoslav partisans in the Second World War and, from 1953, President and ruler of the Federal People's Republic of Yugoslavia.

TOD(D) M.E. *tod(de)* = fox, used now more in Scotland.

TOMMY or TOMMY ATKINS the British private soldier; name supposed to be derived from a specimen guide to filling up enlistment manuals in which the guide form had the name Thomas Atkins.

TOOGOOD, TOWGOOD, TUGWOOD	= too good, like the Scots unco guid.
TOOTH	O.E. *toth* = tooth; reference to one who had prominent teeth.
TORIES	an Anglicized spelling of the Irish *toraidhe* = pursuer. 'The bogs of Ireland afforded a refuge to Popish outlaws, much resembling those who were afterwards known as Whiteboys. These were called Tories. The name of Tory was therefore given to Englishmen who refused to concur in excluding a Roman Catholic prince from the throne'. Thus Lord Macaulay, writing of the reign of Charles II (*History of England*, chapter 2). Referring to this term he said that it did not seem likely soon to become obsolete; it is still used colloquially and in writing, usually in a pejorative sense, to denote members of the Conservative Party.
TORIL	O.Fr. *tor* = bull, here a diminutuve. Cf. Torr.
TORTIS, TORTUS	M.E. *tortusre* = tortoise, in reference to slowness.
TORTOR INFANTIUM	Torturer of infants, see Doctor Acutus.
TOTT	M.E. *totte* = simpleton.
TOUGH, TOW(ES)	O.E. *tok*, M.E. *togh* = vigorous, stubborn.
TRACTARIANISM	the name given to the early course of the Oxford Movement and derived from the *Tracts for the Times*, which were written between 1833 and 1841 by Newman, Pusey, Keble and other High Church leaders.
TRAMONTANE	Ultramontane being the French equivalent.
TRANSLATOR-GENERAL	Fuller thus described Philemon Holland (1552–1637), who translated many Greek and Latin classics.
TRAPNELL	O.Fr. *trop isuel* = too swift.
TRAPPISTS	members of a branch of the Cistercians of the strict observance who take their popular name from La Trappe in France. Begun in 1662 by A. J. Le B. de Rance. The life of the monks is (or was) marked by extreme austerity; silence is imposed for most of the day, and the monks keep their coffins beside them. An interesting reference to the Order is in Robert Hichen's novel, *The Garden of Allah*.
TRAVELL, TRAVIL	O.Fr. *travailler* = to afflict, a reference to trouble.
TREACHER	O.Fr. *trecheor* = deceiver.
TREADWELL	tread well.
TRETT	M.E. *tret* = neat or graceful.
TRICKER	M.E. *trik*, O.Fr. *trique* = trick, in reference to a cheat. Cf. also Trickett.
TRIGG(S)	O.N. *tryggr* = true, trustworthy.
TRIMMER	name self-applied by George Savile, Marquess of Halifax, *temp.* Charles II, to show that he did not hold with either extreme in politics.

TRIPPETT	O.Fr. *tripot* = an evil scheme or trick.
TROJAN	anciently the inhabitants of Troy in Asia Minor. Used as a synonym for brave or hard-working folk.
TROTT	sometimes from A.Fr. *trote* = old woman or hag.
TROUT	O.E. *truht* = trout.
TROYT(E)	O.Fr. *troit* = quarrel.
TRUEBODY	true man.
TRUELOVE	O.E. *treowe* + *lufu* = true love.
TRUEMAN, TROWMAN	faithful, trusty man.
TRUMBLE, TRUMBULL	O.E. *trumbeald* = strong bold.
TRUSHER	trusshare, i.e. a poacher who carried off the hare.
TRUTH	M.E. *trouthe* = faithfulness, loyalty.
TRUTHTELLER, The	a name given to Alfred the Great (q.v.).
TRY(E)	M.E. *trie, trize* = excellent.
TUCKER	occasionally from Fr. *tout coeur* = courage.
TULCHAN BISHOPS	the titular bishops created by the Scottish Presbyterians after the Covenant of Leith, 1572. They were not consecrated as bishops being merely appointees. They disappeared by 1580. The word tulchan comes from Gaelic *tulachan*, hillock.
TUMBLEDOWN DICK	Richard Cromwell; see also Queen Dick.
TUNKERS	from German *tunken*, to dip. The name of a German Protestant sect originating in 1708. So named from their way of bestowing baptism. Also known as Dunkers or Dunkards. The official name is the Church of the Brethren.
TURK	sometimes used as a nickname from the Crusading period (from 1147).
TURNBULL	thought to be a nickname for strength, i.e. from a man who turned a bull. Dr Black (*Surnames of Scotland*) refers to Hector Boece's story of the name as derived from a man who saved the life of King Robert the Bruce by turning a bull which had threatened to gore the king.
TURNPENNY	a person keen on a profit.
TURRECREMATA	the Latin form of the surname of Cardinal Juan de Torquemada (1388–1468), a Spanish Dominican theologian. He must not be confused with his nephew Tomás de Torquemada (1420–98), the Grand Inquisitor of Spain who is held, on reasonable estimates, to have been responsible for burning 2,000 persons.
TURRIANUS	Latin form of surname of Francisco Torres (c. 1504–84), a Spanish Jesuit, versed in patristics (but without critical sense) and a prominent controversialist.
TUTANKHAMEN	the name taken by the Pharaoh, who changed from his original Tutankhaton, because he had returned to

the cult of the old gods. See Ikhnaton. Tutankhamen (c. 1371–1352 BC) was Pharaoh from c. 1361 to 1352. His only importance is the discovery in 1922 by Lord Carnarvon and Howard Carter of his unrifled tomb with all its magnificent treasures.

TURTLE

M.E. *turtel* = turtle dove, or from Fr. *tourtel* (Latin *tortus*) = crooked.

TWIGG

O.E. *twigge* = a slender shoot.

TYRE, William of

(c. 1130–85), Archbishop of Tyre, a historian born in Palestine.

TYSON

O.Fr. *tison* = firebrand.

U

UITLANDERS

foreigners, name given by the Boers in the Transvaal Republic to non-Boers who came into their territories to seek for gold and diamonds. The Boer refusal to give them full franchise was one of the causes of the South African War 1899–1902.

ULPH

O.N. *ulfr*, O. Da. and O. Sw. *ulf* = wolf.

ULTRAMONTANES

literally those beyond the mountains, a term used as far back as the 11th century, and referring to those who upheld the authority of the Pope as against the national churches which compose the Roman Catholic church. Ultramontanism has often been the characteristic of the convert, e.g. Cardinal Manning, who was certainly one of the main instruments in securing the triumph of Ultramontanism in Vatican Council I (1870), when the dogma of the Pope's Infallibility was defined.

UNCLE SAM

the figure which symbolizes the USA. It is said to date from the 1812 war with Great Britain, when a supplier of beef to the US Army was known as Uncle Sam Wilson. The figure is always represented as a tall, white-haired man wearing a long swallow-tailed coat, a tall hat and striped trousers.

UNIAT

a term applied to those churches in Asia and in Eastern Europe which are in communion with the See of Rome, but which retain their rites in their own language and also practices of communion in both kinds, and the marriage of the clergy. There are thought to be 10½ million of Uniats.

UNITARIANS

see Socinians.

UNIVERSAL DOCTOR

Alain de Lille (1114–1203).

UNLUCKY, The

Ez-zogoiby, Boabdil, the last Moorish sovereign of Granada (1491). 'He was ever lamenting his evil star, against which he felt it was useless to struggle. "Verily" he would exclaim after every reverse "it is written in the book of fate that I should be unlucky and that the kingdom should come to an end under my rule"' (S. Lane-Poole, *The Moors in Spain*, 1897, ch. xiii).

UNREADY, The

applied by his contemporaries to Ethelred II (978–1016); *unraed*, strictly interpreted, is better rendered as 'no counsel' or 'evil counsel'. However translated, the description accorded well with the features of the worst reign in English history. Ethelred was ill-omened from the start because although only 10 years old at his succession, he succeeded to the throne only because the legitimate king, Edward the Martyr (q.v.) his half-brother was murdered by Ethelred's mother in order to secure his succession.

UNWIN, HUNWIN O.E. *unwine* = unfriend, enemy.

UPPER TEN or UPPER TEN THOUSAND a slang term for the members of high society. The term was first used of the high society of New York.

UPRIGHT O.E. *upriht* = upright.

URSELL Latin *ursus* = bear, ursel being the diminutive.

URSULINES name given to the oldest teaching order of women in the Roman Church. Founded in 1535 at Brescia by St Angela Merci as a body of virgins dedicated to Christian education, but living in their own homes. The name was derived from the story of St Ursula and her 11,000 virgin martyrs. Strict vows and conventual life were introduced later.

USSELL, UZZELL O.Fr. *oisel* = bird.

UTICA (Uticensis) Cato the Younger (95–46) who was born there. He committed suicide when the Republican cause was defeated. *Victrix causa deis placuit sed victa Catoni* was Lucan's tribute to him in the *Pharsalia*. Addison wrote a tragedy, *Cato*, in which the hero is made to say after he has begun his suicide, 'I fear I've been too hasty.'

UTILITARIANISM a term invented by John Stuart Mill to describe a system of morals designed for the greatest happiness of the greatest number. Jeremy Bentham was the founder of this ethical philosophy which he called Utility.

UTRAQUISTS of both kinds, the practice of the Hussites (q.v.) to receive Holy Communion under both species of bread and wine.

V

VAHID-ED-DIN

(the Black Sultan), Mohammed VI (1861–1926), the 36th and last Ottoman Sultan of Turkey, from 1918 to 1922, who earned his nickname by his intrigues in aid of his personal safety. When his regime collapsed he was rescued by a British warship, and died in San Remo, Italy.

VAISEY, FEASEY, PHEYSEY, LENFESTY

and numerous variants from A.Fr. *enveise* = playful.

VALESIANS

heretical sect founded in 3rd century by one Valesius in Arabia; their main recorded tenet was that castration is necessary to salvation.

VALIANT, VAILLANT

O.Fr. *vaillant* = brave.

VALIANT, The

John V (Jean de Montfort 1389–1442), Duke of Brittany from 1399 to his death, seen as a builder of Breton prosperity, a fact which perhaps explains his strange political manoeuvres.

VALLAMBROSAN ORDER

so named from the parent house at Vallambrosa (made famous by Milton's *Paradise Lost* i. 303) some 20 miles east of Florence. St John Gualbert founded the Order c. 1036, the rule being based on that of St Benedict but with greater austerity: ' . . . angel forms who lay entranced, Thick as autumnal leaves that strew the brooks in Vallambrosa'.

VANDALS

a tribe from the Baltic which ravaged part of the Roman Empire and sacked Rome of its treasures; hence the name for the modern savage who destroys works of art or public utilities.

VANTAGE

M.E. *vantage* = advantage, property.

VARANGIAN

the name of the foreign guard of the Byzantine Emperor. The Varangians were composed of Norsemen and of Anglo-Saxons, many of the latter having volunteered for this service after the Norman Conquest of England. The meaning of the word is variously explained, but the etymology adopted by Sir Walter Scott was the German *Fortganger* or forthgoer, wanderer or exile (Scott, *Count Robert of Paris*, note 3, Varangian Guard).

VAUS(E), VAUX

in some cases from O.E. *fals* = false.

VEAL(E), VEEL

O.Fr. *vieil* = old, or O.Fr. *viel* = calf.

VENERABLE, The

Peter (c. 1092–1156), 8th Abbot of Cluny; 'His moderation and gentleness earned him the veneration of his contemporaries' (*Oxford Dictionary of the Christian Church*).

VENERABLE BEDE   a title used for him within a century of his death. Bede (c. 673–735) was an encyclopedic and biblical scholar, whose book, *The Ecclesiastical History of the English People*, is a prime source for English history. Bede is held in the highest esteem by modern historians, on account of his accuracy; it may be noted that his *History* includes many miracles. In 1899 Pope Leo XIII declared him a Doctor of the Church.

VENTERS   M.E. *venters*, M.E. *aventurous*, i.e. venturous.

VENTRE, VENTURE   M.E. *aventure*. Cf. Ventura.

VERHUEL   Napoleon III, origin of name unknown.

VERITY   Fr. *vérité* = truth.

VICAR OF HELL   the jesting title given by Henry VIII to John Skelton, his court poet, who was Vicar of Diss, Norfolk. Dis in classical lore being King of the infernal regions.

VICTORINES   the canons regular of the abbey of St Victor in Paris; they included many famous scholars and mystics, but the abbey was overthrown in the French Revolution.

VICTORIOUS, The   Parvez, name taken by Khosran II (590–628), King of Persia of the Sassanian dynasty, who overran the Byzantine Empire, capturing Jerusalem and the True Cross, but was worsted by the Emperor Heraclius and compelled to restore all his conquests.

VIETNAM   people of the south; not strictly a nickname, it has acquired considerable currency owing to recent terrible events. The name was given by the Emperor Gia-long of Vietnam in 1802. The French divided Vietnam into Tonking, Annam and Cochin China, which with Laos and Cambodia formed the French colony of Indo-China. Nam-Viet = southern land. Annam = pacified south.

VIGAR, VIGGOR   O.Fr. *vigor* = vigour.

VIGARD   O.Fr. *vigoro(u)s* = hardy, strong.

VIKING   a word derived from O.N. for creek, which with suffix -ing, denoted a dweller in an inlet of the sea. Very early in the Scandinavian tongues Viking denoted a seaman and very rapidly a pirate. In Old English the form *wicingas* was used as in the *Anglo-Saxon Chronicle* under year 879. The Vikings were men coming from the Scandinavian countries from about 800 to 1050 either to loot or, in some cases, to settle in other lands. They constituted a terrible menace to Western Christendom and were responsible for the destruction of Ireland's Golden Age.

VINCENTIAN   a Lazarist (q.v.).

VINEGAR JOE   General Joseph Warren Stillwell (1883–1946), for his sharp honesty.

VIR INCOMPARABILIS   A man incomparable. Thus James Bradley was described by foreign astronomers. Bradley (1697–1762), both divine and astronomer, was the discoverer of the aberration of light. He was an M. A. Balliol College, Oxford; D. D. by diploma Oxford, Astronomer Royal, member of Council of Royal Society.

VIRGIN, VIRGOE, VERGO   possibly from taking the part of the Blessed Virgin Mary in a mystery play.

VIRGIN QUEEN   Elizabeth I of England.

VISITANDINES   or members of the Visitation Order of contemplatives founded by St Francis de Sales and St Jane Frances de Chantal in 1610.

VITENSIS   Victor (late 5th century), Bishop of Vita in North Africa, wrote on the history of Arian persecutions of Catholics.

VOLANT   O.Fr. *voler* = to fly, hence = agile.

VOLTAIRE   the well-known pseudonym of François Marie Arouet (1694–1778), the famous French writer, who adopted the name after the success of his first tragedy *Oedipe* (1718).

VOYLE   Welsh *moel* = bald.

W

WA

dwarfs, term used in Chinese records for the Japanese. 'The *Wei-chih* of about A.D. 292 speaks of the Wa (dwarf) people of regions easily identified as Kyushu and West Japan' (W. Scott Norton, *Japan, its History and Culture*, New York, Thomas Crowell, 1970, p. 8; also R. P. Porter, *Japan*, Newton Abbot, David & Charles, 1919, p.3).

WAACS

members of the Women's Army Auxiliary Corps, raised in the First World War.

WAHHABIS

members of the Moslem Puritan movement founded by Mohammed ibn Abd al-Wahhat (1703–92) which believes in the closest adherence to the original teachings of Islam in the Koran and the Traditions (Hadith). The movement has been associated with the fortunes of the Sa'udi dynasty and has greatly increased with the establishment of the kingdom of Saudi Arabia. Wahhabi is used only by non-Moslems; the name used of themselves by the Wahhabis is Muwahhid, meaning unitarians.

WAKE

'clearly a nickname, trans. by Latin vigil = watchful, alert. The most common early form is Wac, found chiefly in Staffs, Lincs, Leics and Yorks where a Scandinavian origin is possible, probably O.N. vakr = watchful' (Reaney, *Dict. of British Surnames*). For the history of the great medieval family of Wake see *Burke's Peerage*, 1970, where the descent in the female line from the great hero Hereward (q.v.), the last man in England to resist the Norman is given. The title or nickname of the Wake was given retrospectively in the 13th century to Hereward because he was then regarded as the ancestor of the Wakes. For a thrilling account of the Last of the English, see Charles Kingsley's *Hereward the Wake*.

WAKE, The

Hereward, the last man in England to resist William the Conqueror. He held out in the Camp of Refuge on the Isle of Ely until betrayed by traitor monks. The details of Hereward's life are obscure. Charles Kingsley's novel *Hereward the Wake* has a well-reasoned preface as to his hero's parentage. E. A. Freeman in his *Norman Conquest* vol. IV gives a lengthy account of the sources for Hereward's history. He wrote that the name of Wake was given to Hereward in the Chronicle of John of Peterborough whom Freeman terms 'a writer of uncertain date and personality'. *De Gestis Herewardi Saxonis* has the Latin text with the English translation 'from an original manuscript contained in a book compiled by Robert of Swaffham, in the possession of the Dean and Chapter of Peterborough' (1895). The family of Wake, Baronets, claim descent from Hereward in the female line. The subject has been examined by the distinguished scholar, Sir Ian Moncreiffe (*Genealogical Magazine*, June 1967) in which he stated 'The present writer's own opinion is that the Wakes do descend in the female line from Hereward.'

WAKER   O.E. *wacor*, M.E. *waker* = watchful, vigilant.

WALAFRID THE SQUINTER   Walafrid Strabo (c. 808–49) a German theologian.

WALDENSES   a small body founded by Peter Waldo of Lyons in the later 12th century, hence their name. They still exist as a small Protestant church.

WALE   M.E. *wale* = excellent, noble.

WALLER(S)   in some cases from O.Fr. *galure*, *gallier* = a coxcomb, or a man of pleasant temper.

WARE(S)   O.E. *waer*, M.E. *war(e)* = wary, prudent.

WARLIKE, The   Frederick I (1370–1428), Elector of Saxony from 1423.

WARLOCK, WERLOCK   O.E. *waerloga* = traitor, enemy or devil.

WARME   O.E. *wearm* = warm, hence zealous.

WARRIOR QUEEN, The   so styled by William Cowper in his poem, *Boadicea* (now spelt Boudicca), she was Queen of the Iceni in (the later named) Norfolk and Suffolk, and rose in revolt against the Romans. Verulamium (St Albans) Camulodunum (Colchester) and Londinium were destroyed, but Boadicea's army was completely destroyed by the Roman Governor, Suetonius and Boadicea took poison.

WASP(E)   O.E. *waeos* = wasp.

WATCH TOWER BIBLE AND TRACT SOCIETY   See Pastor Russell.

WATER POET   John Taylor (1580–1654), a Thames Waterman who wrote many poems.

WAYNFLETE, William of   (c. 1395–1486), Bishop of Winchester.

WEATHER(S)   O.E. *wether* = sheep.

WEE FREES   when the Free Church of Scotland united in 1900 with the United Presbyterian Church, the minority who did not agree to the union were termed Wee Frees.

WEEPING PHILOSOPHER   Heraclitus, Greek philosopher of the 5th century BC, because he wept for the folly of mankind.

WEEPING SAINT   St Swithin.

WELCOME, WILLICOMBE   from O.E. *cemban*, to comb, the past participle being 'well kempt, well combed'.

WELF   the name of a dynasty which began with Count Welf in Bavaria early in the 9th century. The Welfs were hostile to the Hohenstaufens, and this tradition led to the Italian use of the word in the form of Guelph (q.v.) as a supporter of the Papacy against the Empire.

WELFITT	well fed.
WELLBELOVE(D)	Of obvious application.
WELLBELOVED, The	Le Bien aimé, Louis XV of France, great grandson of Louis XIV whom he succeeded in 1715. Thomas Carlyle began his *French Revolution* with a chapter entitled 'Louis the Well Beloved' and mentioned that when this prince was seriously ill in 1744 'the churches resounded with supplications and groans; the prayers of priests and people were every moment interrupted by their sobs; and it was from an interest so dear and tender that this surname of Bien-Aimé fashioned itself'. Also applied to Charles VI of France (1386, reigned 1380–1422), who had recurrent fits of madness.
WESLEYANS	followers of John Wesley, and members of the Dissenting Church which he founded.
WHALE, WHALL	O.E. *hwael*, M.E. *whal* = whale, 'used of any large fish including the walrus, grampus and the porpoise. The original sense was "roller" and the name may refer to gait or to size and weight' (Reaney, *Dict. of British Surnames*).
WHATMAN, WHEATMAN	O.E. *hwaetmann* = bold, brave man.
WHEAT, WEET	O.E. *hwaet* = active, bold.
WHIGS	described in *Oxford English Dictionary* as of unascertained origin but presumably related to whey, i.e. part of milk which remains liquid when rest forms curds, applied to sour milk. Lord Macaulay (*History of England*, ch.2, Reign of Charles II) thus relates the first use of the term. Some of the Covenanters of Scotland had risen against the government and had with difficulty been put down. 'These zealots were most numerous among the rustics of the western lowlands who were vulgarly called Whigs. Thus the appellation of Whig was fastened on the Presbyterian Zealots of Scotland, and was transferred to those English politicians who showed a disposition to oppose the court, and to treat Protestant nonconformists with indulgence.' The term is used now only in a historical sense, as it was becoming obsolete politically in Macaulay's time (he died in 1860).
WHISSELL	O.E. *hwit* = white + *sawol* = soul. A nickname probably in reference to a very pure or good person.
WHITBURN	O.E. *hwit* + *bearn*, white, i.e. fair child.
WHITE, WITT	O.E. *hwit* = white; reference to fair hair or complexion, the origin of a huge number of surnames, to which may be added the more than usually silly nickname of 'Chalky'. Cf. Whitefoot, Whitehand and Whitehead.
WHITEBOYS, The	a secret society which began in 1761 in Ireland. It was so called because the members wore white shirts over their coats when engaged in nightly excursions. The society was not sectarian, but was a movement of peasantry against the landowners and particularly opposed to the latter's policy of enclosures. Also

known later as Rightboys from an imaginary Captain Right.

WHITE BRETHREN

Catholic reformers of the 15th century who were denounced by Pope Boniface X and brought to nought.

WHITE CANONS

the Praemonstratensians, also called Norbertines, founded by St Norbert (c. 1080–1134) of Prémontré near Laon in 1120. A very severe order.

WHITE CZARS, The

the former rulers of Russia when they were known as Czars of Muscovy.

WHITE DEVIL OF WALLACHIA

the epithet given by the Turks to their great opponent Skanderbeg (q.v.).

WHITE FATHERS

so called from their white habits, the official title being Society of Missionaries of Africa, founded in 1868 at Algiers by Cardinal Archbishop Charles Lavigerie (1825–92). They have done an immense amount in addition to their missionary activity, in work against slavery, for better agriculture in Africa and in scientific exploration. Cardinal Lavigerie's statue facing to the south of the Sahara, stands (or stood) outside the great church of Notre Dame de l'Afrique.

WHITE FRIARS

the Carmelite friars.

WHITEHORN

clearly a nickname referring to a man who possessed a fine drinking horn.

WHITE HOUSE, The

residence of the President of the USA. It is painted white.

WHITE LADIES

the popular name given to some religious orders for women derived from their white habits. Apart from orders which still exist, the name survives in England from places where convents formerly existed e.g. Whiteladies Road in Clifton, Bristol.

WHITELAM, WHITLAM

from white lamb. Cf. also Whitelegg, Whitelock (white or fair boy) Whiteside.

WHITEMEE, WHITEMEY

M.E. *may* = young man or maid, or fair youth, fair maid.

WHITE MONKS

Cistercians, so named from their woollen habits.

WHITE QUEEN, The

Mary Queen of Scots was so called because she wore white when she mourned her first husband, Francis II.

WHITE SISTERS

(1) the Missionary Sisters of Our Lady of Africa, founded by Cardinal Lavigerie 1869 to assist the White Fathers (q.v.) and (2) Congregation of the Daughters of the Holy Ghost, founded in Brittany in 1706.

WHITTLES

O.E. *hwit* + *hals* = white neck. Cf. roinecks (q.v.).

WHORE OF BABYLON, The

an offensive term used by members of the Protestant underworld to denote the Church of Rome. The term comes from Revelation xvii–xix where the harlot city was supposed by post-Reformation fanatics to mean Rome. The language of the Old Testament Prophets makes it clear that the wicked city in the Revelation is Jerusalem, which was completely destroyed in AD 70, whereas Rome – the Eternal City – never has been destroyed.

WIDOW OF WINDSOR Queen Victoria; this phrase was used by Rudyard Kipling and prevented his being given a knighthood.

WIGG(S) O.E. *wicga* = beatle.

WIGHT M.E. *wiht, wight* = agile, strong.

WIGHTMAN, WEIGHTMAN O.E. *wihtmann* = elf-man, or could be 'brave or strong man' (from M.E. *wiht + man*).

WILD, The Edric, a Saxon noble often given as the ancestor of the well-known Weld family of English gentry.

WILD BILL HICKOK James Butler Hickok (1837–76) an American frontiersman and gun fighter, probably best known now from Gary Cooper's portrayal of him in the film 'The Plainsman'.

WILD GEESE, THE FLIGHT OF THE poetic description of the departure in 1607 from Ireland to the Continent of the two Irish Earls Hugh O'Neill, Earl of Tyrone, and Rory O'Donnel, Earl of Tyrconnell.

WILDBLOOD meaning an untamed spirit or a rake. Cf. also Wildbore, Wilber and Wildgoose.

WILDER O.E. *wilder* = wild animal.

WILDING O.E. *wilding* from *wilde* = the wild one. Cf. Wildman.

WILLGRASS O.N. *griss* = wild pig.

WINCHELSEA, Robert of (c. 1245–1313), Archbishop of Canterbury and a theologian.

WIND, WYNDE O.E. *wind*, a nickname for one considered as swift as the wind.

WINE, WYNE(S), WYNNE O.E. *wine* = friend. Cf. Winman, O.E. = friend man.

WINTER O.G. can be a nickname. Cf. Winterman, reference to one cold as winter.

WINTER KING, The derisive term applied (first by the Jesuits) to Frederick V (1596–1632), the Elector Palatine of the Rhine, who married in 1613 Elizabeth, daughter of King James I of Great Britain. He was foolish enough to accept election as King of Bohemia against the advice of his counsellors (26 August 1619) by the Bohemian estates who were in revolt against the Holy Roman Emperor. Crowned in Prague on 4 November 1619 his reign lasted one year, for his army was routed by the forces of the Catholic League in the battle of the White Mountain on 8 November 1620. Frederick fled to Holland where he lived at the expense of the Dutch States-General. Frederick's only importance in history is that his youngest daughter, Sophia, Electress of Hanover (1630–1714), was the mother of George I, the first Hanoverian King of Great Britain.

WISE, WYSE O.E. *wis* = wise.

WISE, The

Albert II, Duke of Austria, also called the Lame (1330–58).

(El Sabio) Alfonso X, King of Castile and Leon 1252–84 (born 1221). Renowned as a patron of learning and literature, he was elected in 1257 by three of the electors as Holy Roman Emperor in preference to the choice of the other four electors who chose Richard, Earl of Cornwall, brother of the English King, Henry III. Alfonso, 'shrewder than his competitor, continued to watch the stars at Toledo, enjoying the splendours of his title while troubling himself about it no further than to issue now and then a proclamation' (Viscount Bryce, *The Holy Roman Empire*, 1912, p. 210). It was Alfonso X who said that had he been present at the Creation he could have made things more simply. This was not the irreverent remark usually supposed. The king, as a student of the then accepted Ptolemaic astronomy, was confused by its numerous cycles and epicycles.

Charles V of France, Le Sage (1364–8).

Frederick II (1482–1556), Elector of the Palatinate.

Frederick II, Elector of Saxony (1544–56).

Frederick III (1463–1525), Elector of Saxony from 1486, hid Luther in the Wartburg Castle.

John V of Brittany (1399–1442), also called the Good.

Leo VI, Emperor of Byzantium, reigned 886–912, also known as the Philosopher, wrote a good deal, including a *Manual of the Art of War* which described the Byzantine army in detail.

Sancho VI (died 1194), King of Navarre; he succeeded in preserving his country by his skill in diplomacy.

Yaroslav, Grand Prince of Kiev, who died in 1054, did much to prevent feuds among the royal house, and under his rule the first Russian laws were set out in writing.

WISE KING

Solomon, the third King of Israel, son of King David. Details of his wisdom are given in I Kings iv. 'He was wiser than all other men.'

WISEMAN

O.E. *wis* + *mann* = wise, discreet man. Also used of persons skilled in magical arts. Cf. Wishart.

WITT(E)Y

O.E. *wit(t)ig* = wise and also in M.E. = witty.

WIZARD OF THE NORTH

Sir Walter Scott (1771–1832), Scotland's greatest man of letters. The Waverley novels were for a considerable time published anonymously.

WOLF

a nickname from O.E. *wulf*, for the animal.

WOOD, WODE

in secondary instances from O.E. *wood*. M.E. *wode* = frenzied.

WOODBINE WILLIE

the Rev. G. A. Studert Kennedy, an Anglican priest, an evangelical preacher who was a very popular Chaplain to the Forces in the First World War. His nickname came from a brand of cigarettes which he distributed to the men in the trenches.

WOODCOCK	originally from O.E. *wuducoce* = woodcock, applied to mean a simpleton or dupe. Cf. Woodey.
WOODFULL	O.E. *wude* + *fugol* = a bird of the woods.
WOODIWISS	O.E. *wuduwasa* = faun or satyr.
WOODROFF	O.E. *wudurofe* = woodruff. It had strongly scented leaves and the nickname could have been given to someone who used perfume, or the reverse.
WOOLSEY, WOLSEY, WOOSEY	O.E. *wulfes aege* = wolf's eye.
WOOR(E)	O.E. *wogere* = wooer, suitor.
WORKER, The	(L'Ouvrier) Albert Alexandre Martin (1815–95), the first working man to hold a post in French Government. He supported the revolution in 1848, and was sentenced to life imprisonment for his part in the rising. He was released in 1859 under an amnesty.
WORLD BURNER	Jehansuz, name given to Ala-ud-Din of Ghor (in north-west Afghanistan) who drove out the Ghaznavids in 1152, the descendants of Mahmud of Ghazni who became ruler of Afghanistan and other (Indian) territories in 997. Mahmud made the hitherto obscure town of Ghazni into a splendid city. It was, of course, sacked by Ala-ud-Din, hence his name of Jehansuz.
WORLEDGE, WOOLIDGE	O.E. *weorthlic* = worthy, noble, distinguished.
WORM(S)	O.E. *wyrm* = snake, dragon.
WORSHIP	O.E. *weorthscipe* = worship, honour.
WRAFS	members of Women's Royal Air Force.
WRAITH	O.E. *wrath* = angry, fierce.
WREN(N)	O.E. *wrenna* = the wren.
WRENCH, WRINCH	O.E. *wrenc* = trick, wile, and M.E. wrench.
WREY	O.E. *wrigian* = to turn and M.E. *wry(e)* = awry, i.e. twisted or crooked.
WRIDE, WREATH	O.E. *writhan* = to twist, as of unreliable person, colloquially a 'twister'.
WRONG	O.E. *wrang* = crooked (as applied to a person).
WROTH, WROATH	O.E. *wrath* = angry.
WRY-MOUTHED, The	Boleslaw II (1086–1138), Prince of Poland.
WYCLIFFITE	a Lollard (q.v.).
WYKEHAM, William of	(1324–1404), Bishop of Winchester, founder of New College, Oxford and Winchester College.

X

XANTHOPOULOS

Callistus Nicephoris (c. 1256–1335), a Byzantine historian.

XAVERIAN BROTHERS, The

A Roman Catholic society founded in Holland in 1846 and named after St Francis Xavier, the great missionary.

Y

YANKEE DOODLE	the contemptuous term used by the British regular soldiers to describe the American colonists. In the end after the British surrender at Yorktown in 1781 the American band played the tune Yankee Doodle.
YAPP	O.E. *geap* = bent
YAVUZ (THE GRIM)	Selim I (c. 1470–1520), Sultan of Turkey 1512–20.
YONWIN	O.E. *geongwine* = young friend.
YORK, William of	(died 1154). Archbishop of York, his name being William Fitzherbert.
YOUNG, YONGE	O.E. *geong* = young.
YOUNG BOSNIA	name of a group before 1914 in Bosnia-Herzegovina, very active among Yugoslav students in Prague, Vienna and Zagreb to inculcate revolution in the province which had been annexed to the Austrian Empire in 1908.
YOUNG EUROPE	an organization founded by the Italian patriot Giuseppe Mazzini (1805–72) in Switzerland for which he was expelled from that country in 1836. At the same time he had founded another society, Young Switzerland.
YOUNG GERMANY	movement of thought led by Heinrich Heine (1797–1856) in the mid-19th century.
YOUNG IRELAND	an Irish political group which was formed c. 1842 to advocate separation of Ireland from England and the revival of Irish culture. The members formed in 1847 the Irish Confederation but this was suppressed in 1848 because it had advocated an Irish rebellion.
YOUNG ITALY	Giovine Italia, an organization founded by the Italian patriot Giuseppe Mazzini (1805–72) with the object of gaining national independence.
YOUNG KING, The	Henry (1155–83) the 2nd son of Henry II of England, so called because crowned in his father's lifetime, but died of dysentery before his father, fortunately, as he would have made a bad king.
	The title was used of the young Stephen Dusan (Dushan) who was crowned in 1322 with his father Stephen Decani or Defanski (Stephen Uros III) King of Serbia. Dusan dethroned his father in 1331 (the latter died on 11 November 1331) and Dusan after some victories had himself crowned as Czar or Emperor of Serbs and Greeks on Easter day 1346. He died in 1355.
YOUNG OTTOMANS	a party among the Turks in the later 19th century who worked for constitutional reform under Abdul Hamid II. They preceded the Young Turks (q.v.).

YOUNG PRETENDER   Prince Charles Edward, elder son of Old Pretender
                          (q.v.).

YOUNG TURKS   a party formed in Turkey in the early 20th century to
                          bring about constitutional reform. The autocratic
                          sovereign, Abdul Hamid II (1876–1909) was dethroned
                          in 1909 as a result of the movement for parliamentary
                          government instead of absolutism.

YOUNGER, The   Apollinarius, Bishop of Laodicea, see Apollinarianism.
                          Edmund Calamy (c. 1635–85), English Puritan.
                          Cyrus, a Prince of Persia, younger son of Darius II,
                          King of Persia. In 404 BC, his elder brother became
                          King as Artaxerxes II, and Cyrus planned to seize the
                          throne. He was defeated and killed at Cunaxa in
                          Babylonia in 401 BC. The account of his expedition and
                          the retreat of his 10,000 Greek troops to the Black Sea
                          is given in Xenophon's *Anabasis*.
                          Hans Holbein (1497–1543), German painter, the son
                          of Hans Holbein the Elder (q.v.), he visited England
                          and painted portraits of Henry VIII and of many
                          notables of his court.
                          St Melania (c. 383–438) granddaughter of St Melania
                          the Elder (q.v.), she fled with her husband, Pinian,
                          to Africa and then joined St Jerome at Jerusalem where
                          she died.
                          Isaac Penington (1616–79), a great figure in the
                          history of the Quakers. He was the eldest son of Sir
                          Isaac Penington, Lord Mayor of London, 1642–4.
                          Pepin II of Heristal (died 714), a member of the
                          Carolingian dynasty, and great-nephew of Pepin I.
                          William Pitt (1759–1806), second son of the Great
                          Commoner (q.v.), William Pitt, Earl of Chatham. He
                          was Prime Minister at the age of 25 in 1783 and
                          continued until 1801. He was Premier again in 1804–6.
                          Gaius Plinius Caecilius Secundus (c. born AD 61 or
                          62), the Younger Pliny, nephew and adopted son of
                          the Elder Pliny (q.v.). Pliny was governor of Bithynia
                          in 111 or 112. His *Letters* have been preserved and he
                          has a place in church history because of his dealings
                          with Christians in his province.
                          Lucius Annaeus Seneca (c. 4 BC–AD 65), the son of
                          Seneca the Elder (q.v.). The Younger Seneca was a
                          Roman statesman, philosopher, satirist and writer of
                          tragedies. He was forced by Nero to commit suicide.
                          He had held at first some influence over Nero, but the
                          latter became more and more irked by him.
                          Sir Henry Vane (1613–62), to distinguish him from
                          his father. Arrested after the Restoration of Charles
                          II, he was tried and executed on Tower Hill, 14 July
                          1662.

Z

ZEALOTS

a Jewish political party in New Testament times who believed in violent resistance to Rome. One of the Twelve Apostles was Simon the Zealot, who may have belonged to this party. Also a party with the same principles but often called Sicarii or dagger men.

ZWINGLIANISM

name given to the Protestant views of Ulrich Zwingli (1484–1531), a Catholic priest who embraced Protestant views independently of Luther. On the Eucharist, Zwingli denied any carnal presence of Christ in the Eucharist, the latter being purely symbolical. Zwingli resided at Zurich. He carried several of the Swiss Cantons into Protestantism but was killed in a fight with those who disagreed with him. See George Potter, *Ulrich Zwingli*, Historical Association, 1977.

INDEX